For Reyn —

Hope your amble down "Waffle Street"
proves entertaining & edifying.

Best,
Jimmy
Adams

WAFFLE
STREET

THE CONFESSION AND REHABILITATION
OF A FINANCIER

JAMES ADAMS

Sourced Media Books
San Clemente, CA

Sourced Media Books
20 Via Cristobal
San Clemente, CA 92673
www.sourcedmediabooks.com

ISBN–13: 978–0–9841068–5–1

Printed in the United States of America.

This publication is designed to provide entertainment value and
is sold with the understanding that the publisher is not engaged
in rendering legal, accounting, or other professional advice of any
kind. If legal advice or other expert assistance is required, the services of a competent professional person should be sought.

—From a Declaration of Principles jointly adopted by a
Committee of the American Bar Association and a
Committee of Publishers and Associations

For Rebecca

DEBT

Etymology: Old French *dette,* ultimately from Latin *debita,* plural of *debitum,* from neuter of *edebitus,* past participle of *debere;* to owe.

—noun

1. Something that is owed or that one is bound to pay to or perform for another: a debt of $50.

2. A liability or obligation to pay or render something: My debt to her for advice is not to be discharged easily.

3. The condition of being under such an obligation: His gambling losses put him deeply in debt.

4. Theology. An offense requiring reparation; a sin; a trespass.

CONTENTS

ACKNOWLEDGMENTS

The author wishes to thank the following individuals:

- His parents, Jim and Jane Adams, for providing feedback on several economic essays.
- Benjamin Gibbs, for suggesting the book's title.
- Gregory Osmond, for introducing him to Amy Cook at Sourced Media Books.
- His wife, Becky, for her unflagging support throughout this quixotic endeavor.
- Jean-Baptiste Say, whose reputation this volume hopes to reclaim.

BOND^{n}1

—noun

1. Something that binds, fastens, confines, or holds together.
2. Law. A written promise of a surety.
3. Finance. A certificate of ownership of a specified portion of a debt due to be paid by a government or corporation to an individual holder and usually bearing a fixed rate of interest.

BOND^{n}2

—noun

1. A serf or slave.

PREFACE

William Edward Preston, Junior, was born on September 18, 1899 in Perth Amboy, New Jersey. In 1908 his father, tired of his twenty years as a butcher, sold his business to a local competitor and relocated his family to a 135-acre farm in Morganville, Marlboro Township, New Jersey. William Sr. relished his newfound life as a produce farmer. He not only harvested his crops but also managed their distribution to consumers in New York City.

William Jr. assisted his father in his agricultural endeavors until he enlisted in the Army in 1917. Upon arriving in France, he trained as an aircraft mechanic and was fortunate enough to capture a private photograph of General John J. Pershing, commander of the American Expeditionary Force during World War I. In 1918, Preston survived a bout of Spanish influenza (which would go on to kill at least 50 million less fortunate people), and returned home to New Jersey after the armistice was declared in November.

While he could have resumed work on the family farm, William instead elected to go to work for the manager of a small, private savings bank in New York City. In 1923, he married Alta

Mae Walling, a girl two years his junior. The newlyweds resided in the Flatbush section of Brooklyn for a brief period, then relocated to Keyport, New Jersey after their first child was born in 1924. William continued to work for the bank until 1925 but sought greener pastures after his manager departed. He eventually landed at a much larger financial institution, situated at 55 Wall Street: The National City Bank of New York.

Founded in 1812, National City Bank of New York (not to be confused with Cleveland-based National City Bank) had grown to in excess of $1 billion in assets by 1919. In 1921, Charles E. Mitchell was elected president of National City Bank. In a separate action, he also became president of its investment banking affiliate, National City Company. Under Mitchell's leadership, both the commercial bank and investment bank grew at a torrid pace. By 1930, National City Bank (the commercial bank) had established 100 branches in 23 countries outside the U.S., making it the second-largest commercial bank in the United States. National City Company (the investment bank) had become the world's largest underwriter of stocks and bonds.

Mitchell capitalized on his unique position as the only U.S. bank with a considerable overseas presence to underwrite bonds on behalf of Latin American governments. He used his large domestic sales force to distribute the debt to American retail investors.

William Preston, Jr. was one of the salesmen, selling the bond certificates for cash right out of his briefcase. Eighty years later, his children recounted that their father "never really enjoyed hawking those Latin American bonds—he never felt they were a safe bet. But he made such good money selling them, how could he not? After all, he had two kids to feed."

As fate would have it, Preston's instincts were eventually vindicated. Many of the securities he sold defaulted as the Depression spread from the United States to Latin America in the early 1930s. Fortunately, he was able to retain his employment with National City Bank, becoming a commercial loan officer in the foreign credit department.

For his part, "Sunshine Charlie" Mitchell remained chairman until 1933, when he was arrested and indicted for tax evasion. Though acquitted of all criminal charges, he paid the government a million dollars in a civil settlement. For Mitchell, the sum was not terribly onerous; National City had paid him in excess of a million dollars in each of the years 1927–1929.

William Preston was never indicted on civil or criminal charges for his role in the proliferation of dubious securities. He did, however, perform several acts of restitution to the community. In an era when bankers were reticent to extend credit to anyone, he was able to keep several small businesses alive by authorizing their credit lines. He counseled friends in managing their businesses as the banking crisis unfolded in the early 1930s. In one expression of gratitude, Preston's wife Alta was given a mink coat by a fur clothing retailer who had narrowly avoided financial ruin thanks to William's admonition.

William retained his role as a loan officer for National City Bank for the remainder of his career. While not an avid churchgoer, he was considered to be a man of integrity. He succinctly described his moral code with the phrase, "I carry the Golden Rule in my pocket." Indeed, the Prestons consistently used their means during the Depression years to ease the suffering of the less fortunate. Alta frequently kept a large pot of soup on her stove in their Keyport home; anyone who solicited a meal was never refused. Word of their generosity spread. Homeless people marked the sidewalk outside their residence with chalk to indicate the presence of a compassionate matron. On several occasions, the Preston girls found their winter coats missing. Alta had given them away to less fortunate children in the neighborhood.

The Golden Rule, as originally stated by Jesus, reads, "Therefore all things whatsoever ye would that men should do to you, do ye even so to them." Colloquially, we truncate the expression to "Do unto others as you would have them do unto you." A Wall Street version might read: "Never sell a customer a stock or bond that you wouldn't buy for your personal account." Of course, that ethic would be laughed off a trading desk in a New York minute. But it's the version that William must have realized that he violated by selling Argentine debt to hapless clients early in his career.

Here's another scripture I frequently ponder: Exodus 20:5. Context: God is delivering the Ten Commandments to Moses on the slopes of Mount Sinai. "For I the LORD thy God am a jealous God, visiting the iniquity of the fathers upon the children unto the third and fourth generation of them that hate me." Now this may not seem immediately relevant, but here's the thing: William Edward Preston was my great grandfather, and I followed in his footsteps as an unwitting participant in a global financial debacle.

Old Testament verses notwithstanding, I don't blame William for my own recent mishaps in the capital markets. I am, however, frequently tempted to ascribe my unfortunate interest in finance to a congenital defect that he has bequeathed upon me. Unlike my progenitor, I never had any compunction about the morality of my actions during my seven-and-a-half years as a bond market professional. Nonetheless, I have come to realize my own complicity, however small, in the financial meltdown.

While my accidental culpability has never caused me to lose sleep, I believe that when we become aware of past transgressions, it behooves us to make penance wherever we can. And so I am compelled to repent in the only way I know how—with a narrative.

This book is my best effort at atonement.

Chapter 1

PINK SLIP

"The sense of helplessness which unemployment brings to a man is an affliction of the spirit even heavier than the material loss which accompanies it." —Henry Clay

If initial appearances were any indicator, Friday, January 16, 2009, was well on its way to being an aberrantly upbeat day in the capital markets. Bank of America confirmed it would receive $138 billion of government aid to mitigate losses related to its purchase of Merrill Lynch. Citigroup reported an $8.3 billion quarterly loss as its management announced plans to split the sprawling financial conglomerate in two. Bank of America and Citigroup shares rose 12% and 17%, respectively, as investors were heartened by the government support and restructuring plan.

Over the course of the trading session, news of more trouble in the real economy broke. Electronics retailer Circuit City announced its imminent liquidation, which meant that the economy could potentially lose another 34,000 jobs. Bank of America also offered a decidedly melancholy outlook on its earnings call. CEO Ken Lewis explained that higher unemployment levels meant higher losses on BofA's credit card loans. If history was any guide, the projected eight percent unemployment rate meant that the bank would likely write off in excess of eight percent of its credit card portfolio. Lewis's only semi-sanguine remark was an expression of hope for "early signs of stabilization" in the second half of 2009. As the market digested the likelihood of continued (and accelerating) loan losses, Bank of America and Citigroup shares both plummeted. BofA closed down 14% from its opening level; Citi dropped 9%. Another day in paradise. It was a story I had seen many times over the previous eighteen months: rays of light quickly consumed by the vicious circle of souring debts and rising unemployment.

The only thing that really made this day any different from the others since June 2007 was a phone call I received at 10.30 a.m. The head of our marketing department asked if I had a few minutes to talk to him. I had been working fairly closely with him on some investment strategies that we could pitch to potential clients. I could only assume that he wanted me to brief him on my progress with some of the marketing materials.

While climbing the staircase which bridged our trading floor to the offices upstairs, I was intercepted by my direct supervisor, who gently placed his hand on my back and joined me in my ascent. I suppose it's a testament to my naivete, but I didn't realize something was awry until I finally stepped into the marketing director's office and found the company compliance officer seated on the sofa in his office. "Great," I thought. I knew I was going to get reprimanded for not filling out some authorization form before distributing a pitchbook to a prospective client. Or worse, I might be upbraided for incessantly checking for status updates on Facebook. I knew my habit was unprofessional, but after all, that program is so uncontrollably addictive.

"This isn't good news, is it?" I asked sheepishly.

"I'm afraid not," he replied.

"How long have you been with the firm?" he asked.

"Since March of 2006 . . . that makes it almost three years."

"Wow. Time has really flown. You know, in that time, you've done consistently great work for us." He paused. "And it really kills us to do this."

I don't exactly remember how he began his next sentence. It was along the lines of, "As you know, our assets under management have declined and revenues have consequently fallen."

I knew then that my days at the firm had come to an abrupt end. I was reassured that my termination was in no way performance related. After all, I had survived two previous rounds of layoffs. But given the eleven-hour days that I had been working on the aforementioned new products, I considered myself a fairly integral part of a resurgent marketing effort and wasn't anticipating being cut. (Admittedly, I could have abbreviated my workday had I not spent so much time reading economic theory, but I was helplessly drawn to it in a sincere effort to understand why the global financial architecture was rapidly crumbling.)

My only prior experience with a layoff had been three years before. At the time, I was employed by a large, publicly-traded life insurance company that was merging with a competitor. I had been involved on a high-profile deal that had recently closed, and I was told that my severance was not a reflection of any ineptitude. Despite the reassurance, I took the layoff very personally, cycling through the customary stages of grief: incredulity, despair, anger, and acceptance. My return to emotional normalcy took about four months. I was a man who took his career very seriously. Perhaps I even defined myself by the rate of my ascent on the corporate ladder. Clearly, I had a lot to learn about life.

As the director continued to express his regrets about my departure, I found my sense of shock gradually supplanted by another sentiment: relief. I couldn't understand it. To date, this had unquestionably been the best experience of my career. The company was replete with smart, good-hearted people, with whom I relished working. Senior management had afforded me tremendous opportunities for professional growth. I was planning on being with the firm for another twenty years. So why did I feel this way?

It's a funny thing when your coworkers hear that you've received a layoff notice. They react in one of two ways: 1) they are quick to wish you well in your next endeavor, or 2) they cease to acknowledge your existence. Women with whom I had previously enjoyed casual, flirtatious banter were suddenly reticent to even make eye contact. The phobia must have been born of a conviction that pink slips are as contagious as shingles.

I was given a week to pack up my belongings, transition my responsibilities to colleagues, and say my goodbyes. Maybe I should have, but I didn't feel awkward as I sorted through the miscellany of documents in my cubicle. Still, it was a little disappointing to think that in some female eyes, I had gone from being the office eye candy to its resident leper. But even leper colonies have their advantages. In my case, the newfound solitude afforded me a lot of time to contemplate my sense of peace.

I knew my odds of finding a job (let alone a decent-paying one) in this environment were quite low. Even more unexpectedly, I found myself not *wanting* a job in this industry. It didn't add up. It wasn't that my passion for finance had dissipated, or that I was disappointed by the severity of the recent volatility. After all, I had been in capital markets since August 2001. I cut my teeth in the corporate bond market during the Enron, Tyco, and WorldCom debacles. I had watched the domestic airline industry implode from the vantage point of an institutional investor. I was a veteran. As much as you can be at age 31, anyway.

But the turmoil seven years ago had, for the most part, been contained to a few miscreants in the energy trading and telecom sectors. Bernie Ebbers, Dennis Kozlowski, and Jeff Skilling were undoubtedly bad guys, but they weren't reflective of corporate America in general. Relative to the financial events of late 2008/ early 2009, the corporate accounting scandals were a pleasant dream by comparison. Something was different this time. Very different. Pillars of the financial system had toppled like helpless dominoes. Those that remained were severely cracked, and the thought of spending another year watching the government spackle them in a vain effort to restore their structural integrity held little appeal.

The thing that made this market so different from recent history was that there was no way to win, anymore. The economic foundation was shifting so drastically from week to week that you could no longer place an intelligent wager. Our chief investment officer had succinctly described it as an "Ike Turner market." I couldn't help but concur. It really was like being in a relationship with a temperamental lover: moderately uplifting one day, then terribly abusive the next. Common sense told me that it didn't pay to play a game whose rules were constantly being changed. You just had to sit it out until the rules had been credibly rewritten. So that's what I decided to do. Watching from the sidelines was a lot more appealing than showing up for work every day just to receive another concussion.

The best way for any girl to rebound from a major heartbreak is to begin dating a new guy. Ideally, someone very different from the last fellow she dated. After you catch the leather-jacket-clad bad boy you fell for running around with another girl, you start to think your mom was right when she advised you to accept the more subtle advances of the clean-cut guy in your homeroom. Some part of me still wanted to believe that if I could just be patient, maybe my mercurial boyfriend, Mr. Market, would eventually become a nice guy. But in my heart of hearts, I knew that fidelity would never be his strong suit.

There were other reasons for a hiatus. Over the past seven years, my career path had caused my wife and me to relocate to three different cities. Including intra-city moves between apartments and houses, we had packed and unloaded all of our possessions more than six times. The logistics of the transfers became increasingly depressing with every move.

During our first two relocations, the thoughts of life in our new homes sustained us and seemed to make the sofas lighter as we loaded them into the U-Haul. By the fourth move, however, we found ourselves handicapping the time until my next assignment in corporate America. While sincerely longing to establish a genuine homestead, we had seemingly been consigned to the fate of bivouacking for the rest of our married life. I wasn't in the Army, after all. But perhaps this was the lot of financial mercenaries, as well.

$$$$$

The investment profession is comprised of two classes of practitioners: 1) product manufacturers and 2) product distributors. Hedge funds, insurance companies, and mutual funds are product manufacturers. In the industry, they are referred to by the umbrella term, "asset managers." Their personnel usually have titles like "chief investment officer," "portfolio manager," or "securities analyst." Financial product distributors come in the form of stockbrokers, financial planners, and life insurance agents. They receive brokerage commissions for selling mutual funds and insurance policies; advisory fees are earned for placing money on behalf of clients.

Although stockbrokers and insurance salesmen have modest licensing requirements, no such examinations are necessary to work as an asset manager or financial advisor. And except in the case of insurance companies, asset management companies have no liability for the performance of the securities that they manage. Likewise, distributors are not on the hook for the performance of the asset managers' products that they sell or recommend. In short, being an asset manager or financial advisor is akin to practicing unlicensed medicine, dentistry, or law with no chance of ever being sued for malpractice. Except that you can make more money.

If you tell me what aspect of financial services that an individual works in, I can give you a pretty accurate general idea of what kind of person he or she is and what his or her school days were like. Asset managers tend to be intellectual, math-oriented, introverted types who dress rather casually. During high school, future asset managers populate chess clubs, student newspapers, quiz bowl teams, and the Model United Nations. They are often teachers' pets. In their leisure reading, they embrace the fantasy and science fiction genres, primarily because 23rd-century space chicks are more interested in a man's brains than in his ability to throw a football. The blossoming asset manager has a high intelligence quotient but a generally limited capacity for scoring chicks. In short, these people are on the receiving end of a lot of wedgies.

Stockbrokers and financial planners, on the other hand, are extroverted, well-dressed types. They are smooth talkers. In high school, they held student government offices that entailed no real responsibility but nonetheless made them look respectable to college admissions officers. They served as captains of football and lacrosse teams and dated girls on the homecoming court. They gave a lot of wedgies to the sci-fi crowd, who would eventually pay psychologists a lot of money to mollify the consequent emotional damage.

My own high school experience was a contradiction in terms. I was an unapologetic participant on the quiz bowl team (PA state champs, 1994!), but I also played four years of lacrosse. Though I became team captain my junior year and was named MVP my senior year, I was made to endure the requisite freshman hazing outside a McDonald's on the return from a road trip to Baltimore. In an act of Providence, the upperclassman spared me the ignominy of having my underwear retailored with a lacrosse stick. Instead, they were content to duct tape me to the front of a Ronald McDonald statue in a semi-prostrated position. Eighteen years later, I can still vividly recall several kids in the jungle gym adjacent to the restaurant pointing and laughing at the spectacle of me being taped to America's preeminent corporate icon. While my boxer shorts emerged from the incident with all threads intact, my dignity didn't fare so well. But all things considered, I was a pretty lucky fellow.

I entered Wake Forest University in the fall of 1995 intent on pursuing a degree in history, which had been my favorite subject in high school. During my second semester, I took a macroeconomics course and was absolutely intrigued. I remembered how much discussion in my high school history classes revolved around economic events. Everything in politics, it seemed, boiled down to money.

Macroeconomics is the study of the behavior of national economies. It is concerned with the wealth of countries. **Finance,** in contrast, is the study of getting rich yourself. An ability to speak in macroeconomic jargon enables you to sound sophisticated while bantering with your buddies at fraternity parties. Pursuing a degree in finance enables you to convince the girls at the party that you are on the fast track to becoming a rich man without the nuisance of attending medical school. When it came time to declare a major, the choice was clear.

After completing my finance degree, I spent the first five years out of college in the investment departments of two life insurance companies. As a credit analyst, I poured over the financial statements of corporations to determine whether or not we should purchase their bonds. (A **bond** is a debt instrument issued by a borrower to a group of lenders.)

Admittedly, it wasn't particularly glamorous work, but I loved it anyway. How could I not? I got paid to read all day and pause occasionally to place a forty-million-dollar bet with somebody else's money. It was the perfect gig for an intellectually curious man who could temper his bravado with a healthy dose of skepticism.

Along with my colleagues in the corporate bond group, the investment departments were staffed with commercial loan officers and mortgage securities traders. The commercial loan officers lent money to real estate developers while the mortgage securities traders purchased and sold pools of residential loans that had been "securitized" into mortgage bonds.

While nearly everyone in the investment department could fairly be described as a nerd, mortgage traders unfailingly proved the geekiest of the lot. They take pride in being versed in the high level math necessary for modeling mortgage prepayment patterns. Mortgage traders considered guys like me dumb brutes because corporate bond math only requires basic algebra. They're right, of course, but that sort of lame bragging really makes you want to give them a wedgie.

The only people below the mortgage guys on the insurance company social totem pole were the actuaries. Those guys would kill for a mortgage guy's social finesse. Contemplating the typical high school experience of an actuary presents a legitimate theological conundrum. That is, when you consider what his social life must have been like in grades 9–12, you don't leave much room in the universe for a merciful God.

This model for projecting future financial career paths based on high school experiences may strike you as terribly simplistic and unreliable. In a future edition of this book, I will include a full-blown statistical analysis to substantiate my thesis. In the meantime, you'll just have to have my claims anecdotally corroborated by your nearest actuary. Just don't press for details when memories of his senior prom result in inconsolable sobbing.

After a long day of trading bonds and teasing actuaries, most of the nights during my insurance years were devoted to educational pursuits. I spent the first five months of 2002, 2003, and 2004 studying for the Chartered Financial Analyst (CFA) examinations. After successfully passing each of three six-hour tests and completing 36 months of qualified work experience, I received my CFA charter in late 2004. According to the CFA Institute, I had demonstrated a knowledge of economics, statistical inference, financial accounting, investment analysis, and portfolio management. Most importantly, I had earned the right to affix "CFA" to my name on business cards. The Institute promised that the title would afford me instant credibility in financial matters for the rest of my life. Of course, should I ever neglect to pay $300 in annual dues, the Institute also promised to censure me for unauthorized usage of those three letters.

A year after completing the CFA program, I enrolled in the executive MBA program at the University of North Carolina-Chapel Hill. The dean assured us that our degree would greatly increase our marketability in the corporate world, notwithstanding that prospective employers would [correctly] interpret "executive program" as a thinly-veiled euphemism for "night school."

I genuinely liked my professors and classmates, but I can't say that I approached the curriculum with as much zeal as the other students. That's not to say that I didn't enjoy studying business—I always have. But shelling out fifty grand to analyze companies in the halls of academia seemed ridiculous given that I had already spent the past five years doing it professionally. But as much as I could complain, my access to the UNC network paid immediate dividends after my layoff from the insurance company in 2005. Thanks to their career services department, I landed my dream job.

The corporation I will call "Alpha Managers" (due to my severance agreement) had started in the early 1980s as an investment advisor to commercial banks. The firm's competitive advantage laid in its expertise in valuing mortgage-backed securities before the vast majority of market participants had figured out how to do so. Its early successes soon enabled the firm to branch out into discretionary asset management—i.e., the firm was making trades on behalf of its customers without having each one individually approved by the client. By the time I joined the firm in early 2006, Alpha Managers' assets under management had crested $30 billion.

We managed separate accounts for large institutional investors, both domestic and international: state and corporate pension plans, banks, insurance companies, even sovereign wealth funds. We also ran several pools of commingled assets, including two mutual funds, several hedge funds, and a few limited partnerships comprised of Japanese banks.

My assignment in the firm's product management group was to service $20 billion of those assets by representing our trading desk to clients, investment consultants, and Wall Street brokers. I provided verbal and written commentary on the performance of forty bond portfolios whose strategies covered nearly everything under the sun. Occasionally, I participated in marketing efforts by designing pitch books and visiting prospective clients.

The work itself was extremely interesting, but the best part of the job was being surrounded by so many intelligent, ethical people. I cannot overemphasize what a pleasant anomaly this was. As far as most financiers are concerned, the phrase, "What shall a man give in exchange for his soul?" is not a rhetorical question. I'm willing to bet that sixty percent of the personnel on any New York trading desk can provide a ready answer in terms of square footage in the Hamptons.

When housing prices began to drop in early 2007, mortgage bonds soon began to follow suit. Initially, I explained to our clients that the declining bond prices were primarily the effect of selling by investors that had borrowed heavily to finance their positions and were now forced to repay their debts. The market would rally, I declared, as soon as the waves of forced selling had subsided. As the months passed and mortgage bond prices continued to tumble, fulfillment of my prophecy appeared increasingly implausible. I'm not sure my reassurances sounded any less pathetic than Linus's promise to Charlie Brown that the Great Pumpkin would arrive with gifts on Halloween night—if only the believers proved patient enough.

As the economic situation continued to deteriorate, many of the bonds we had purchased began to incur severe principal losses as overextended homeowners neglected to make their mortgage payments. Many of our investors terminated their accounts, taking their now severely-depreciated portfolios with them.

Two years of watching our clients flee and chronicling what appeared to be the last days of capitalism had exacted a terrible emotional toll. For the first time in my life, I had lost my capacity to speak about anything with genuine conviction. When apprised of my severance from the firm, I didn't feel terminated; I felt emancipated. The millstone of mortgage debt had finally been cut loose from my neck.

My wife took the news of the layoff much harder than I did. Only twelve hours before, we had both agreed that it was time for us to start a family. Money wasn't going to be an immediate concern; we had accumulated enough savings to service our expenses for a long time. Nonetheless, her dream of becoming a stay-at-home mom seemed to have been summarily dashed. I knew she didn't hold me personally accountable for the setback, but I still felt that I had somehow disappointed her. For the time being, she would continue in her position as a nurse manager while I would assume more responsibilities around the house.

My first day as a kept man had a seemingly auspicious beginning. Just after my wife had left for work, a man knocked on my door and introduced himself as a neighbor from down the street. He had locked himself out of his car and needed a ride to a friend's house. This was the silver lining to the layoff, I thought. I had been so busy with my job and my evening MBA program that I had largely neglected my social life. If nothing else, a little time off work would provide an opportunity to make some new friends in the community.

When she returned home from the hospital, I delivered a report to my wife on my new station as a domestic. Rather than providing me with a grocery list, she had given me carte blanche to purchase whatever items I deemed prudent. I had neglected to procure our usual sundries, returning instead with six cases of ramen noodles which now sat on our dining room table. Although neither of us had eaten ramen since college, I explained to my wife that our new cash flow constraints should emphasize frugality over nutritional content. She politely demurred. Additionally, I also had to account for crashing our computer's hard drive and getting swindled out of twenty-eight dollars by a man posing as our neighbor.

I retired to our upstairs loft and nestled in my recliner. I picked up the latest issue of *The Economist* and began reading about the financial crisis. For the first time in nearly a decade, the financial press had become leisure reading rather than a work requirement. It didn't matter. Now, more than ever, I was captivated by the riddle of the markets.

$$\$\$\$\$\$$

Imagine an island inhabited only by two men, each of whom owns a small plot of land. One of the men uses his land to grow coconut trees, while his neighbor elects to cultivate pineapples. For several months, each man lives entirely in isolation, consuming only his own production. Understandably, he tires of eating the same kind of fruit day in and day out. Then one day, the men get together and decide to trade a several coconuts in exchange for a few pineapples. An economy has just been born.

An **economy** is a system of production arrangements and production exchanges. On the island, each man labors on his farm to produce one type of fruit. By exchanging some of his production with the other farmer, he may consume both kinds of fruit. The production of pineapples by one farmer creates an opportunity for the other man to sell his coconuts. Obviously, the farmers could not eat the fruit without first planting and harvesting it. Ergo, *production is the cause of consumption.*

Demand, in the economic sense, is not equivalent to a capricious materialistic desire. If all that were required to procure an item was mere longing for ownership, every sixteen-year-old kid would be driving a new Ferrari. Rather, true demand is driven by the willingness to work in order to supply more goods.

On our island, the supply of pineapples constitutes the demand for coconuts—i.e., if the pineapple farmer wants to eat more coconuts, he must first grow more pineapples to give the other farmer in exchange. Neither farmer will exchange his produce unless the other man has also produced something of value. The only alternative means of acquiring the coconuts is to borrow or steal them. If the coconut farmer lends the coconuts, he will only do so with the agreement that the pineapple farmer repay him in the future. That is, he will trade his own production today for a claim on the other man's production in the future. But whether it occurs in the present or the future, the creation of value is always the basis for demand. *Production is the cause of prosperity and wealth; consumption is the effect.*

The first modern economist to state the proposition that the production (or supply) of a good creates the foundation for demand was a French businessman named Jean-Baptiste Say. First published in 1803, Say's *Treatise on Political Economy* asserted that "a product is no sooner created, than it, from that instant, affords a market for *other products to the full extent of its own value.*" In personal correspondence, Say later wrote "as the amount for which we can buy is equal to that which we can produce, the more we can produce the more we can purchase."

This concept—that the very power to consume depends *entirely* on the power to produce—is known as **Say's Law**. As the fundamental proposition of economics, Say's Law is sometimes referred to as "The Law of Markets." Colloquially, it is often expressed as "you can't get something for nothing." While an obviously immutable principle, it is one which nearly everyone attempts to violate at some point in his life.

In our two-man, two-product island economy, the farmers can directly exchange their production with each other in a barter system. Under a currency system, the farmers add an intermediate step: they exchange their production for money. **Money** is anything for which someone is willing to trade his production. In a more developed economy (e.g., one with hundreds of producers and products), the presence of money greatly facilitates the exchange of production.

Money serves as a **medium of exchange** by which people indirectly exchange their separate productions. One person produces, then sells his goods or services in exchange for money, and subsequently uses that money to consume someone else's production. In Jean-Baptiste Say's words, "money performs no more than the role of a conduit in this double exchange [of production]."

Produce ▶ Sell Production (for $) ▶ Consume Production (with $)

In addition to serving as a medium of exchange, money also represents a **store of value**. That is, money should retain its purchasing power over time, or at least not lose it very rapidly. Lastly, money is a **unit of account**, meaning that money can be used to measure the amount of a good or service. For example, a dollar could measure a loaf of bread, a half gallon of gasoline, or a liter of soda. A unit of account provides a means of expressing prices, costs, and profits in a common language. We can even express time in units of money. Assuming a laborer receives $15 per hour for his wages, then four minutes of his labor is also worth one dollar.

Any commodity which can function as a medium of exchange, store of value, and unit of account can serve as money. Gold and silver have served as money in many societies. Money has also taken the shape of alcohol, tobacco, and even livestock. But regardless of its form, it is only a mechanism of trading one production for another. As Say explained, "money is but the agent of the transfer of values."

After exchanging their production for money, many people do not immediately spend their money on consuming the production of others. The excess of their production over their consumption is known as savings. That is,

Production − Consumption = Savings.

Savings represent a decision to defer one's consumption until a later point in time. In the interim, savers can do two things with their money: hold it or invest it. Everyone should maintain a reasonable amount of cash on hand for emergency needs. But generally speaking, a large cash hoard does the saver no good. He is not enjoying consumption, and he is not putting his savings to work in his behalf.

To the extent that people choose to save rather than consume, the supply of **capital** increases. Capital is savings that has been (or is waiting to be) recycled into investment. Just as with any other good, the price of capital is determined by the amount of its supply relative to demand. The price of capital when it is loaned to a borrower is known as the **interest rate** on a loan. A higher savings rate increases the supply of capital, putting downward pressure on interest rates. That is, the more money that some people save, the cheaper it becomes for other people to borrow.

When savers lend their money, they transfer the power to consume to a borrower, who then spends the money. Broadly speaking, borrowers try to invest the funds on assets that will assist in the production of other goods and services. A bakery may purchase a more efficient oven, or a factory may purchase software which increases its manufacturing efficiency. Spending on vocational training (e.g., medical school tuition) can also be an investment. But whatever the form it takes, investment spending should follow one general rule: increase productivity.

By producing, saving, and channeling savings into productivity-enhancing forms of investment, we increase our capacity to consume in the future. Jean-Baptiste Say described spending on current wants as "unproductive consumption," while investment spending was "reproductive." Inasmuch as savings are reinvested in these reproductive uses, output per worker increases, and the economy grows. An economy's total output is measured by multiplying the average productivity per worker by the number of workers. The total output is usually referred to as the **gross domestic product**, or **GDP.**

Total Economic Output (GDP) =
Output per worker x Number of Workers

Aside from increasing productivity, the only other means of raising an economy's output is to increase the workforce population. As with other items, labor can be imported or manufactured domestically. The former process is known as "immigration," and the latter is known as "childbearing." Forgive the pun, but it is wholly true that childbearing represents the ultimate form of reproductive investment.

While Jean-Baptiste Say is traditionally given credit for first articulating the principle that production must always precede consumption, any good rabbi can tell you that the concept dates from antiquity. Moses recorded it 1,500 years ago in the third chapter of Genesis. After Adam and Eve partake of the forbidden fruit and become aware of their nakedness, God dispenses a series of punishments. First, the tempting serpent is sentenced to crawl upon his belly and eat dust all the days of his life. Second, Eve is cursed with acute labor pains. Lastly, Adam is informed that the ground has just been cursed for his sake.

In that last curse, the salad days of capricious dining from every tree in the Garden of Eden come to an abrupt halt. Henceforth, God declares, "in the sweat of thy face shalt thou eat bread, till thou return unto the ground." Exiled from the Garden, Adam is now consigned "to till the ground from whence he was taken." Until the end of the earth, man and woman must labor for their sustenance. East of Eden, there is no such thing as a free lunch.

So the last thing man learns prior to his expulsion from paradise is the grand, immutable principle of economics: Say's Law. Although God didn't actually state that "production is the basis of consumption," it is clearly the doctrine being imparted. Regrettable though it may be, Adam's condition has been shared by all mankind ever since the Fall: someone has to bake bread before anybody is going to eat a sandwich.

$$\$\$\$\$\$$

When I was previously laid off in 2005, I was given several months to look for new work. Thus, I was able to start a new job at Alpha Managers on a Monday morning after spending the previous Friday at the insurance company. This situation, in contrast, constituted bona fide unemployment. I had a few leads on some good-paying gigs in the bond market but absolutely no desire to pursue any of them. A headhunter contacted me regarding a job in corporate finance, but I had scarcely submitted my resume before the position was filled by another candidate.

After a few days of catching up on leisure reading and running errands, I found myself thoroughly bored and decided to search out the county unemployment office. I couldn't find any government bureau under "Unemployment" in the White or Yellow pages. I turned to the blue government pages and eventually found a listing for the "Employment Security Commission." That struck me as the appropriate euphemism for "where to get your handout," so I gave them a ring.

After ten frustrating minutes of navigating automated telephone menus, I decided to see the Employment Security Commission for myself. A ten-minute drive brought me to the front door of the office where two signs prohibited the possession of knives, firearms, and nunchucks. I entered the foyer half expecting a sepia-toned room full of men wearing trench coats and fedoras queued up for a bowl of soup.

Instead, I saw ten people lined up to speak with a husky woman situated behind a large reception desk. I took my place at the end of the line and glanced around the office. To my left, thirty people sat at tables in an austere lobby. To my right, unemployment claimants met with counselors under hanging placards which read "Placement Services," "Workforce Investment Act," "Veterans Services," and "Career Resource Center." Despite the close proximity, I couldn't hear any of the conversations.

The receptionist handed me a form which I quickly filled out, submitted, and took a seat at a nearby table. The place was eerily quiet, particularly given the large number of claimants in the waiting room. To my surprise, many of them were accompanied by their spouses and small children. Maybe the family had only one car, or perhaps the dependents had simply come to offer moral support for their breadwinner during a stressful time. I wouldn't say that a pall hung over the place, but there was clearly a general feeling of sobriety. No one read or made idle chat; they just sat there.

I desperately wanted to know everyone's story, but I was constrained by the solemnity of the place. The melancholy demeanor of my fellow claimants left me with the distinct impression that any playful banter would not have been appreciated. These people needed this money to feed their families. I, on the other hand, needed it for . . . why did I need it, after all? I had just received two months of severance pay, my wife earned good money as a nurse manager, we had no debt at all, and I could live off my cash savings for many years.

Just as I had begun to contemplate my need for state handouts my name was called. I informed the woman behind the desk that I desired to file an initial unemployment claim, and that I was utterly clueless about the process. She was thoroughly patient and helpful. I was advised that my severance package would disqualify me for unemployment benefits for the next eight weeks. Before my discouragement could fester, she threw me an unexpected lifeline.

"Now there is a way around this regulation," she said. "If you are pursuing continuing education, this requirement is waived and you qualify for immediate benefits."

Continuing education? I was intrigued. My expression must have conveyed my interest, because before I could solicit further information about this convenient loophole, she was already explaining how to exploit it. If I presented proof of enrollment in a class at the local technical college, I could return tomorrow with full eligibility to have my claim paid. Given my previous salary, I would qualify to receive $450 per week. And as fate would have it, Community Tech was located only several hundred yards from the State Employment Commission. I don't know whether it had been situated there by design or sheer coincidence.

I left the office and headed down the road in pursuit of higher learning. I had no idea what sort of curriculum would be required or what the classes would cost. In any case, it didn't seem that I had much to lose by investigating the opportunity.

As I traversed the campus in search of the Continuing Education facility, I remembered a conversation I had with my late grandmother in my middle teenage years. In the most respectful tone I could muster, I posited the immorality of taking state handouts—in her case, Social Security. "I paid into it for decades," she had coolly replied.

Fifteen years later, I stood condemned by my own impudent remark. To make matters worse, the state hadn't even deducted unemployment insurance premiums directly from my paycheck; my employer had paid them on my behalf.

According to the registrar's office, I was mistaken in my assumption that my beeline from the unemployment office to Community Tech was anomalous. As a matter of fact, most of their new enrollees had also been laid off recently; few of them were fortunate enough to receive severance packages. The registrar handed me a class registration form and a course catalogue. On its cover, a man constructed a wooden frame for what appeared to be a large bookcase.

Inside, I discovered a veritable cornucopia of scholastic opportunities. The course offerings ranged from the vocationally-oriented (carpentry, medical coding, real estate appraisal) to the liberal arts (history of western art, applied acoustic guitar), to the recreational (scrapbooking, wine appreciation, salsa dancing).

While a number of the classes looked genuinely interesting, I suspected that only a handful would satisfy the Employment Commission requirements. To my complete shock, I was told that enrolling in any single class offered in the course book would make me eligible for unemployment benefits.

"What about this one?" I pointed to a course description: "Make treasure from trash? In this fun and creative class you will learn to make keepsake treasures using recycled materials. Discover your creative side, have fun, and save a little space in the landfill by reusing cast-off items to make art with a personal touch."

"Now there's no way a 'garbage art' class could possibly be construed as continuing career education," I asserted.

She assured me that as far as the state was concerned, it was totally legitimate. Ten minutes later, I had enrolled in a six-week sewing course. (Yoga had been my first choice, but those classes had quickly filled.)

"You're absolutely sure that this will enable me to receive my unemployment checks?" I asked, still incredulous.

"It counts," the registrar affirmed. "Are you so surprised?"

"You bet I am. In my eight years in finance, I've never seen a real arbitrage before."

$$\$\$\$\$\$$

Arbitrage represents an opportunity to make risk-free profits without any investment. It is the Holy Grail of finance. Arbitrage profits are made by exploiting the pricing differential of identical goods in different markets, without using any of your own capital. It works like this: borrow cash to purchase the good in the market where it is underpriced. Simultaneously, enter into a contract to sell the good in the other market, at which it can be sold at a higher price. In essence: buy low, sell high with no risk of loss.

In the 19th century, the Rothschild family frequently arbitraged the gold market. One family member borrowed gold in London, which was immediately sold for cash. At the same time, another Rothschild agent purchased the same amount of gold at a lower cash price in Paris. The Parisian gold would then be delivered to the family's creditors in London. The family reaped a handsome profit without ever risking any of their own capital. If you perform a Google image search on Rothschild European estates, you can quickly gain an appreciation for the immense profit potential of arbitrage.

Typically, true arbitrage opportunities arise only from knowing something that no one else does. By placing five brothers in different financial centers, the Rothschilds created a unique information network unparalleled in Europe which readily lent itself to the practice.

Currency exchange rates, oil futures contracts, and stocks of merging companies can all be arbitraged. Unfortunately, in the digitized age, genuine arbitrage opportunities are typically very small and quickly exploited by the Wall Street dealer with the brawniest computer. The only way to consistently make large arbitrage profits is by trading stocks on inside information. Insider trading ensures risk-free arbitrage profits but concurrently creates a risky legal situation for the parties involved.

Arbitrage opportunities are the magical leprechauns of finance—you will receive a big pot of gold if you can just find one. Everybody wants to believe in them, and a few people actually do. Unfortunately, arbitrage opportunities, like leprechauns and free lunches, are never seen by anybody sober. Nevertheless, finance professors and hedge fund managers use the word indiscriminately, because using French terms is an easy way to make yourself appear sophisticated to your audience. Technically speaking, arbitrage denotes "no money down, risk-free profits." In contemporary Wall Street parlance, it has come to imply any trade which involves the purchase of one asset with the simultaneous sale of another.

Despite the abuse, I can't blame the Street for casually throwing the word around at client conferences. "IBM's cash bonds are cheap to their five-year credit default swaps; there's clearly an arbitrage opportunity" sounds a lot more dignified than "Hey, a leprechaun just ran down that hole. If you're fast enough, you can still catch him."

In my case, the leprechaun and pot of gold had taken the form of a kindly middle-aged bureaucrat and the North Carolina State Treasury, respectively. The trade would work like this: Buy class time for $59. Sell class time back to the state for $1,800, thereby netting a tidy $1,741 in profit. Execute the trade again next month.

After completing my course registration, I promptly returned to the State Employment Commission offices. As I strode through the door, I was intercepted by a hefty bureaucrat in sweat-stained trousers.

"Can I help you?" he asked gruffly.

"I'd like to officially apply for unemployment benefits," I said.

"It's too late for that today," he snapped. "This office closes at 5 P.M. sharp." He cast a derisive glance at my course registration form as if to indicate that he knew that I had just spent the past hour gaming the state welfare system.

"It's 4:15," I said casually. As far as I was concerned, if the state wanted to compensate me for reinventing myself as a seamstress, I wasn't going to refuse.

"We quit taking applications an hour before closing time. If you really want a check, be here at 8:30 A.M. tomorrow," he said disdainfully.

$$$$$

I returned for my orientation session the following morning. After a half-hour wait, I was ushered into a back room and seated around a conference table along with ten other claimants. We were shortly joined by an administrator who briefed us on the nuances of the claims-filing process. As she started to speak, I noticed a framed poster of FDR signing the Unemployment Insurance (UI) Act. "1935–1995: UI is 60!" it declared.

The administrator explained that Employment Security Law required all claimants to actively seek work before they can draw unemployment benefits. For each week of benefits claimed, we had to file a weekly certification verifying face-to-face contacts with two different prospective employers. If these criteria were met, the state would deposit money on a bank card the following Monday morning. As far as I could tell, my account would still be credited even if I didn't actually intend to accept the job offer.

If we did gain part-time employment, we were permitted to work up to 23 hours a week so long as our wages did not exceed our earnings allowance. Most importantly, we had to maintain meticulous records of our work search claims for the next five years or the IRS would have a field day should our tax returns ever be audited. After enumerating all of the procedures and caveats, she proceeded to with an illustration. "Now, let's say you apply at McDonald's . . ."

As she went on to explain the nuances of unemployment insurance, my thoughts drifted away from the lecture. Her hypothetical scenario had completely sidetracked me. I tried to imagine myself filling out a McDonald's application. It seemed so cliché. Then again, I didn't have any better ideas. So that's what I did. I applied to work at McDonald's.

Nothing on the McDonald's menu is gourmet cuisine, but I've always loved it, anyway. Economists, on the other hand, might describe the fare as an **inferior good**, meaning that the public generally consumes more of it during periods of macroeconomic distress. And so it was in the last quarter of 2008. American Express Co. reported a 79% drop in quarterly net income, citing higher loan loss provisions and a 10% decline in customer spending. In contrast, Mickey D's reported an 11% increase in its fourth quarter operating income, driven by a five percent increase in same-store sales (a key performance metric for retail establishments). It's too bad for AmEx that Ronald only accepts Mastercard and Visa.

Despite the occasional litigation over excessively hot coffee, I can never recall McDonald's integrity being seriously called into question. The main knock on the company is that its menu will inexorably, albeit slowly, kill you. The health risks were brought to the attention of the general public by Morgan Spurlock in a 2004 documentary entitled *Super Size Me*. Spurlock, as director-cum-protagonist, physically demonstrates the perils of eating all of his meals at McDonald's for thirty consecutive days. To no one's surprise, he gains 24 pounds and utterly comprises his circulatory system in the process. The backlash generated by the film precipitated a prompt discontinuation of the Super Size option, wherein a customer could dramatically increase the size of his soda and fries in his combo meal for a mere 39 cents. A great victory against excessive American consumerism had been won.

It's too bad Spurlock didn't make a documentary about the perils of the consumption of McMansions by overextended homeowners. I will forever maintain that paying 99 cents for a double cheeseburger (that's only two-tenths of a cent per calorie) represents a much better deal than paying $500,000 for a 4,000 square-foot house (that's $125 per square foot). Consuming too much of the former may result in cardiac arrest, but excessive consumption of McMansions may result in a nationwide financial crisis.

As I was out running errands, I happened upon the McDonald's outlet where I had dined, at least bi-weekly, for two-and-a-half years before my company relocated its office. It wasn't the healthiest diet, but then again, a three-dollar lunch tab was hard to beat—as was the two-minute stroll across the meadow which separated my office building from the restaurant. A lake was accented by a fountain, an omnipresent gaggle of geese, and an occasional turtle or jumping fish. Inasmuch as 21st-century corporate America can be, it was positively bucolic. Notwithstanding the occasional misstep into a goose dropping, I found the brief amble to be quite relaxing.

I hadn't dined at this particular franchise since our office had moved seven months ago, and I was excited to reacquaint myself with an old haunt. I still recognized most of the faces behind the counter. I presented myself at the register with the same element of swagger that a sailor displays to a dockside paramour after returning from a long deployment at sea.

After receiving my food and exchanging pleasantries with a Latino attendant who had recognized me, I asked for an application.

"Que?"

"Could I get an application please? For employment."

She paused. "What?" I had spoken clearly, but she was obviously puzzled.

I didn't know much Spanish, but figured it was worth a shot.

"Uh, *uno applicacion, por favor?*"

"For . . . you?"

"Yes."

Startled, she turned to look behind her before quickly resuming eye contact. "Just a minute, please." She retreated to the back of the restaurant and quickly convened a powwow with three other employees. After two minutes of talking and casting furtive glances in my direction, the woman returned with a two-page job application and the contact information for the local franchisee.

I called the store owner the next day. An amicable woman, Jane and her husband Max had been McDonald's franchisees for twenty-two years and currently owned seven restaurants in the area. Prior to being bitten by the entrepreneurial bug, they had both been public school teachers. Over the course of our conversation, I realized that Jane and Max were undoubtedly in a more favorable financial position than most of the principals at the firm that I had just been dismissed from. I had nearly forgotten you could get rich without ever once trading a mortgage bond.

She inquired about my background. I gave her a brief synopsis, concluding that I was tired of the capital markets and was now contemplating doing something else with my life—maybe even becoming a McDonald's franchisee. I needed to find out if I had the chops for real work before forever consigning my career fate to the movements of numbers on a computer screen.

Jane laid it on the line for me. You could certainly do well owning a McDonald's store, but it was clearly a lot of work. As in, sixteen-hour days, seven days a week—and a lot of personnel-related headaches. Yes, the current recession would mean good times for Mickey D's for the foreseeable future, but Ronald had no panacea from the vicissitudes of commerce. In addition to negative publicity from the *Super Size Me* muckraking, Jane had seen a fair amount of hard times during her tenure. She asked me what, if anything, I knew about the restaurant business.

I had to confess that I had never worked in foodservice per se, but I tried to preemptively squelch Jane's concerns about my inadequacies by feeding her some line about my having briefly worked in the "food logistics industry." Translation: I spent the summer after my junior year of high school in my father's warehouse salvaging forklift-damaged pallets of yellow mustard, onion rings, and other foodstuffs.

"Oh, I see," she said, her voice intonation conveying unveiled skepticism. Ultimately, Jane referred me to the store supervisor, to whom she had delegated all hiring decisions.

I spoke with him the next day. "We're always looking for people," he said. Encouraged by the demand for my services, I filled out my application with great alacrity and dropped it (and an updated resume) off at the restaurant the following night. I didn't hear anything over the weekend, so I left the manager a voicemail on Monday evening. I kept myself pretty occupied the rest of the week running long-overdue errands. By Friday, it finally dawned on me that I hadn't heard back yet from the store manager. I took the neglect rather personally.

Later that night, I found myself watching a YouTube video of a presidential town hall meeting in Florida. President Obama fields the last question from a second-semester college student, who dreams of a post-collegiate career in broadcasting. Julio has been laboring at his local McDonald's for the past four-and-a-half years and laments his inability to find another gig. What will the president do for him?

That lucky jerk, I thought. I had five more years of formal education than Julio but couldn't even land a face-to-face interview with his current employer. You would think that cleaning broken cases of Hellman's mayonnaise from a warehouse floor would leave me qualified to do *something* in this economy. Private high school, college, and the Chartered Financial Analyst curriculum evidently hadn't. And neither had MBA school.

I turned from the computer to glance at my MBA diploma. On one hand, I was grateful to have completed the program before the school implemented a $15,000 tuition hike. On the other hand, when the advanced degree on your resume doesn't even get McDonald's to return your phone calls, you have to wonder if a full refund isn't in order. If, however, I did land a fast food gig, I desperately wanted to arrange a little field trip for the introductory finance class.

I had a delectable vision of thirty graduate students crowding into a McDonald's, where I was diligently scrubbing the grill. The professor would say something like this: "Here is an alumnus of the same MBA program that you are currently enrolled in. He currently earns $6.50 an hour, works a fifty-hour week, and 50 weeks out of the year. Assume he pays no taxes. Now assume that upon graduation, you get the same job that he has. Given the $70,000 you pay for your degree, what is the payback period on your investment?"

I finally heard back from the store manager a full week after I had submitted my resume, which had apparently been misplaced by one of the night shift crew members. He asked me to complete an online version at the McDonald's website and assured me that he would be in touch within 48 hours. After our conversation, I returned to the Employment Security Commission to submit my final leg of paperwork before my benefits commenced. I never turned it in.

After a one-on-one meeting with a benefits counselor, I bumped into an office manager who introduced himself as the employment supervisor for veterans' benefits. He graciously agreed to answer a few of my questions about state employment conditions, ushering me into an office where a wall plaque attested to his prior service in the Marine Corps.

He informed me that the North Carolina Employment Security Commission's coffers had been depleted by the unanticipated surge in unemployment claims. It was so bad, he said, that the state would soon be forced to turn to Washington for additional funds. I solicited his economic prognosis for the state. The economy had to get better soon, he reasoned. When I pressed him to justify his sanguine outlook, he could only offer that the alternative was too unpleasant to seriously consider.

As the supervisor continued to outline his agency's budgetary woes, I could feel the enthusiasm for my arbitrage opportunity begin to wane. I thought back to the faces of the people in the lobby. They needed the money to pay rent and feed their kids. In contrast, I had recently paid off my mortgage and had no dependents. My wife still had a good job as a nurse. Granted, the past two years of my job had proved extremely taxing, and I did feel somewhat entitled to a break from the mayhem. But unemployment insurance had been established during the depths of the Depression in order to help needy families get by. The original intent had never been to furnish a paid vacation for people of means.

Worse, I couldn't help but feel a growing sense of culpability for my role in the economic downturn. There was no way to spend the state's money without feeling guilty for having accepted it in the first place. Before the supervisor concluded our meeting, I had already decided that I'd accept the McDonald's job. Assuming, of course, that they'd offer it.

$$$$$

Perhaps it's impossible to find a perfect metaphor for the economy, but I prefer to think of it in anatomical terms. In the human body, millions of cells constitute tissues. Organs, in turn, are comprised of various tissues. Each organ contributes a unique product to the rest of the body. The liver and kidneys produce hormones, the pancreas generates insulin, and so forth. The output of each organ is introduced into the blood stream, which then transmits the output to the other organs. By distributing each organ's production to the other organs, blood plays a crucial role in the body's production processes. Blood, *while producing nothing itself*, provides the means by which the various components of the body can interface. In the absence of blood, the lungs and pancreas would have to directly touch in order to exchange oxygen for insulin.

Whereas organs are comprised of tissues made from cells, industries are made up of companies, each of them consisting of numerous workers. Each industry produces a unique set of goods required by other parts of the economy. The "Real Economic Output" is the sum of the production of each of the cells, or workers. Each industry's output is distributed through the "bloodstream" of money flow. That is, money is simply the mechanism of introducing each worker's production into the body of commerce. An economy's "Money Supply" is analogous to the amount of blood in the body.

In economic terms, money is exactly like the circulatory system. It creates nothing by itself but is the indispensible conduit by which each worker's output is ultimately transmitted to other workers. In the absence of a monetary system, each worker would have to barter with another worker in order to exchange his output. It would be horribly inefficient.

Blood pressure is an important means of assessing the health of the blood flow. Many factors can affect blood pressure, but for purposes of illustration, consider just two: blood volume and heart rate. All else equal, a larger amount of blood in the body places greater stress on the arteries, causing blood pressure to increase. (Conversely, loss of blood will trigger a decline in blood pressure.)

When the body exerts itself through cardiovascular exercise, the lungs and other organs increase their production. The heart rate rises as the body circulates a fixed amount of blood at a faster pace in order to distribute the higher level of output. The blood courses through the arteries at a faster rate, causing arterial stress. The result: higher blood pressure. After the athlete finishes her workout, organ production slows and the blood pressure declines.

Just as blood pressure rises when blood is added to the body or the heart rate increases, the "Price Level" of the economy's goods and services will rise as money is added to the economy or each dollar circulates at an increased rate. A rise in the Price Level is known as **price inflation**. A decline in the Price Level is known as

price deflation. The rate at which a dollar circulates through the economic bloodstream is referred to as monetary "Velocity."

The relationship between an economy's output, money supply, price level, and velocity is captured by the **Equation of Exchange**:

Money Supply x Velocity = Price Level x Real Economic Output

The Equation of exchange is generally abbreviated as: MV = PY

Let's consider a few illustrations of the interplay between these four factors.

As a child matures, his organs grow as the body produces more tissue. Accordingly, the body will generate a larger quantity of blood to service the greater flow of output from each organ. If the body failed to increase the amount of blood in circulation, the adolescent would display low blood pressure. Likewise, if an economy's output grows without a comparable increase in the money supply, the Price Level will fall—i.e., deflation will result. (MV = P▾ Y▴)

Deflation means that a dollar now purchases more goods and services than it used to. This is a great condition if somebody owes you money. The dollars that you will receive from your debtor will now buy more things than they did when you originally made the loan. Of course, deflation is not so much fun if you owe money. You can think of deflation as a *tax on borrowers*.

In the late 19th century, the United States experienced deflation for this very reason: the U.S. economy grew at a faster rate than its money supply. Deflation was the major political question in the 1896 presidential election, because falling prices raised the real debt burden on Midwestern farmers who were making mortgage payments on their property.

The farmers turned to the Democratic nominee, William Jennings Bryan, who promised to create some inflation to help them repay their debts. Bryan lost the 1896 race. He lost again four years later, and again in 1908. However, it's not fair to label Bryan as a born loser, as he achieved a measure of success in 1900 with the publication of L. Frank Baum's *The Wizard of Oz*. (He served as the inspiration for the Cowardly Lion.)

Now imagine the maturing child's body's blood supply rises at a faster rate than his organs are growing. He will have more blood servicing a smaller number of organs; the excess fluid will generate a higher blood pressure. Similarly, an economy whose money supply rises at a faster rate than its real output will experience a higher price level. The result: inflation. Inflation means that the dollar's purchasing power has declined because it takes more dollars to purchase the same amount of goods. ($M \blacktriangle \ V = P \blacktriangle \ Y$)

Inflation is a borrower's best friend, because it's easier to repay a loan if there's more money floating around. On the other hand, inflation really stinks if you are a lender, because your debt will be repaid in devalued dollars. You can think of inflation as a *tax on savers.*

While 19th-century America experienced frequent deflationary episodes, inflation has been the predominant condition during the 20th century. The most memorable episode occurred during the mid- to late-1970s. The United States government had accumulated a large amount of debt in order to fund a bevy of government welfare programs and a war in Vietnam. Rather than overtly raising tax rates on its citizens, the Federal Reserve simply printed more money, which it then used to purchase the government debt.

Because the increase in the money supply outpaced the rate of economic output, each dollar purchased fewer goods. Between 1973 and 1980, the dollar lost 55% of its purchasing power. Anyone who had been saving cash for a rainy day—or even a haircut—was decimated. The tragic result was an entire nation groomed like Lhasa Apsos.

If inflation increases too quickly, businesses and laborers will no longer accept "money" in exchange for their production as its value becomes increasingly dubious. Alternatively, if deflation occurs too rapidly, people will hoard their cash instead of spending or investing it. Many economists used to suggest that the inflation/ deflation problem should be approached by setting an inflation target and then printing the amount of money required to generate that rate given the anticipated level of economic growth. If only it were that simple.

In the first place, economic growth is difficult to project because you don't know beforehand exactly how much workforce population and productivity growth will occur over a given time period. Even if economists could predict economic growth with absolute certainty, there's another issue: *all of the components of the exchange equation interact with one other, so the problem is fundamentally unsolvable.* The big wild card in the system is the velocity of money—how many times (on average) that a dollar moves through the marketplace over the course of a year.

The primary driver of monetary velocity is **cash preference**. Cash preference, also known as "liquidity preference," indicates the desire of consumers and businesses to hold cash, rather than spend or invest it. As people cling to more of their money, its velocity falls as the cash moves through the economy at a slower pace. On the other hand, if the cash preference declines, then money will circulate at a faster velocity.

When people anticipate that inflation will rise because the government is increasing the money supply faster than the economy is growing, they are more inclined to spend their dollars rather than hoard them. If a computer is going to cost more in six months, you are more likely to purchase it now because you expect that your money's purchasing power will deteriorate in the interim. The fear of rising prices encourages you to spend your dollars today because they will be worth less in the future. In other words, your cash preference is low.

As consumers or companies reduce the amount of time that they hold money before they spend it, the velocity of money increases. Money is now changing hands at a faster rate; the higher velocity enables inflation to become a [partially] self-fulfilling prophecy. That is, the very expectation of inflation can result in higher prices. (M V▲ = P▲ Y)

While inflation expectations tend to lower cash preferences, expectations for a slower economy produce the opposite effect. If your job security becomes increasingly uncertain, you will think twice before parting with any cash. Consequently, the velocity of money slows during recessions, creating modest downward pressure on consumer prices. $(M \ V \blacktriangledown = P \blacktriangledown \ Y)$

Every few decades, economists forget how the interplay between production, money, and inflation actually works. I'm not sure why, but they seem to have an insatiable need to develop these alternative explanations rather than to embrace the one that readily accounts for centuries of economic phenomena. Fortunately, medical doctors are not so anxious to reinvent the wheel when it comes to physiology. I can't imagine suffering from chronic pain and seeking advice from prominent physicians, only to discover that none of them knows for sure which one of my organs introduces oxygen into my bloodstream.

$$\$\$\$\$\$$$

I tried to put McDonald's out of my head by spending the next two days running errands and catching up on leisure reading. As much as I tried, I was unable to convince myself that eagerly anticipating my next interaction with the manager was fundamentally different than a homely girl waiting next to the phone on the off chance that her crush might call.

Besides quick service restaurants, I had only considered one other alternative career move. I had excelled at making door-to-door sales during college; perhaps I still had a knack for them. Whenever my fraternity was faced with a budget deficit, we turned to selling doughnuts. While most of my frat brothers considered the endeavor a terrible chore, I relished hawking glazed Krispy Kremes in female dormitories.

Watching a calorie-obsessed fitness freak gradually acquiesce to my repeated entreaties was particularly gratifying. "Just look— no, smell—these warm doughnuts," I'd say, provocatively waving the open box in front of the poor coed. As her resolution began to dissolve, I laid my trump card: "Why, you've practically *earned* them with all that time you just spent on the treadmill. Please don't deny yourself the pleasure. We both *know* you want them."

While I did more than my share of helping to replenish the fraternity coffers, money was the least gratifying element of the job. The best part was envisioning a customer's inevitable remorse after singlehandedly devouring the full dozen, despite having promised herself that she would save half of the box for her girlfriends. No wonder the devil approaches his job with such alacrity.

Friends told me that I had aged pretty well in the eight years since I had been out of college. Nonetheless, I had serious qualms about resuming campus doughnut sales. An eighteen-year-old freshman who opens her door to discover a thirty-something man holding a large plastic bag (which she doubts is full of doughnuts) would probably shoot him with pepper spray before he could even make his sales pitch.

If I couldn't hack it in door-to-door sales, perhaps there was another viable alternative. Earlier in the day, I had driven past an adult novelty retailer that had opened just a few weeks ago. A window sign indicated that they were still in a hiring phase. I'm ashamed to admit how seriously I actually considered applying. Ultimately, I was dissuaded by a window display featuring a leather-clad mannequin clutching a riding crop. It was too reminiscent of the bond market.

Before my ruminations could lead me any further into a morass of self-pity, I had an epiphany. When thrown back into the dating pool, the natural response is to immediately turn to the most familiar names in one's black book. This is a mistake. The best bet for a solid romantic adventure is to look up an ex-girlfriend that you haven't thought about in years. No passion reignites so quickly and passionately as the one that got away.

Surely the same principle applies to dining establishments, I reasoned. McDonald's had sufficed as lunchtime fare during my corporate years, but only because I had forgotten how sublime dining out could really be. As I reflected on my fond memories with an old college flame, I knew exactly what had to be done.

I would reintroduce myself to my long lost true love: the Waffle House.

$$\$\$\$\$\$$

The storied history of the Waffle House deserves to be told by a Herodotus, Livy, or Flavius Josephus. In their absence, I'll try to do it justice.

In 1955 (the same year that McDonald's opened its first franchise store), Joe Rogers, Sr. and Tom Forkner opened the first Waffle House in Avondale Estates, GA, an Atlanta suburb.

Rogers wanted to create a "good food, fast" dine-in experience. Unlike McDonald's, all Waffle House food would be cooked fresh, made-to-order, and delivered to the table by a friendly waiter.

Despite the increased demands of order customization, Joe was determined to rival the meal preparation time of drive-in restaurants. Rogers was also insistent that Waffle House stores operate around the clock and remain open every day of the year. Furthermore, customers could order anything from the sixteen-item menu at any time of day. For anyone who wanted them, cheeseburgers were served at 5 A.M. and waffles would come out of the iron at midnight.

Rogers's formula worked beautifully. By 1960, there were four Waffle Houses in metro Atlanta. Shortly thereafter, the company began to franchise its stores and established 27 restaurants by the late 1960s. Today, Waffle House boasts 1,600 locations across 25 states. While its stores are still primarily concentrated in the Southeast, Waffle House has locations as far north as Pennsylvania and as far west as Phoenix. Metro Atlanta now has over 200. The chain is so popular in Georgia that major intersections frequently have two stores situated on opposite sides of the same street.

The brick exterior of the Waffle House is accentuated at the top by a bright yellow façade which bears the restaurant's name in black lettering. Many locations have double-length parking spots to accommodate truck trailers and recreational vehicles. No store has a drive-through window, although servers will gladly prepare take-out meals for a ten percent surcharge.

Inside, one wall is lined with four booths, each of which can accommodate four patrons. The four-and-a-half-foot "high bar" offers barstool seating for six customers directly in front of the grill. Eight chairs line the adjacent "low bar," whose top is three feet from the floor. Another row of three booths connects the high bar with the wall opposite the first row of booths, making a grand total of 42 seats. The interior walls are decorated with pictures of menu items. A photograph of a steak attests that that Waffle House is the world's leading seller of T-bones (over 10,000 a day), no mean feat for a restaurant chain primarily renowned for its breakfast fare. Another proclaims that the company has served over 450 million waffles since 1955.

Besides its eponymous feature menu item, Waffle House is renowned for its "world famous hashbrowns." The hashbrown potatoes may be cooked "in the ring," i.e., inside a circular steel cookie cutter roughly four inches in diameter. Alternatively, they are "scattered" on the grill without the constraint of the ring.

The scattered hashbrown experience is typically augmented with a variety of toppings. The plate can be: SMOTHERED with onions, COVERED with cheese, DICED with tomatoes, CHUNKED with ham cubes, PEPPERED with jalapenos, CAPPED with mushrooms, and/or TOPPED with Bert's famous chili. (Bert was a Waffle House employee that won a chili cookoff in 1983. The company appropriated his recipe shortly thereafter.) The company claims that variously combining these additives creates 1,230,458 ways to prepare hashbrowns. As I haven't done any permutation math since high school, I'll have to trust them on this one.

The most common add-ons are onions and cheese—that's "scattered, smothered, and covered" in Waffle House vernacular. More intrepid diners (including your narrator) order their hashbrowns "all the way," meaning that all seven additives are concurrently piled on the plate. In addition to being incredibly delicious, nutritionists should note that this meal represents all four food groups, a fact I used to justify my indulgence in a double plate at the beginning of every shift for two months.

Outside of placing its trademark yellow icon on interstate exit signs, Waffle House doesn't employ official advertising campaigns. It doesn't need to. Its cult-like following has spread by word of mouth. Many devoted customers have even held their wedding ceremonies at their regular store. In lieu of tossing rice, the custom is to throw grits at the newlyweds. Etiquette dictates that the grits are not cooked beforehand.

Waffle House reciprocates the customer love. The company's website and calendars feature regular customers who have dined at Waffle House stores every day for decades. "Regular" patrons who dine there every day of the week receive a 10% discount; some stores even extended the discount to "weekday regulars" that neglected to visit on Saturday or Sunday. (I hold that to be a particularly magnanimous gesture.)

The company also maintains a 24-hour Customer Call Line at 1–877–9–WAFFLE. If you ever have a dire need to unravel the enigma of a "waffle sandwich" at 3 A.M. on a Tuesday, you can speak to a live operator who will happily field your question. (I did this, myself, recently. It turns out that it's an otherwise-standard ham and cheese sandwich which is grilled inside a waffle iron.) If you are dying for more Waffle House lore, you can tour the company museum at the original restaurant location in Avondale Estates. It is primarily used for internal corporate events but public tours are available by appointment.

Guided campus tours given to high school seniors offer no real clue as to how or where the enduring memories of the college experience will be produced. Eight years after my graduation, I can't think of any particularly memorable incidents at the gymnasium, student union building, assembly hall, or classrooms. Categorically, the only anecdotes worth relating all happened late at night.

As all bona fide Southerners know, there is no better way to conclude a night of carousing than to pile six friends into a car at 2 A.M. and head to the local Waffle House for a plate of hashbrowns. In such a setting, the banter inevitably proves three times as entertaining as a typical dinner conversation at the university cafeteria. In the first place, at least two people in your party are still likely to be inebriated, and therefore amenable to tomfoolery. More importantly, your server is accustomed to waiting on imbeciles like you and your friends, meaning that the ramifications of any obnoxious behavior are relatively limited. (One notable exception: while he typically enjoyed a lively repartee with Waffle House waitresses, my brother was nearly expelled from a Winston-Salem store for turning a pecan waffle into a fashion accessory.)

Infatuated by such reminiscences of my glory days, I hopped in my car and made a ten-minute drive down the road. As are most Waffle House outlets, the restaurant was situated just a few yards from the interstate exit. I had driven past the diner on many occasions since moving to town three years ago but had never ventured inside. In fact, I hadn't eaten at any Waffle House location in several years.

I parked my car and entered the restaurant. A waitress and a cook attended to a handful of patrons, who were scattered across the counter seats and booths. I asked the waitress, Mary, for a word with the manager. She informed me that the best time to catch him was the following day at 2.30 P.M. I asked if she knew about any available jobs.

"The Waffle House is always hiring," she said.

"What do you mean, 'always'?"

"I mean the managers are constantly looking for more folks. Cooks, servers, whatever."

Call Barack Obama. I had just solved the nation's rising unemployment problem.

"Really? In that case, I'd like an application."

"Sure, let me get one for you." She reached under the counter and produced a pale green piece of paper not much bigger than a 3 x 5 index card. I accepted it and quickly scanned it over.

"There's no writing on the back side of this," I observed.

"Yeah. Is that a problem?"

"No. I just thought it would be a little longer."

She assured me I was holding all of the requisite paperwork.

I surveyed the restaurant again, trying to get a better feel for the establishment.

"Are you hiring at this store or are your available positions only at other locations?"

"We're looking for people at all of our area stores."

"Really? How many are there around here?"

"There's three alone inside the city limits." I turned to see a grizzled man holding a cigarette with two inches of ash reclined in the corner booth.

"Oh," I said. "I thought there was just the one."

He shook his head in a gentle, reproving nod. He leaned forward and drew on his cigarette.

"You see, you got Waffle Houses all around the capitol area." He then proceeded to list the city and street of each outlet within a 60-mile radius—twelve in all. I had to admit, I was pretty impressed. I didn't even bother to memorize my wife's social security number. He was certainly a devoted customer. Or else . . .

"You don't work for Zagat, do you?" I inquired.

"No, I work for Roadway Trucking. Why?"

"Just wondering."

I thanked the waitress for her time, nodded respectfully to the Connoisseur, and exited the restaurant. I returned home, laid the application on my kitchen counter, and took another look. It *was* decidedly succinct. Under "education," all I had to do was circle a number indicating years of schooling. Oddly, the last number was "14." I wasn't quite sure what that meant. Did it connote completion of two years of post-secondary education, or did circling indicate repeating the second and fifth grades? In any event, there were no pesky boxes in which the applicant would have to report completion of an MBA program. I circled "12" and moved on.

Like the McDonald's form, I was asked to report any recent criminal convictions. Unlike the McDonald's application, however, there were no specific inquiries about sex offenses. Did Waffle House have greater respect for employee privacy than McDonald's, or did sex crimes simply not raise their ire? I decided it best not to dwell on the question too long.

I returned at the appointed time the following day. The manager was not in, although the assistant manager, a forty-something woman named Debbie, agreed to meet with me. After a brief review of my application, she invited me to join her in the corner booth where the Connoisseur had been seated the previous day.

"So you're looking for work, huh?"

"I am."

"You ever work in a restaurant before?"

"No." I confessed, trying to keep a confident demeanor. I braced myself for a thorough scrutinizing.

"What were you doing at your last job?" She paused, eyeing me. "You have had a job before, right?"

"You know that international banking crisis that's been in the news lately?"

"Yeah."

"Well, it's kind of my fault. I mean, not the whole thing, but I was one of the people involved."

"Oh?" Her eyes widened. "What were you doing?"

"You know those bad mortgages?" She nodded. "My firm bought a bunch of them for banks. And for pension funds. And for mutual funds. And for some other people. And now I'd like to do something completely unrelated to mortgage bonds. Or any kind of bond." I lowered my head, hoping that my gesture of contrition might curry some favor.

Debbie looked at me with wonderfully sympathetic eyes. "You're one of those millions of people that just lost their job recently, aren't you?" I nodded solemnly.

"Well, you can start at 8 A.M. Monday. Wear a white shirt, black pants, and black shoes. The shift runs until 2 P.M."

I was ecstatic. My confession had surely softened her heart and swept away any doubts she may have been harboring. On the other hand, maybe the Waffle House would hire anybody. Debbie explained that I would be in a training program for the next few weeks and cautioned me against being complacent in the face of a steep learning curve. (That's not exactly how she put it, but you get the idea.) I reassured her that the restaurant would receive my full intellectual commitment. I figured if I paid any attention to what I was doing, I couldn't do any more damage to restaurant patrons than I had done to institutional investors. As long as I wasn't going to cook and there wasn't a bond in sight, what could possibly go wrong?

After administering a few more instructions, Debbie let me go. I waved goodbye to my new colleagues and returned to my car with a spring in my step. On the way out, I stopped to examine the music catalog of a juke box situated near the store entrance. I had forgotten that every Waffle House has one. How cool was that? For all its supposed sophistication, the bond market didn't even have a juke box. I spent the drive home daydreaming about squandering my tips on Randy Travis songs. I didn't even particularly care for country music, but the idea was liberating nonetheless.

While trying to remember how many tunes I could purchase for a dollar, I realized that I had neglected to ask Debbie a very important question. Though the application had said something about "above average wages," I had no idea what I was going to be paid, or how much I could expect to earn in tips. Then it dawned on me—I didn't care about the money. What really mattered was that I had officially put the bond market behind me and had begun a new chapter in my life.

Chapter 2

SCATTERED, SMOTHERED, AND CLUELESS

"When the going gets weird, the weird turn pro."
—Hunter S. Thompson

My family members were universally supportive of my sabbatical from the capital markets. "Finally, you're doing something I actually understand and can wholeheartedly endorse," my father crowed. I had expected as much from him. This was a man who agreed to accompany my mother on her frequent 400-mile treks to visit me at college on the sole condition that he could patronize the Waffle House. (At the time, the company had no stores in my home state of Pennsylvania.)

"I think it's terrific," my mother said. "You're going to find out what the real world is really like."

My brother found the situation deliciously ironic. "You'll be waiting tables on a lot of college-aged jerks. You remember how obnoxious we were back then."

"I remember how obnoxious *you* were," I said.

My sister, a usually serious type, broke into uncontrollable laughter. "You have no idea what the heck you're getting into, do you?" she sneered.

"Probably not," I conceded.

"That place is going to kick your butt," she prognosticated. I had to acknowledge that she was probably right.

Despite her jibes, my sister did have one major concern: the Waffle House still had a smoking section in nearly all restaurants whose state laws permitted it.

"Cigarette smoke is really bad for you. You can get heart disease that way," she warned.

"The bond market will kill a man faster than second-hand smoke," I retorted.

One other voice haunted me. Three years ago, the director of the career development office at my graduate school had issued an ominous warning to a roomful of MBA students. "Don't ever take a step backwards in your career," he cautioned. "It can permanently impair it."

At the time, I had received his comments as words of wisdom. Now, they seemed like a fetter restraining me from enlightenment. Every time I moved ahead two steps ahead in my path to the corner office, the rug had been pulled from beneath my feet. I was sick of playing by the rules. Besides, I wasn't taking a step back down the corporate ladder; I was throwing myself down four flights of stairs. It was time to see if fate would respond better to some reverse psychology.

$$\$\$\$\$\$$$

I showed up for my first day wearing the only white polo shirt in my closet and a pair of black cotton pants that I hadn't worn in at least six years. I took a seat at the low bar and completed a packet of paperwork. After I returned it back to Debbie, a man in his late twenties introduced himself as Matthew, the store manager. He invited me to accompany him to the employee break room where I was joined by another new employee. A hefty man in his mid-twenties, Tim had previously worked as a cook at a local country club where he had earned $20 an hour. As a new "grill operator," Tim would be making less than half of his previous wage.

Like Tim and I, Matthew had also fallen on hard times. Prior to Waffle House, he had been a construction supervisor in Florida. The money had been great, although his employer was "crooked as hell" and eventually went under. Matthew was perfectly amicable, though I could tell by his repeated stares at the Jupiter Yacht Club crest on my polo shirt that he was anxious to discover my history.

"And what did you do at your last job?" he inquired.

"Well, you know how most of the homes you built were sold to people that really couldn't afford them?"

"Yeah."

"Well, my last shop gave them the money to do that."

"Oh." He thought for a few seconds, then shot me a broad smile. "Well, I bet it was fun while it lasted, right?"

"Sure was," I said.

Matthew grew increasingly warm towards me after this brief exchange. Evidently, our shared culpability for the economic meltdown had endeared me to him. But instead of reminiscing about "the good old days" and lamenting his current situation, he gave one of the best workplace pep talks I've ever heard in my life. As French author Antoine St. Exupery once admonished, "the best way of building a ship is not to order people to collect wood and assign them tasks, but rather to teach them to long for the endless immensity of the sea." And that's what Matthew did. He painted an alluring portrait of life at Waffle House, a veritable siren song.

"You can make a lot of money here," he began. "And I'm not playing with you boys. I'll be honest, it was hard for me when my last company went under. I didn't know what to expect when I came aboard. But let me tell you something. If you work hard, and you produce, you do have opportunity. I started out just like you guys not that long ago, and now I'm the store manager." He proceeded to relate numerous anecdotes about how the company consistently rewarded its top performers with managerial positions. In many cases, managers even went on to run their own franchises.

Matthew praised the business acumen and dedication of the company's founders. As someone who has heard a lot of canned speeches delivered by corporate managers, the sincerity of his tone was completely unfamiliar to me. He had genuine respect for the men running his company—in particular, CEO Joe Rogers, Jr.

A voracious consumer of his company's products, "Joe Junior" dines at the Waffle House nearly every day of the year. He is renowned for dropping into his stores unannounced, where he spontaneously pours customers' coffee, grills waffles, and washes dishes. Joe requires that all Waffle House senior executives work holidays, including Christmas and New Year's. In his view, the demands placed on rank-and-file employees should not exceed those placed on upper management.

I was wholly unprepared for this sort of praise of executive management. In the corporate world, nobody talks about senior company officers in such a flattering manner—unless, of course, they're present. As Matthew continued extolling the virtues of the top man, I got the distinct impression that Joe Junior would have to immediately resign should Waffle House ever list on the New York Stock Exchange. In my experience, a man with that much humility could never thrive in a corporate boardroom.

The only coffee-pouring anecdote about a CEO that I ever heard had been markedly less flattering. Rising from his chair in the middle of a conference meeting, the president of an insurance company beckoned his secretary from her desk down the hall. When she arrived at the conference room, he directed her to prepare his coffee, notwithstanding that the service cart had been situated directly behind him all along. In the time required by this superfluous act of her fealty, the CEO could have simply poured his own cup and consumed half of it.

After wrapping up the grand corporate vision of Waffle House, Inc., Matthew concluded his speech where he started it: with an appeal to greed. If we were motivated, he claimed, we would soon be living high off the hog like Debbie. Yesterday, she had raked in a hundred dollars worth of tips during an eight-hour shift. After including her $2.13 hourly wage, her average earnings were better than fifteen bucks an hour. Furthermore, because most of her tips were in cash, the IRS would be none the wiser if she elected not to report some of them.

As someone who normally expresses tremendous skepticism at any promotional pitch, I was surprised by how much Matthew's speech won me over. I normally carried less than fifty dollars of cash in my wallet, so the idea of physically holding in excess of a hundred bucks at one time was quite alluring. More importantly, I really liked the idea of being able to give the tax man the slip. It was only after I bothered to do the math on the drive home that it dawned on me. Even if I worked really hard, my income would never amount to more than a fifth of what it had been just a few weeks before.

$$$$$

During our first week on the job, Tim and I divided our time between watching training videos in the back room and shadowing our trainers on the breakfast shift. Despite a generally mirthless demeanor, Debbie proved a patient mentor. I followed her to each table, placing the silverware as customers arrived and fetching drinks after they had placed their orders. Most of the table waiting process was fairly prosaic. The real difficulty, I learned, was in memorizing prices and properly calling in orders to the cooks.

Unlike most contemporary restaurants, Waffle House does not utilize computers to facilitate communication between servers and cooks. Instead, servers stand on a specified floor tile and verbally relay the orders for their table. This is a three-step process. First, all of the meats are aggregated. The server calls "PULL," followed by the requisite number of cheesesteaks, hamburger and sausage patties, bacon strips, and so forth. The grill operator then retrieves the requisite meats from the refrigerator and places them on the grill. Secondly, hashbrowns are ordered with a "DROP" and the appropriate number of servings. Lastly, the server yells "MARK" and indicates the particulars of each dish to the grill operator.

The cook marks the plates using a proprietary system wherein condiment packets represent meat and eggs. Mayonnaise indicates bacon or sausage, depending on its position; ketchup signifies a cheesesteak; a butter cup indicates a T-bone, and so forth. The arrangement of the packets indicates the temperature of the meat and how the eggs are cooked. Any egg or meat plate not marked for hashbrowns is assumed to be receiving grits. Waffles are always called last.

Similar orders must be consolidated as much as possible. For example: three customers order scrambled eggs. One of them would like cheese in his eggs and a bowl of grits, while his two companions prefer hashbrowns in lieu of grits; one of them wants wheat toast. The proper call is: "Mark order scrambled on three. Make one cheese raisin; make two a plate; make one of the plates wheat." The grill operator then calls back the order to the server to verify that he has marked the plates correctly. At no time during the process does the grill operator view the order ticket.

It's really an ingenious system in many respects. It eliminates the need for a computer, while leaving the server in control of the order ticket so that he can tally the meal cost and make any subsequent additions. Unfortunately, the process has a drawback— namely, a large number of idiosyncrasies on the menu. For example, you must always remember a regular order of bacon is comprised of three strips. However, when bacon is being added to a sandwich (e.g., to a cheeseburger) only two strips are required. In that case, the server requests a "half order" of bacon. The BLT sandwich is the exception to the rule, as it receives a full order. Of course, the "bacon lover's" BLT receives five strips—an order and a half. Got all that?

At the end of every shift, each server submits a test, which requires him to write the abbreviation and price of nearly every menu offering. Initially, it's a laborious process because you are constantly referring to a master pricing sheet. But committing this information to memory has tremendous value to a server, who does not want to be forced to consult the pricing sheet during the middle of a busy shift. Even once you master the ordering system (which took me well over a month), it's still difficult to place an accurate order call on nights when you're operating on five hours of sleep.

After the breakfast crowd subsided, Debbie told me to take a seat at the low bar as she retreated to the back room. She returned a minute later with a large black binder under her arm.

"Read this," she said, placing *The Waffle House Way* on the counter. "For the next four weeks of your training program, this is your Bible."

"Is it okay if I pretend it's the Qur'an?" I asked. "The paperwork I filled out yesterday said that Waffle House doesn't discriminate on the basis of religion."

She looked confused. I explained that the Qur'an was the primary text of Islam, a religion whose adherents numbered in the billions. I neglected to mention that a devout Muslim would not assume a vocation that involves serving prodigious amounts of bacon and pork sausage.

"You can call it whatever you want, so long as you read it," she said.

$$\$\$\$\$\$$

I spent the next two hours immersing myself in the 200-page training manual. The first few pages outlined general principles for creating a quality dining experience. The manual alleged that regardless of how well the food was prepared, servers who neglected to bathe on a regular basis might endanger their gratuities. I also learned that delivering a customer's check along with his food provided a subtle hint to pay his bill as soon as he was finished eating. By encouraging faster table turnover with this tactic, Waffle House would garner more revenue, and I would earn more tips.

Beyond explaining rudimentary serving skills, *The Waffle House Way* imparted optimal temperatures for brewing iced tea, grilling hashbrowns, and maintaining the chili pot. The manual committed me to memorizing each of them and concluded each chapter with exercises to test my knowledge. There was even an "honesty pledge" for me to sign. I wondered if anyone, anywhere, in a capital markets job ever had to make such a vow. My brain, for one, cannot conjure a mental image of a Wall Street bond trader making a public commitment to professional integrity without a conspicuous smirk on his face.

Matthew abruptly broke my study session by informing me that the franchise owner would be in later that afternoon to inspect the premises. Accordingly, the grill operator and servers would have to clean the store from top to bottom before his arrival. I was assigned to wash windows.

"I hate to do this to you," Matthew said to me, "but we all need to be looking as hygienic as possible when this guy shows up. So that means you have to wear appropriate headgear during the review. Unfortunately, the visor we ordered for you hasn't arrived yet, so I'm afraid you're going to have to wear this for the time being. Sorry, but it's the only alternative."

He was right to have made the preemptive apology. A wedge-shaped paper cap is the kind of item that you only wear if you lose a bet or you're too senile to be cognizant of your appearance. As a normally very fashion-conscious fellow, I was taken aback by how few reservations I had about donning it. After all, if you're going to swim in a freezing pool, you might as well jump headfirst into the deep end.

No sooner had I emerged from the employee break room sporting my new accoutrement than a regular customer named Bert decided to critique it.

"What're you wearing that funny hat for?" he snickered.

I had to concede that I looked pretty lame. The wedge cap made me look more like a 1950s-era soda jerk than a contemporary Waffle House employee. On the other hand, it wasn't really fair that a man wearing camouflage pajama pants and tan combat boots should call my fashion sense into question.

"Well, Bert," I said, "management told me to 'keep it sexy' when they agreed to hire me, so I'm trying to fulfill that mandate as best I can." I strode to the front door and began washing its panels. After thirty seconds of cleaning, I turned around to find Bert staring blankly at me from the high bar. My remark had obviously disarmed him, and it was clear that he was thinking really hard about what I had just said. Apparently, Bert did not realize that it's impossible to denigrate a man who no longer considers dignity to be any sort of a virtue. I smiled at him and sprayed a few more squirts of cleaning solution onto the glass.

I'm sure that it loses luster for people that have been doing it for thirty years, but for me, washing windows and sweeping floors proved an unexpectedly sanctifying experience. I had spent the previous twenty-four months cleaning up bond market messes via conference calls, lengthy emails, and five-page memoranda. Cleaning up physical messes, rather than financial ones, was a welcome change of pace. On the surface, it may seem less glamorous, but at the end of the day, what difference does it make whether you're cleaning up after a mortgage trader or a trucker? At least the latter would tip you in cash and not bust your chops every time you interacted with him.

Undoubtedly, the best part of my new job was a culinary perquisite. During our shifts, we could eat nearly any menu item that we wanted at no charge. Pork chops, steaks, or chicken would cost us a few dollars, but for everything else, the price was free and quantities were unlimited. All you can eat hashbrowns? That passes for nirvana in most parts of Arkansas.

The only problem with this otherwise unbelievable amenity was the ambiance in which said hashbrowns were consumed. Employees were required to eat in the back room of the restaurant, whose decorations consisted of soda syrup bladders, a rusty CO_2 tank, two industrial sinks, and a wall calendar extolling the loyalty of a twenty-year regular customer. Over the course of twenty years, he had consumed an estimated 6,000 waffles and 15,000 cups of coffee.

Accentuating the Spartan décor was the omnipresent odor of cigarettes. When the room wasn't profuse with the smell of live Newport menthols, it was caked with the smell of stale smoke. After several days of nearly choking to death, I decided to cast the situation in different terms. Instead of considering the carbon monoxide exposure as an express lane to heart disease, I decided to think of it as an amenity. Purchasing two packs of cigarettes would have set me back ten bucks, so I figured that consuming a pack's worth of secondhand smoke probably had a five-dollar retail value. In a week's time, my eyes and lungs had adjusted to the adverse conditions. Given that all of the other employees smoked, asking them not to do so in my presence would have been a major imposition. I only expressed my disdain on one occasion as a pregnant coworker ignited a cigarette in front of me.

"When are you due?" I asked.

"In another four months," she responded.

I cast a scornful glance at her Newport cigarette and watched her follow my eyes as I let them deliberately wander to her protruding belly.

"I'm just trying to get rid of my last carton," she said, blushing. "Honest."

"Of course," I said. "It would be a shame to let good tobacco go to waste."

$$\$\$\$\$\$$$

Despite my occasional misgiving about their smoking habits, I was genuinely enjoying time with my new colleagues. They were very patient with me as they imparted skills like judging whether a pot of coffee was fresh or stale based on its smell. Most of them were quite incredulous at my claim that because I never drank coffee, I didn't even know how to brew a pot. In short order, I earned a reputation as a serious eccentric. Rumors began circulating that I had been through some serious hell in the financial markets which had left me in a state of cognitive disrepair.

Despite my general ineptitude, my only work-related injury during the training period was a minor cut on my index finger. I had been eavesdropping on an economic conversation, causing me temporarily lose my concentration as I diced salad tomatoes. Oddly, listening to middle-aged smokers discuss a precipitous drop in the Baltic Dry Container Index and the declines in their retirement accounts proved much more painful than the laceration.

As expected, the juke box turned out to be a small treat, containing a robust selection of country, pop, and hip hop. If no one placed any coins in it for more than twenty minutes, it began to play spontaneously Waffle House-themed ditties. Some of them were shameless marketing propaganda like, "Why would you eat your grits anyplace else?" Other tunes took a more comedic approach: "Last night I saw Elvis at the Waffle House." (Within weeks, I would come to realize that a cameo appearance by the King would rank fairly low on a list of absurd late-night happenings at Waffle House.)

I was impressed by the broad swath of appeal cut by the juke box's country music tunes. Old and young, male and female, black and white all deposited coins to hear, "She Thinks My Tractor's Sexy" or the Dixie Chicks's "Goodbye, Earl." I would never have expected to witness a young black man dressed in gangbanger attire enthusiastically singing along to "Forever and Ever, Amen."

"I didn't take you for a Randy Travis fan," I said playfully. "Do have him on your iPod?"

"Oh, no, I'm not," he said, blushing. "I never even heard this song before."

I had caught him redhanded. "That's funny, I swore I heard you reciting the lyrics like you were already familiar with them."

"Well," he stammered, "I picked up the tune after a minute or two. I gotta admit it's kinda catchy."

I turned from him and began bussing a table where a woman in her mid-twenties was finishing her meal.

"Thank you, Brother," she said as I removed a plate.

"I'm sorry, I don't recognize you from any family reunions," I responded.

"Oh, I don't think we're biologically related. I call everyone 'Brother' because I'm a communist."

"Really? I thought that 'Comrade' was the preferred term."

"That's true, but I prefer 'Brother' because it expresses the same sentiment with a more familiar term."

"I see. Do you happen to know if the Soviets addressed their political dissidents as 'comrade' after they tossed them in the gulag?"

She smiled. "That wasn't *real* communism. People always mess up when they try to implement good ideas . . . even capitalists," she said with a wink. "People are fundamentally bad. That's why Thomas Hobbes advocated a powerful state—to keep people in line."

"It's certainly true that free markets only work when there is some base level of trust among the participants," I said. "But the power of the state can never coerce people into moral behavior. That's a deeply repugnant notion, even if it was advocated by American presidential advisors like John Kenneth Galbraith."

"Well, how would you make people decent?" she asked.

"I would defer to George Washington. In his farewell presidential address, he asserted that religion and morality are indispensable supports to political prosperity. A republic works best when its citizens are taught correct principles in their families and are then left to govern themselves. When the majority of the people are fundamentally decent, then the only necessary role for government is the protection of property rights."

"Amen, Brother."

I continued. "People forget that Adam Smith, the father of capitalist thought, was a moral philosopher first and an economist second. He believed that the free market was the best mechanism for improving the aggregate well-being of society."

She stared at me for a while before venturing an opinion.

"Jimmy, you're too much of a philosopher to be working at the Waffle House."

"And here I thought I was working at the Waffle House *because* I was a philosopher."

The Communist smiled and advised me that she would return for another meal within a few days.

I had high hopes for her. While the statist doctrines of Hobbes and Marx had caused some minor cognitive impairments, it appeared to be nothing that Adam Smith and a few plates of hashbrowns couldn't remedy.

$$\$\$\$\$\$$$

Adam Smith is generally recognized as the founding father of **Classical economics**. Classical economists believe that individuals should be left free to pursue their own economic self-interests with minimal interference from the state. Prior to Smith's time, economies were typically managed under mercantilist philosophies which held that governments should play a protectionist role by encouraging most exports and discouraging certain imports.

In contrast, Smith held that markets are best left to regulate themselves. This belief is sometimes referred to as laissez-faire, a French expression meaning "let it be." Smith's novel ideas on free enterprise and free international trade were expressed in the seminal *An Inquiry into the Wealth of Nations*, published in 1776. The classic tome on capitalism, *Wealth* revolutionized economic thought and inspired much of Jean-Baptiste Say's *Treatise on Political Economy*.

But while he was the intellectual parent of laissez-faire capitalism, Smith was first and foremost an ethicist. Seventeen years prior to writing *Wealth*, he had penned *The Theory of Moral Sentiments*, a treatise on the nature and motives of morality.

Smith argued that despite man's natural inclination to selfishness, all human beings possess an innate concern for the welfare of others. Morality, he explained, consists of the development of this natural endowment of sympathy. Sympathy encourages people to cultivate good relations with their fellow human beings and provides the basis for social order. (If this philosophy sounds vaguely familiar, it's probably because you heard some version of it expressed in Sunday school. "To love our neighbor as we love ourselves is the great law of Christianity," *Sentiments* asserts.)

The Wealth of Nations served as an economic corollary to the broader philosophical views espoused in *Moral Sentiments*. Its great philosophical contribution is that voluntary economic transactions benefit both buyer and seller. That is, no one will purchase a good or service unless he assigns a value to that good above the price he is paying. Similarly, sellers will not continue to offer their goods unless the sales price exceeds their cost of production. Furthermore, laborers in the employ of the sellers also benefit from wages earned in the production process. Led by an "invisible hand," each of these economic actors pursues his own **self-interest**, concurrently benefiting himself and society as a whole.

Consider a contemporary illustration. The Waffle House offers the "All-Star Special," which is arguably the greatest breakfast value in the continental United States. For just $6.30, diners can enjoy two eggs, toast, and their choice of grits or hashbrowns AND waffle or biscuit and gravy AND two sausage patties or three bacon strips. It's almost too good to be true. The customer parts with his dollars because he values the food more than his cash. For its part, Waffle House offers the meal because its cost of production is below $6.30, so the company turns a profit on the sale. Waiters serve the All-Star because we value the (anticipated) tips resulting from our labor more than we prize our leisure time. Everyone wins: customer, business owner, and laborer. Despite acting in their own self-interests, a universally beneficial outcome is attained. It's pretty amazing when you think about it.

By offering its customers a delicious breakfast at a reasonable price, Waffle House revenues have increased precisely because its stores attract a loyal customer base that relies on the restaurant chain to produce an affordable, quality product. The same condition holds for the servers: on average, increased attentiveness to customer desires yields higher tips. Customers, in turn, will receive better service as they patronize the store more frequently and reward servers with large gratuities.

In the aforementioned example, each participant (Waffle House, waiter, customer) is acting in his own self-interest *by serving other people*. In Smith's view, these sympathetic actions are fully consistent with pursuit of individual self-interest and form the basis of economic interaction. Commerce requires cooperation, which is fundamentally grounded upon sympathy and trust.

In the absence of sympathy and trust, however, the wheels of industry grind to a halt. You will not patronize a restaurant if you are unwilling to entrust the cooks with your food preparation. The restaurant, in turn, is reluctant to serve customers that it believes may walk out without paying. Waffle House will not hire a cook without having faith in his ability to properly prepare a meal. Similarly, the company would be hard up to find willing cooks if prospective employees believed that their payroll checks wouldn't clear.

To Adam Smith, a free market implies "free of excessive government interference." To a **selfish** person, the free market means "free of scruples." While self-interested behavior benefits all parties in a free economy, selfish behavior does not. Selfish behavior is personal aggrandizement *at the expense of other persons.* Unlike self-interested behavior (which benefits all parties—capitalist, laborer, and customer), selfishness is a zero sum game.

In the short term, selfish behavior seems to pay off. A restaurant can temporarily fatten its profit margins by deliberately overcharging its customers, a worker can steal from his employer, and a customer can save a few dollars by neglecting to tip.

But while selfish people may reap short-term economic benefits from their behavior, selfishness has an immediate drawback: it renders one fundamentally incapable of experiencing true joy. Instead, selfish people experience a debased version of happiness derived from the accumulation of whatever good they presently covet. In the long term, of course, selfishness catches up with the offending party. The unscrupulous restaurant will see its business erode, the dishonest employee will eventually be fired, and the stingy customer will receive increasingly mediocre service.

Unfortunately, contemporary society conflates selfishness with self-interest, forgetting that capitalism—as envisioned by Adam Smith—is a fundamentally *moral* economic arrangement. As long as individuals behave in a self-interested (rather than selfish) manner, more economic freedom enables greater levels of happiness and higher standards of living.

In contrast, state-managed economies produce widespread misery and low standards of living for one simple reason: no one has any economic incentive to serve anyone else. As far as I can tell, Russia only produced two worthwhile goods during eighty years of Communist rule: crude oil and Tetris. (Sorry, matryoshka dolls don't count.)

In addition to making reproductive investments in machinery that was productivity enhancing, Smith explained that much of the gain in living standards in a capitalist system arises from the intelligent **division of labor**. As the types of work performed become increasingly specialized across a broad pool of workers, the volume and quality of output both increase.

Smith observed these productivity gains when he visited a pin factory. He estimated that by dividing the manufacturing process across ten specialized laborers, the men were able to produce between 240 and 4,800 more times as many pins than if they had made them independently of each other. It makes you wonder what those guys could have accomplished with a really large grill and a few truckloads of uncooked hashbrowns.

$$\$\$\$\$\$$

A typical Waffle House shift operates with half the number of employees as Adam Smith's pin factory. Labor tasks are divided amongst five employees: two grill operators and three waiters. The former group is responsible for food preparation; the latter, for its distribution. Like most other restaurants, the Waffle House has "side work" assignments for its servers. In addition to our table waiting duties, servers are expected to refill napkin holders, replace empty condiment bottles, sweep floors, bus tables, and so forth. They are also charged with serving as dishwashers and cashiers.

Having no previous retail experience, I had never operated a cash register before. But as far as I could tell, our machine operated differently from the registers which I had encountered as a customer at other restaurants and retail outlets. Normally, the process goes as follows: 1) The clerk rings up each individual item on your tab. 2) He punches a button to calculate the total, which appears on the register screen. 3) You hand the clerk an amount of currency and/or coin equal to or exceeding your total, which he then keys into the register. 4) The amount of change due appears on the register display.

Our register wasn't quite that fancy. For some reason, it only had a step #2, so the onus of calculating the check total and the correct amount of change fell entirely to the register operator. For this reason, most servers used a calculator, which they kept in their apron pockets or on the counter next to the register. Unfortunately, as I discovered during one of my first customer checkouts, they weren't terribly dependable.

No sooner had I started to sum the tab than I realized the keypad had been totally compromised by waffle syrup. The "3" and "7" keys would not return to an upright position after I pushed them; the number "5" key refused to depress altogether, despite my repeated efforts to force it down with a knife butt. I decided to resort to manual addition before my customer's visible impatience increased any further.

I showed up for work the next day proudly brandishing my Hewlett Packard model 12c financial calculator. Since acquiring her eight years ago during my first week on the job as a junior credit analyst, the HP 12c had remained with me throughout my entire bond market career. She had seen me through all three levels of the Chartered Financial Analyst exam, two years of business school, and countless hours of capital market mayhem. In her past life, the HP 12c had been used to calculate capital gains on sales of forty-million-dollar blocks of corporate bonds. Now she was consigned to spending her latter days computing taxes on nine-dollar restaurant tabs.

As a new recruit, I wore a pocketless cook's apron in lieu of the pocketed version worn by tenured servers. Regrettably, the absence of an apron pocket meant that I had to keep my beloved calculator on the cashier's counter. It was the last place I ever saw her.

A few hours after my shift ended, I realized that I had neglected to bring the HP 12c back home with me. No matter, I thought.

No one would want it to take it, anyway. The machine operated via "reverse Polish notation," meaning that the keys had to be punched in an unconventional sequence to perform even basic arithmetic. It had taken me several weeks to master this skill, so I presumed that a casual thief would be deterred by the sheer frustration of trying to operate it. I thought wrong.

Although I realized that any investigation into the calculator's whereabouts would likely prove utterly futile, I decided to ask around anyways. I began my inquiry with Betty, a wonderfully pleasant server in her late forties. Upbeat and gregarious, she always sent departing customers off with the phrase, "Have a blessed day."

It was evident that she really meant it. Even when she was tired, I never heard Betty utter a cross word about anyone. Which isn't to say that the job didn't wear her down on occasion. During her four-year stint, she had quit her job on five different occasions. But despite her repeated public resignations, she always showed up for her next shift, anyway. You have to admire that kind of tenacity.

In recognition of Betty's faithful service as a "five-star waitress," the district manager had presented her with a single star pin, which Betty promptly affixed to her hat. And while the bright red star undoubtedly differentiated her from the other servers, it seemed to proclaim Communist partisanship rather than five-star waitressing.

"Betty, did you happen to see a Hewlett Packard calculator in the store this morning? I can't find it anywhere."

"Oh, you mean that real fancy looking one that you had yesterday? I had never seen a calculator like that before," Betty said.

"Yeah, she was a real beauty," I said morosely. "So you haven't seen anyone using it to run amortization schedules?"

"I can't say that I have, hon. Then again, if I knew what you were talking about, I could give you a definite answer." She paused for a minute, studying my features.

"You don't look like the typical Waffle House guy," she said finally.

"Oh? Why is that?"

"You just don't have the *Waffle House look*."

I had never been so insulted. French aristocrats have dueled with less provocation.

"What's that supposed to mean?" I could feel a grin slowly creeping across my face.

"I didn't mean anything bad by it. You just look more like a scientist to me. Or maybe the vice president of a corporation."

"Betty, we just met. Don't you think it's a little soon to malign my character?"

"I didn't mean nothin' by it. I think scientists are great. But what are you doing here?"

"I'm on work release."

"From jail? A guy like you? I don't believe it."

"From the bond market. It's a lot like jail, but the uniform's less comfortable and we don't get any yard time."

She shook her head. "Whatever you say, honey."

'Honey.' I really liked that. She called everyone "honey," but it still made me feel special.

$$\$\$\$\$\$$

I couldn't be entirely certain why I failed to project the "Waffle House look," but an objective review of my attire offered a few clues. I had substituted a white button-down shirt for the polo shirt I had worn during my first three days on the job, which probably made me look more corporate than I had intended. Following a company policy mandating black shoes, I had worn the same Brooks Brothers cordovan leather pair that had served me for seven years in the bond market. I thought they added a classy touch to the uniform.

Another server had pointed out that that my feet would fare much better with a cheap pair of dark cross-trainers supplemented by Dr. Scholl's inserts. He was right of course, but at the time I was in an extremely frugal mindset. After a few weeks, I came to see the wisdom in his advice. I broke down and bought the cheapest pair of black sneakers I could find.

The impetus for my purchase was not sore feet. Rather, the smooth sole of my dress shoes had crossed paths with a wayward onion ring the night before. Hearing the patrons laugh at me as I picked myself off the floor was all the motivation I needed to shell out a few bucks for an oversized pair of skateboarding shoes. They looked absolutely ridiculous. I consoled myself with the thought that I probably looked better standing erect in a fifteen-dollar pair of skater shoes than lying down on the floor of the Waffle House wearing my eight-hundred-dollar Oxfords.

Wearing my button down shirt didn't prove to be a great idea, either. In short order, it was totally compromised by coffee and chili stains. Coupled with the loss of my financial calculator, I had consecrated about $140 worth of personal items during my first week of work. In that same period of time, I had put in twenty hours at an hourly wage rate of $6.55 (as a trainee, I was ineligible for tips and was therefore paid the minimum wage). After seven days, the privilege of employment at Waffle House had cost me about ten bucks.

After two weeks under Debbie's wing, my training period was over. Matthew presented me with a charcoal gray short-sleeved button-down shirt bearing the company logo on the left sleeve and an American flag on the right. "Wear this with pride," he said, handing me a black visor and a bright yellow nametag bearing the Waffle House logo and a windblown American flag. The bottom half of the tag read: "JIMMY, Salesperson, Team Member Since 2008." It was slightly larger than my old business card, which had read: "James Adams, CFA, Vice President, Product Management Team." How far I had come.

"You're ready for action now," he declared.

"I certainly hope so," I said.

I wondered why my tag stated that I had begun my employment the previous year. As I scrutinized it, I realized that my name hadn't actually been engraved. Matthew had simply printed off a label and taped it over my predecessor's name. It seemed like kind of a bad omen. In any event, I was grateful for the inaccuracy. If customers perceived I had some tenure, maybe I would garner more credibility. I sorely needed every ounce of it that I could muster.

Most restaurants experience most of their volume during two spans of rush hours: an 11 A.M.–1 P.M. lunch rush and a 5 P.M.–9 P.M. dinner rush. By 11 P.M., most of the patrons have headed home and the employees have begun to clean the establishment. The restaurant is typically vacated by midnight and will not reopen its doors for another ten hours. In contrast, Waffle House does most of its sales during a 9 A.M.–12 P.M. breakfast rush and a late-night rush from 11 P.M.–3 A.M. At no time does the store ever close.

Given these unconventional rush hours, the most prudent way to acclimate a tenderfoot server to Waffle House is to start him waiting tables during a "second shift" which runs from 2 P.M.–9 P.M. (First shift runs from 7 A.M.–2 P.M.; third goes from 9 P.M.–7 A.M.) For the next two weeks, Tim and I were assigned to work second shifts along with Mary, the waitress who had given me the application form during my initial visit to the store. I hadn't seen her since then and was anxious to ingratiate myself with the girl who had facilitated my career transition.

I supposed that we didn't have much in common. She was finishing her senior year of high school, which made her too young to consider any of my bond market anecdotes the least bit entertaining. But in my naive optimism, I supposed that I could surmount our age disparity and her mercurial disposition by applying some timeless Dale Carnegie principles. In *How to Win Friends and Influence People*, the author posits that the fastest way to make others warm to you is to encourage them to talk about themselves as you make a sincere effort to learn about their interests.

"Read any good books lately?" I thought it a safe opener.

"I *hate* to read."

"Really? 'Hate' is a strong word."

"I prefer movies. The only book I've read recently was *The Caramel Seduction*."

I hadn't encountered that title in the *New York Times* book review, so I had to ask.

"Oh? What's it about?"

"It's erotica."

"You don't say. I thought it might have been a biography of Milton Hershey or some other confectionary mogul."

"There's no one named 'Milton' in this book," she said reprovingly.

"Of course," I said. "'Milton' is a name best suited to economists, not Casanovas."

She stared blankly at me for a few seconds through the thick lenses of her tortoise shell glasses. When she finally solicited my literary interests, I had the distinct impression that she wasn't asking out of politeness, but out of a desire to ascertain the cause of my idiotic suppositions.

"I don't read much fiction," I said. "I mostly read the financial press, books about history or economics, and the occasional theological treatise."

"Sounds boring. You mean you don't read any novels?"

"Hardly ever. The last novel I read was *Atlas Shrugged*."

"Is that erotica? 'Cause that's a good title for a romance novel." In truth, Ayn Rand's magnum opus does contain three or four love scenes. But something told me I would regret encouraging her in this line of dialogue.

"I'm afraid not. It's more of a libertarian screed against the perils of socialism and government bureaucracy."

"And you liked reading that?"

"It wasn't too bad. But I thought that the author's earlier work, *The Fountainhead*, was a much better read."

"*The Fountainhead*? Never heard of it. What's it about?"

"It's about an architect."

"An architect? Those guys that draw buildings?"

"That's right. This architect refuses to compromise his professional integrity despite being incessantly buffeted by his adversaries. It's an inspiring tale of surmounting obstacles and staying true to a vision, no matter what."

She placed a finger on her lip for a few seconds, a pensive look on her face. Maybe we could have a stimulating conversation after all.

"So does the architect seduce anyone?"

I removed my visor and gently pressed my forehead against a nearby refrigerator. Two thoughts came to mind: 1) it was going to be a long night; and 2) Dale Carnegie had obviously never worked at a Waffle House.

$$\$\$\$\$\$$$

While I made vain attempts at literary banter with Mary, Tim was learning the finer points of grill operation from a mustachioed Waffle House veteran. Despite being a pack-a-day smoker, Edward Jarvis barely showed thirty-five of his nearly fifty years of age. An otherwise average build was accentuated by broad shoulders and sinewy forearms.

Edward was one of the store's only two "master grill operators." The designation indicated a complete knowledge of the plate marking system, all menu items, abbreviations and prices, and the experience of having cooked $3,200 worth of food over the course of a ten-hour shift. He was also a "relief manager," meaning that he was authorized to change out the cash register drawers at the end of each shift.

Edward was leagues brighter than anyone else in the store. In addition to managing the grill, he provided trenchant (albeit usually ribald) commentary on all customer and employee activity. After watching him deliver endless innuendos and colorful euphemisms over the next five months, I eventually concluded that his talents would have been better applied to writing bawdy fortune cookies than cooking omelets.

As the resident alpha male, Edward was quick to reprove words or actions that were inconsistent with good service, although he was generally willing to overlook infractions that had no direct bearing on the customer's experience. Alternatively, if he concurred with another's sentiment, he sanctioned it with a deep, low "yeeeeaaauuuh." Three full seconds and a subtle head bob were required to expel the guttural affirmation.

Edward's extremely gruff voice made it exceptionally difficult for me to understand him. To say the least, his grave intonations and my penchant for daydreaming made for an interesting workplace dynamic. Half the time, I was unaware that he was addressing me. When he did have my undivided attention, I couldn't readily interpret his dialect.

"Jimmy, hand me that bama ring."

"The what?"

"The bama ring. The one you just pulled out of the dish washuh."

I passed him the only item I saw. Apparently, "bama ring" was Wafflespeak for *bain marie*, which is a fancy French term for a translucent plastic bucket used to hold waffle batter or condiment packets.

In the majority of cases when communication did miraculously occur, I was usually being issued a reprimand.

"Jim-may, you're makin' too many visits to the stock room. One minute you're getting paper towels. The next minute, you're headin' back for ketchup. Then for straws. Make a list and save yourself two trips. Aren't you a college boy? Use your head, Man."

When he wasn't chastening me for superfluous energy expenditure, he was expressing incredulity at my inability to locate any given item in the store, even when it was situated directly in front of my face. I explained to him that I had the exact same problem when I combed through the refrigerator at my house. My wife considers my idiosyncrasy to be a sort of charming defect. Edward didn't find it quite so endearing.

Edward had been a frequent armchair psychoanalyst in his youth but eventually yielded to paternal counsel that such endeavors were useless.

"My father taught me that the surest and fastest way to go crazy in this world is to spend your time trying to figure out why a mofo is doing this, or why he's doing that," Edward said. "There are more strange cats out there than there are hours in the day, so you can't afford to speculate on the brain waves of every wild animal that comes down the pike."

Edward had earnestly tried to follow this admonition, but apparently his interaction with me caused him to fall off the wagon. He just couldn't believe that someone with my educational credentials could be so utterly clueless when it came to the practical aspects of life.

I explained that in my previous career, I had dealt exclusively in abstractions. When researching a company, I preferred to study its Securities Exchange Commission filings rather than its annual reports because I felt that the pictures contained in the latter would compromise my objectivity. I didn't care how a company's widget looked, smelled, or tasted. I only cared how much cash the firm generated by selling them. The only reality I was concerned with had been a completely intangible one.

"If you're so good at abstract thinkin'," Edward said, "Did you see the big crash coming?"

"I expected a slowdown, but not necessarily a crash."

"Is that a yes or a no?"

"No, I guess not, Edward."

He directed me to follow him to a booth that had recently been vacated.

"Can you see all these syrup stains?" he asked, pointing to the table.

"Yes."

"Outstanding. Even though you can't find anything else in the store, you're still more valuable in here than you were at your last job. Now grab a wet towel and get to it."

I wiped down the table, trying to recall an occasion in high school or college when I had seen the Socratic Method employed so brilliantly. The Connoisseur sipped coffee in the same corner booth where I had first encountered him. He scratched several lottery tickets, stared into space, tapped the ashes off his cigarillo, poured some creamer into his coffee mug, then began scratching more tickets. He repeated the cycle three times over the course of an hour before finally punctuating it with an amble to a nearby gas station. He promptly returned with another fistful of lotto tickets and resumed scratching.

Several of my coworkers had recently apprised me that the Connoisseur's affinity with the Waffle House was not entirely driven by his appreciation for our cuisine. The district manager (who oversaw our store and two others) had purportedly offered him free coffee in exchange for keeping an eye on the employees during second shift. I was advised that any mischief would summarily be reported to the higher-ups.

I couldn't help but think that this arrangement was completely unnecessary. In the first place, customers only have to pay $1.30 for a bottomless cup of coffee, so it would take a truly desperate person to sell out for less than that sum. Second, if any associates were actually stealing cash from the register, a manager would know within hours because the cash register was balanced at every shift change. Drawer shortages were immediately recorded, and the shortfalls were deducted from the paychecks of all salespersons working on that shift.

I was cleaning orange juice that had spilled behind the coffee machine when the Connoisseur finally broke his silence.

"Didn't you used to be a stock broker?"

I paused for a second, carefully weighing my response. I didn't know if he was making honest conversation out of boredom or practicing his subtle form of espionage.

"No, sir. I have never been licensed to sell securities." I resumed wiping the counter.

"Well, I heard you used to do stocks."

"I worked in the bond market. I never touched stocks during my career." I dropped my dishtowel and turned towards him.

"Stocks are for children," I said. "You can do a lot more damage with bonds."

I explained to the Connoisseur that bad investments aren't really dangerous unless large institutions are borrowing vast amounts of money to buy them—that's when things get particularly nasty. My only saving grace was that I hadn't actually bought the bonds myself; I had just been a press secretary for those that did.

"Well, it's not your fault then," the Connoisseur asserted. "You were just doing the job you were assigned."

"Isn't that the 'Nuremberg defense?'" I asked.

"What?"

"The Nuremberg trials. After World War II, the Nazi leaders were charged with war crimes in an international court. They pleaded innocence on the basis that they were only following orders."

"Oh. Well, you don't look like a war criminal to me."

"That's tremendously reassuring. Do I look like a white collar criminal?"

"Not anymore you don't. Waffle House shirts have gray collars." He nodded at my new uniform.

Maybe the Connoisseur was right. Perhaps serving good food to the taxpayers that were footing the financial bailout caused by guys like me was a legitimate form of restitution. Perhaps my new uniform symbolized redemption from my past transgressions.

I had barely finished thanking him for his kind words when Edward reminded me that my sidework assignment for the evening included cleaning the restrooms.

"Since things are pretty slow at the moment, you might as well get started now," he said, handing me a bottle of disinfectant. Redemption, indeed.

$$$$$

In addition to purloining financial calculators, employees were occasionally known to take toilet brushes—even used ones—from the store without permission. In their stead, management had furnished me with old dish towels which were to be immediately discarded after usage. I put on a rubber apron and latex gloves, grabbed two of the towels, and headed into the ladies room.

I emerged from the lavatory ten minutes later.

"Well, that was a thrill," I said to Edward. The experience had given me legitimate reason to wonder how women ever earned their reputation as "the fairer sex."

"You must not get out of your house a lot," Edward replied. "Haven't you ever had a real thrill before?"

"I guess you could say so. I jumped out of an airplane on five occasions."

I briefly related my experience in the Wake Forest "Demon Deacon Battalion" during my freshman year of college. I had participated as a "walk-on" cadet, meaning that in exchange for not receiving any pay, I was able to participate in the ROTC program without signing a formal contract with Uncle Sam. It also meant that my name was not sewn on to any of my uniforms, and that none of the Army officer cadre took a particular interest in ensuring that I received the same training as all of the other cadets.

My deficiencies as a soldier were quickly made manifest during my first field training exercise at Fort Bragg. I was the only cadet in the battalion with no clue on how to clean an assault rifle. One upperclassman was kind enough to do it on my behalf, notwithstanding his irritation by my use of the word "gun." In the Army, I was told, a soldier can only refer to his M–16 as a "weapon" or a "rifle." I went along with the terminology. But for all intents and purposes, it still seemed a lot like a gun.

Later that weekend, I had the opportunity to use my "weapon" on the firing range to qualify for marksmanship certification. About halfway through the qualification, I felt my stomach beginning to rumble. I ignored the sensation and shot a few more times at my designated paper target. As I was calculating the number of remaining rounds in the magazine, my innards began to spin in earnest. There was no more disregarding nature's vociferous call; Army food had gotten the best of me. Fortunately, my supervising officer was kind enough to let me adjourn to the latrine.

I had been in the latrine no more than five minutes when I heard my fellow cadets assembling to board a bus to return to the barracks. The senior officers had started a head count. It was only a matter of time.

"Hey, where's Adams?"

"Uh, I think he's in the latrine, sir."

"Well, tell him to hurry up. We're all waiting."

There are undoubtedly worse things in life than contending with an acute case of diarrhea when a surly Army sergeant bangs on your bathroom stall and demands that you finish immediately, forcing you to waddle thirty yards into a busload of fifty people who are aware of your plight and are thoroughly enjoying themselves at your expense. But I can't think of any right now.

I had anticipated this scenario when my stomach made its first outcry on the firing range. But my prescient awareness of the ridicule utterly failed to prepare me for the humiliation when it finally came. On the other hand, the illness did provide a perfect alibi for my failure to qualify as an expert marksman.

At the end of my freshman year, I was summoned to the captain's office. The results of the "cadet competence" poll were in. The Captain bluntly informed me that I had been voted the worst cadet in the entire battalion. The news didn't come as a big shock. What *was* surprising was that the captain went on to ask me if I would like to take three weeks out of my summer to attend Airborne School at Fort Benning, Georgia. I wouldn't receive any pay for attending, but there were a few perquisites, namely, "three hots and a cot."

"You can't beat that!" the captain said enthusiastically.

He was a lousy salesman. My mother's cooking was undoubtedly better than whatever the Army chefs would prepare, and lodging in the barracks would be less commodious than my bedroom at home. But I was flattered that the ROTC officers thought I still had the potential to be a good soldier. Granted, my Army career had gotten off to a shaky start, but I had been given an opportunity to redeem myself. I thought back to a biography of General Custer that I had read in the fifth grade.

Like me, Custer had also been at the bottom of his class (albeit at West Point). Despite the rough start, he went on to become a distinguished cavalry officer during the Civil War and the nation's preeminent Indian fighter. I was heartened by his example. The book had also mentioned that Custer's illustrious military career ended abruptly at some place called Little Bighorn on what you wouldn't call a high note, but I tried not to dwell too much on that point.

A week after my talk with the captain, another cadet apprised me that unless we sent a cadet to Fort Benning for the last three weeks of June, our battalion would lose a slot at jump school for the next few years. Apparently, the ROTC cadre had already made the offer to every other cadet in the battalion before finally extending the opportunity to me. So much for delusions of military grandeur.

Thirteen years after the fact, I still remember my time at jump school quite vividly. Most days were spent running, practicing parachute landing falls in sawdust pits, and standing around waiting for orders. By the end of three weeks, I had gotten pretty good at all three activities. The two constants were the heat and the humidity. We were told to drink copious amounts of water to prevent heat exhaustion. One soldier who neglected to follow this counsel collapsed outside the mess hall one morning after physical training (PT).

That was all I needed to see. Unlike so many youngsters, I was going to learn from other people's mistakes, rather than become dehydration's next victim. I decided to drink two canteens of water the next morning before we began our PT session. I was a wise man.

As we jogged the mile from the barracks to the PT area, my sense of wisdom gradually yielded to feelings of intense bladder pressure. There is nothing like running that exacerbates the need to go. Each step sends a shock up the leg, and you get the sensation that barbarians are taking a battering ram to your crotch. Tomorrow, I decided, one canteen of water would suffice. In the interim, I needed to get to a bathroom. Badly.

My platoon sergeant would have none of it. Despite my repeated implorations, he refused to let me visit the latrine until after we had finished PT and our morning run. I would have to wait it out for another fifty minutes. I was doomed.

I had heard stories from other soldiers about what to do in these types of situations, which occur fairly often during long hikes in basic training. The consensus was that the best option was to keep moving along with the group, relieve yourself in your trousers as surreptitiously as possible, and hope that nobody noticed. So that's exactly what I did.

Everything was going along according to plan until I reached the chin-up bar. After knocking out three repetitions, a sergeant from another platoon confronted me about the conspicuous spot on the front of my fatigues. He commanded me to drop from the bar and began his interrogation.

With a completely straight face, I did my best to assign the blame for my incontinence to my squad sergeant, who was too incredulous to be angry with me. He instructed me to run back to the barracks, change, returning in time for our group run. Aside from some brief ribbing, the incident didn't create too much of a stir. It was a small price to pay for a substantial quantity of relief.

Within a week's time, I was standing in the doorway of a C-130, eagerly anticipating the rush of my fourth jump. After my chute deployed, I checked the direction of my drift and adjusted the angle of my body to prepare for the imminent landing. The Sergeants Airborne had instructed us to never look at the ground before landing; staring at it causes you to extend your legs, greatly increasing the chance of a broken bone. Instead, we were to focus on the horizon and brace for impact. Confident in my landing preparations, I permitted myself to relax and enjoy the panoramic view of the Georgia skyline for a full minute. As I was relishing the view, I felt my body mildly lurch forward. Had the wind just shifted?

My question was summarily answered with a prompt face plant into the Drop Zone. The tilled soil of the field had partially broken my fall, but my head was throbbing nonetheless. Through the fog of my headache, I vaguely remembered that the first thing that the jumpmasters had trained us to do after hitting the ground was to detach our parachutes from our harnesses.

As if on cue, a gust of wind suddenly swept across the earth. My chute promptly inflated, dragging my body across the field at what felt like twenty miles per hour. After struggling for a few seconds, I was finally able to roll onto my back and engage the chute releases. I turned onto my side and began spitting out a mouthful of dirt.

As I rubbed my forehead in a futile attempt to assuage my headache, everything suddenly became very dark. I looked up to discover the frame of a horribly large, muscular sergeant, whose physique was broad enough to completely obstruct the noonday sun. He demanded that I pack my chute into its stuff sack and clear the area, giving me ten seconds to do so. I staggered around, desperately trying to comply with his orders while he impugned my masculinity with the aid of a bullhorn.

I'm sure the whole spectacle must have been terribly amusing to a casual observer. At the time, I could only ruefully contemplate paying a very steep price for three hots and a cot. But after one more jump, I was finally awarded my coveted silver wings and returned home. I had no reservation about promptly returning my uniforms to the ROTC office when I resumed college in the fall. I had come to interpret my ineptitude with firearms, adversity with bodily functions, and less-than-dignified parachute landings as God's less-than-subtle way of telling me that he simply hadn't fashioned me for a life in the military. Between my inability to see things directly in front of my face and my mind's penchant for incessantly wandering, I was a sniper's dream come true. Instead of serving waffles in North Carolina, I would have undoubtedly been a grease spot in Fallujah by now.

Had I been a more competent soldier, I could have served a valuable role in the economy as a member of the Armed Forces. As *The Wealth of Nations* explains, governments should protect physical property (including, of course, life) by providing for the national defense and providing a justice system. Adam Smith asserted that governments should also enforce private contracts and protect intellectual property by granting patents and copyrights to inventors and authors.

The defense of private property is absolutely essential to a functioning free market. When each economic actor knows that the wealth generated by his production will be protected by the law, he will become more productive. In the absence of this guarantee, businesses and individuals will be far less willing to risk their capital in the reproductive investments which promote economic growth.

Instead of a military career in which I would have protected American capital, I eventually opted for finance, a vocation in which I allocated capital on behalf of savers. And while finance has historically been a more lucrative endeavor, it is certainly no more prestigious than soldiering. Yes, you get to wear expensive suits and use fancy terms like "LIBOR," "swap spreads," and "convexity hedging." But you don't get to shoot at any bad guys without concurrently guaranteeing yourself a prison term. And, unlike the Army, should you happen to wet your pants during your financial market workday, your colleagues on the trading desk won't let you live it down after 24 hours. (I never actually saw anyone lose control of his or her bodily functions during my eight years in the bond market, but I'm sure a few probably came close on several occasions.)

Edward seemed to appreciate my Army anecdotes, but he still felt that my parachuting experiences needed some spice.

"So, of the five times that you jumped outta that plane, were you naked on any of those occasions?"

"No, Edward, the Army made us wear camouflage uniforms."

"Well, when you jump out of a plane in the buff, *then* you can call it a thrill. Don't hardly count if you was wearing clothes at the time."

I couldn't quite follow his line of reasoning. But, as I would soon learn, Edward was consistent in his belief that nudity was a prerequisite for any worthwhile endeavor.

Chapter 3

ONE FLEW OVER THE WAFFLE HOUSE

"Banking was conceived in iniquity and born in sin."
—Josiah Stamp, director of the Bank of England

After two more weeks working second shift, Debbie approached me with a proposition that would radically alter the course of my life. According to the grill operators and other servers, I had made substantial progress with my table waiting skills. If the reports were indeed accurate, she believed I was ready for reassignment to the 9 P.M.–7 A.M. third shift on Thursday, Friday, and Saturday nights.

The initial leg of the shift wouldn't be markedly different from the second shifts I'd grown accustomed to, but I would have to be prepared for a considerable spike in volume after the local bars closed at 3 A.M. Because of the brisk pace, this offer was extended to only the most competent servers. In fact, Debbie said, I should think of this opportunity to earn large tips from profligate drunkards as "something of an honor."

I appreciated her flattery. Despite my initial fumbles, my rapid ascension up a steep learning curve had been recognized. I would soon learn, however, that being asked to work third shift was not an honor in the same sense as being asked to speak at a Rotary luncheon. Rather, manning the Waffle House on early Saturday mornings with two cooks and two other servers is honorable work in the sense of 250 Texans defending an old Spanish mission against a Mexican army force ten times their strength. Third shift isn't about servers earning tips any more than a firefight is about soldiers receiving combat pay. Like a gun battle, third shift is about one, and only one, thing—survival.

To my knowledge, no motion picture has ever attempted to recreate the social dynamic of a Waffle House at 2 A.M. on a Saturday morning. Fortunately, the penultimate scene of Oliver Stone's Vietnam War epic, *Platoon,* provides a suitable proxy. Cinemaphiles will recall that a hopelessly outnumbered U.S. Army battalion watches helplessly as its position is overrun by hundreds of frenzied North Vietnamese troops. In desperation, the commanding officer finally instructs the Air Force to expend all of its remaining ordnance inside the perimeter of his firebase. The scene concludes with the terrain being wholly consumed in the fiery blaze of a napalm airstrike.

I can't tell you how many early Saturday and Sunday mornings I spent entertaining fantasies of a squadron of F–4 Phantom jets strafing the restaurant in similar fashion. If you can imagine Waffle House employees and patrons in the roles of the American soldiers and Vietnamese belligerents, respectively, then you have a pretty accurate depiction of my weekends.

At 2:30 A.M., the restaurant doors explode. Within fifteen minutes, sixty barflies and club hoppers occupy a diner with seating capacity for only forty-two persons. I and two other harried servers struggle to placate them as they drunkenly clamor for service. Plunging into the maelstrom, I ask myself which part of my job description contains the phrases "crowd control" and "hangover mitigation."

A young man boasts of the beauty of a lady that had recently given him her cell phone number. His colleague is unimpressed.

"Yeah, she had a tight little body, true dat. But the girl is missin' way too many teeth," he responds.

The Casanova goes on to extol her other virtues (the list is decidedly brief) and argues to his confederate that bicuspids are overrated to begin with.

I glance down to discover an obese girl I waited on 45 minutes ago is cradling her face in her crossed arms next to a half-eaten plate of cheese eggs. I lean over the counter, trying to ascertain whether or not she is still breathing. Before I can get close enough to gauge vital signs, she erupts, flailing her arms wildly.

"Security!" she blurts out. "Look, Man, if you're going to harass me like this, I ain't payin' for my raisin toast."

No sooner have I begun to offer my apologies than her face collapses back into her forearms. I retrieve two orders of scrambled eggs from the grill, passing by another narcoleptic customer who is snoring audibly. I deliver the eggs to a girl with ubiquitous tattoos and eight visible body piercings. She offers me a large tip in exchange for desecrating her companion's double cheeseburger while she adjourns to the restroom. I politely decline the offer.

A white man contends with two black women that his struggle to obtain company health insurance benefits for his gay partner is every bit as important as Rosa Parks's quest to desegregate public buses. The girls demur, and a civilized political discussion quickly degenerates into threats of fisticuffs.

"Security!" the corpulent patron yells again.

For many a drunkard, deciding what to eat is no small feat, and placing a correct order is practically a Herculean task. As I wait on a man in a camouflage t-shirt which regrettably fails to cover his navel, the value of menu pictures immediately becomes manifest. "I'll have a cheesesteak," he says emphatically, while tapping his index finger on a photo of a different menu item.

"You mean you'd like a Texas bacon egg and cheese sandwich?" I ask.

"Yeah, I want a cheesesteak," he says.

I invite him to examine the menu more closely.

"Yes, that's what I pointed to," he said. "A cheesesteak sandwich."

"Would you like the sandwich that comes with bacon and fried eggs and American cheese served on Texas toast?"

"Yeah. Y'all don't call that a cheesesteak sandwich?"

"We call it a Texas bacon egg and cheese sandwich."

"Really? 'Cause 'cheesesteak' is a lot easier to say. Bacon egg and cheese is too many syllables, Man."

I concede the point and turn to his friend, who is comparably inebriated. As he struggles to customize his hashbrown order, our dialogue quickly degenerates into an Abbott & Costello sketch.

"Make 'em scattered, covered, and sluthered."

"I'm sorry, did you just ask for 'sluthered' hashbrowns?"

"Yeah, Man—just like it says on the menu. Sluther it with that . . . stuff."

"Onions?"

"No, no onions. Just sluther 'em for me."

"Sir, smothered hashbrowns contain onions. That's what 'smothered' means."

"That's what I said, Man. Cover and sluther them, just hold the onions."

I turn to the last man in the booth, who appears to have some semblance of sobriety.

"Do you know what he's talking about?" I ask.

"He's just tied on one too many beers. Today is his birthday."

"That's cool. Did NASA give him the day off work?"

I decide to call in an order of scattered and covered, hoping that he's too intoxicated to notice the difference by the time his plate arrives.

Distracted by a group of college girls performing a horrid cover of a *Destiny's Child* song, I inadvertently scald a customer's hand with a plate containing a cheesesteak sandwich.

I apologize profusely and provide him with burn ointment from our first aid kit. His check is discounted by ten percent, the maximum amount permitted by company policy.

"You know," his friend says reprovingly, "this man is a keyboardist. His fingers are his livelihood. He should probably sue you."

I hand him a five-dollar bill out of my pocket, considering the payment a cheap insurance policy against getting my tires slashed.

Other customers show greater magnanimity when I fumble a delivery. While placing several drinks on a table where two couples are seated, I knock a glass of Coke onto the booth seats. The young man barely vacates his seat before the soda splashes.

"I'm awfully sorry," I apologize. "It's a good thing you've got such fast reflexes."

"No sweat Jim," he responds. "Wouldn't a been no harm even if the pants had gotten soaked. The odds are real good that my trousers and drawers are coming off in about ten minutes anyhow."

His male companion howls in laughter as his date playfully slaps him. I thank him for his patience, and for creating such a delightful mental image. For some reason, my brother's collegiate hijinks of hellraising at Waffle House no longer struck me as particularly humorous.

I stave off a gaggle of hungry, impatient customers by excusing myself to attend to the cash register. Ringing up the second tab, I discover that the credit card machine has just run out of tape. For the rest of the night, all customers must pay cash. The news is not well received.

The only effective means of fighting the mob is an extremely potent air conditioning unit. When the barflies get really out of line, we set the thermostat to the low 60s. Generally, the frigid temperature shifts their focus from harassing servers to maintaining their own body heat. Still, there are some nights when nothing short of the concentrated blast of a fire hose would squelch the din.

Edward barks a series of contradictory orders at me. If I am ringing out a customer at the register, I should be taking an order. If I am taking an order, I should be picking up food from the grill. If I'm picking up an order, I should be ringing out a customer. Things aren't any easier for him at the grill, where he is swamped in a flood of orders.

"Wait staff, drop your own waffles!" he cries, indicating that the responsibility for pouring batter into the waffle irons now lies with the servers. This command is the military equivalent of "fire at will!" or, more accurately, "every man for himself!"

In the four feet of space separating the high bar from the grill, servers call in orders and pick up food as grill operators mark plates and drop hashbrowns onto the grill. The frenzy is reminiscent of a commodities exchange; I can only marvel that the plates emerge unscathed. Seemingly, the laws of probability would dictate that several of them should be dashed to the floor in pieces.

As the melee escalates, we keep all of the waffle irons constantly filled with batter (whether or not waffles have been ordered) just so we will have them on hand to readily placate impatient customers. I call in an order, pour batter into two irons, then return to the floor to attend to a customer. I retrieve the waffles when a timer sounds three minutes later, noting that the elapsed time is the same length as the round of a prize fight. It certainly feels like I've been in one.

By 4:30 A.M., all customers have vacated the premises, and the store is eerily quiet. The recent decadence is attested to by a floor strewn with used napkins, hashbrowns, bent silverware, syrup splotches, and the occasional afro pick. Within another hour, the early Sunday morning crowd trickles in. Many of these patrons carry Bibles and say prayers over plates of food that others had cursed only a few hours before. I refill their coffee as subtly as possible so as not to interrupt their scripture study.

As they read psalms, I am floored by the irony of our store's hasty transformation from Bacchanalian festival to house of worship. I remember St. Paul's admonition that believers should not keep company or eat with drunkards, which raises two questions. Does it violate the spirit of Paul's teaching if the believers and drunkards dine in the same establishment within forty minutes of each other? More importantly, was there a Waffle House in ancient Corinth that inspired this piece of doctrine?

$$\$\$\$\$\$$

Relative to the Friday and Saturday night ruckuses, Thursday shifts were downright sedate by comparison. Absent the frenetic rush of a bar crowd, customer flow was much more manageable, enabling me to consistently deliver food within five minutes after taking an order. The confluence of greater customer satisfaction and sobriety won me much larger gratuities. On Friday and Saturday nights, I typically wrote between 50 and 55 tickets and left the restaurant with eighty dollars in tips. On Thursdays, I only averaged about 30 tickets but usually earned closer to $90 or $100.

Occasionally, an extended lull in activity provided me with sufficient time to eat a quick meal during the middle of a shift. Tim had graciously prepared all of my food during our training period, but his goodwill expired shortly thereafter. Left to cook my own hashbrowns, I always came up short in my attempts to emulate his performance. Reticent to burn yet another batch early one Friday morning, I solicited his help.

"Not now, Jimmy. I'm watching something go down."

Ten minutes ago, an old Lincoln sedan had pulled into the parking lot, prompting me to grab napkins and silverware to set a place for the driver when he entered the store. He never did. The reason became evident as a jeep pulled up next to him and a fistful of cash was passed through his window. In return, the Lincoln driver handed the other man a brown paper bag.

"Looks like the Waffle House just got a drive-through window," Tim chuckled.

As the cars drove away, he turned to the grill and began my tutorial.

"It's not that hard to cook hashbrowns. Now grab a spatula and listen. Drop one ladle of oil on the grill for every scoop of hashbrowns. After a few minutes, put the cubed ham on the grill. Just before the ham is done cooking, flip the hashbrowns and add in all the toppings you want. When they're finished, mix in the ham cubes, then put the cheese slices on top."

It sounded easy enough, but my finished product proved woefully inadequate on several fronts. The ham was undercooked; and while the hashbrowns had gotten hot enough to burn, they hadn't been sufficiently warm to melt the cheese I had placed on top of them.

"I don't know, Tim. These hashbrowns don't look as good as the ones you make."

In an apparent rejoinder to my comment, Tim began to flail his tattooed arms and recite rap lyrics. I understood them to mean something to the effect that his culinary prowess warranted my adulation. Or that Rome wasn't built in a day. Or that I was just stupid.

"Yeah, I clearly messed up. So what should I do with the plate?"

"What do you mean? I'm the grill operator on this shift, and that's part of my reported food cost. If we throw 'em out, that money's gonna come out of my pocket. So you're eating them or nothin', boy."

This seemed terribly unfair. In the bond market, no money managers are required to eat their own cooking—no matter how sick their customers get.

It took me a few more weeks of trial and error until I could properly implement Tim's instructions. In the interim, I expanded my repertoire by asking Edward to teach me how to make a bacon, egg and cheese sandwich. Under normal circumstances, I suppose it's a fairly easy skill to learn. However, the endeavor becomes markedly more difficult when your tutor intersperses his instructions with commentary on *Friday the 13th* films.

"Where do these clowns think they're gonna run to? Jason grew up in the woods 'round Crystal Lake. The boy knows every tree. Now, they're innocent victims, no question 'bout that. All I'm saying is that if they're stupid enough to really think they can escape by running into the forest, then Jason is doing the world a small favor by taking them fools out of the gene pool."

The grill's spatula was too large to be of any use in the frying pans, so making eggs over easy required a cook to flip them in the air with an adroit flick of the wrist. This isn't a skill you pick up overnight. As fascinated as I was by Edward's application of Social Darwinist concepts to horror movies, his remarks proved an unfortunate distraction. After two unsuccessful attempts at turning the eggs, I finally got them airborne and landed them both inside the pan.

"Edward, I did it!"

"Third time's da charm," he said, smiling. "If the circus can teach a bear to ride a bicycle, I can teach you to fry eggs."

"No doubt, Edward."

"No doubt suh."

I noticed a small aperture between the flames and the grill. Glancing down, I could see several discarded egg shells and overcooked bacon strips.

"Edward, would you mind if I throw my eggs down this little chute here?"

"No problem suh, that's what it's there fo'. Just make sure you throw the yolk in the pan, and the shells in the trash."

He grabbed my shoulder lightly, spun me towards him, and looked me straight in the eye.

"If you throw the yolk in the garbage, and the shells in the pan, you're gonna be eating a crunchy-ass sandwich."

"Yes, Edward, I suppose it would be crunchy."

"Yeaauuuh. Of course, if you want it like that, I ain't gonna stop you."

$$$$$

Besides larger gratuities and free classes at Edward Jarvis University, Thursday nights offered the perk of quality customer interaction. Friday night banter, while colorful, was unfailingly formulaic. "We were at this club/concert. We drank so much beer/liquor. There were these three/four girls. It was so crazy/awesome. In the history of the world, no one has ever done anything as cool as we did tonight, ever." The narrative never deviated much.

Conversely, weeknight patrons always had a unique story. A man in his late twenties debates whether or not to follow his girlfriend to Tampa, where she had recently relocated. A group of Yankees are making a pilgrimage to an old family homestead in a less-traveled part of the state. Or, my personal favorite . . .

A man wearing a trench coat staggers through the door. He promptly seats himself at the high bar and begins casting furtive glances over his shoulders. His eyes are quite bloodshot, but I don't smell any alcohol or smoke on his breath. This is going to be interesting.

"Are you alright, sir?"

"I'll be alright as soon as I get a biscuit in me. I just seen my daddy's ghost."

"When?"

"About five minutes ago."

"Where?" I look out the front windows. "Here?"

That's all the store needs, I thought. A specter lurking in the parking lot. The poor soul had probably died of food poisoning and has now come back to haunt the responsible parties. It's bad enough dealing with churlish drunkards on the weekends. But if the weekday shifts include confronting the supernatural, then I'm going to have to resign my commission.

"No, Man, in my bedroom. I just woke up to find my daddy at the foot of my bed just starin' at me. And he been dead fo' five years."

Thank goodness. The Waffle House was not, in fact, haunted. The man informs me that he has been thinking of his father in recent days. While shocked by the apparition, he is still deeply grateful to have seen his father, albeit in an ethereal state. I now realize he has been crying. In my tenure at the store, he is the only customer whose eyes are bloodshot from tears rather than substance abuse.

The man's sorrows are promptly consoled with a sausage, egg, and cheese biscuit, a dish renowned throughout the South for its palliative effects. Ten minutes later, he is on his way back to bed, another poor soul whose burdens have been lightened in our sanctuary.

I do not use the term "sanctuary" with as much sarcasm as you might suspect. The Waffle House really is a haven for folks at the end of their ropes. People came to us with all sorts of problems, at all times of the day or night. At any given time, we could function as a sort of third-tier emergency room, church, motel, or concert hall. But the particulars are incidental. Our congregants know that no matter what their problem, be it insobriety or encountering a dead relative, they will always leave our stores in a better disposition than when they arrived. Hashbrowns, you see, are the universal salve—a veritable balm of Gilead.

Countless immigrants have found hope in these assuring words inscribed on a plaque inside the Statue of Liberty: "Give me your tired, your poor, Your huddled masses yearning to breathe free, The wretched refuse of your teeming shore. Send these, the homeless, tempest-tossed to me, I lift my lamp beside the golden door!"

Of course, poetess Emma Lazarus had no idea that the promise made in her 1883 sonnet would ultimately be fulfilled inside the four walls of the Waffle House. Where else can you find tired, poor, and tempest-tossed individuals congregating inside a golden door? Verily, the prophecy has come to fruition.

Regrettably, I must acknowledge that "wretched refuse" is a term applicable to at least two percent of our clientele. (On weekends, that number approaches five or seven percent.) But there is respite for all, whether or not the patron deserves it. In short, Waffle House serves as a kind of YMCA for people who don't like swimming or aerobics. Seriously.

At 9:30 P.M. one Friday night, a woman in her late forties enters the store pulling a suitcase behind her. She removes her raincoat, sits down in a corner booth, and orders a cup of coffee. I deliver it and inquire if she will be eating dinner tonight. A bottomless cup of coffee will suffice for the evening, she says, opening a paperback novel.

Within two hours, the novel rests, pages down, on the table, and the woman's head is tilted backwards against the wall. She emits a faint snore through her gaping mouth. I look forward to watching her slumber being abruptly curtailed by a horde of barflies. But when the stampede arrives three hours later, the commotion doesn't cost her an ounce of sleep. I'm not sure whether to be impressed or dumbfounded by the feat. At 6 A.M., she finally resurrects and demands another cup of coffee.

"Aww, this is stale. I'm going to need you to brew a fresh pot for me," she demands.

"Certainly, ma'am. As soon as I get this order of eggs out to another table, I'll take care of that for you."

"No. I need that coffee right now," she says in a surly tone. I brew it for her and ask if she's planning on having breakfast with us this morning. She's not, which just leaves one remaining question.

"Are you partial to *The New York Times* or *The Wall Street Journal?*"

"What difference would that make?"

"We offer a national newspaper as a courtesy to all of our overnight guests. I just need to know your preference."

"I'll have to think about that," she says. "But I'll let you know."

Nothing in this world is more irritating than trying to criticize someone's manners, in a decidedly non-subtle way, only to have your insults go completely over their heads.

Edward, as always, has been monitoring the entire dialogue.

"Jimmy, you shouldn't talk to the customers like that," he admonishes.

"Should I have offered her *The Washington Post,* instead?"

"You got a good point, but she is still a paying customer."

"Are you serious, Edward? She orders one cup of coffee all evening, sleeps in the booth like some kind of vagrant, and then has the nerve to complain this morning because the coffee's not fresh. I came this close to asking her if she wanted me to change the linens in her booth."

Edward smiles. "Well, I won't say you wouldn't be justified in doing that, but it behooves you to keep a cool head about you, no matter what the customahs say or do."

As much as I could complain about a small number of them, I genuinely *liked* the vast majority of my customers, particularly the regulars. There was Fat Albert, a nineteen-year-old retail stock boy who always arrived at the beginning of my shift along with his brother and their mutual friend. The three of them sat at the low bar, where they manufactured sweetened iced coffees, creating a terrific mess in the process.

They were in dire need of finishing school, but nonetheless every receipt of a cheeseburger and every coffee refill was unfailingly acknowledged with a "thanks, Man," or " 'preciate it." After their departure, a very pleasant middle-aged woman came in for eggs and coffee after her shift ended at the local FedEx terminal.

Later in the evening, we received occasional visits from the Spy, a short, rotund fellow that took particular pride in repeatedly advising everyone within earshot that he worked for the government. On two occasions, I overheard him attempting to impress his dinner companions by threatening rowdy customers on the other side of the store.

"I know people that could take care of that guy for us," he'd whisper under his breath.

The only thing that the Spy enjoyed more than steak and hashbrowns was implicating the CIA in every mundane piece of global news. I couldn't help but solicit his information sources.

"Who exactly did you say that you work for?" I asked.

"The government," he said. "Federal government," he added with a wink.

The pace of his response was familiar. "Bond . . . James Bond," he seemed to be saying.

When I pressed for details about his occupation, the Spy informed me that any further disclosure would inevitably culminate with a phone call to my next of kin. I thanked him for his magnanimity in providing such a subtle warning and refilled his Diet Coke.

I came to understand that the Spy lived in the sort of imaginary world that most people abandon during their elementary school years. He wasn't walking into the Waffle House with a prostitute at three in the morning; he was strutting into a Monte Carlo casino with a beautiful woman who may or may not be a Russian double agent. I couldn't decide whether it was pathetic or admirable that a middle-aged man could still have such an active imagination.

The Spy's fashion sense and physique were at conspicuous odds with his swagger. He usually wore sweaters with geometric designs—the horribly gaudy sort that Bill Cosby popularized during the second Reagan administration. He didn't have Daniel Craig's mysterious eyes, chiseled jaw, or bulging pectorals. Instead, big eyes sat above rosy cheeks, and a potbelly protruded below a cluster of isosceles triangles on his sweater. He didn't belong in a James Bond movie; he belonged in an animated Disney film (perhaps as a woodchuck in Bambi's entourage).

Whatever my opinion of him, the Spy was absolutely convinced of his own importance. I never discovered his exact vocation, but I'd bet cash money that he works as a meter maid somewhere in the District of Columbia.

At the bottom of my list of favorite regular customers was a colorful duo of Repo Men.

In my old career, "repo men" were guys that worked on the "repo" desks of Wall Street broker/dealers. A repurchase agreement, or "repo," is a way to borrow money using a bond as collateral. It works like this: I own a U.S. Treasury bond with a market value of $1 million and want to borrow money. Merrill Lynch offers to buy my bond today at a price of $1,000,000, on the condition that I will repurchase the bond from them in three months at a price of $1,010,000. The higher repurchase price represents my interest cost. Effectively, Merrill is lending me money at a three-month rate of 1% ($10,000 / $1,000,000).

Of course, "repo" can also stand for "repossession," rather than "repurchase." In the Waffle House context, Repo Men do not lend money for lower Manhattan brokerages using Treasury bonds as collateral. Rather, they seize collateral on behalf of third-party creditors. On Wall Street, Repo Men rise very early in the morning and take commuter trains to work. At the Waffle House, Repo Men drive pick-up trucks in the middle of the night to their reclamation assignments. In lieu of pressed shirts and Zegna suits, they wear Nascar t-shirts and jean jackets. In fact, the Wall Street and Waffle House Repo Men have only one thing in common: if you don't pay your debts, you can be sure they will seize their collateral. Immediately.

As completely nocturnal creatures, it only made sense that the Repo Men would patronize the only 24-hour establishment in town. I suppose I should have been grateful for their business. I wasn't. The Repo Men were two of the lewdest human beings I have ever met. They almost never ordered food and contented themselves by waxing philosophical in incredibly profane terms.

By "waxing philosophical," I don't mean that they were debating epistemology or metaphysical issues. Rather, their dialogue was generally confined to matters of professional ethics—e.g., "if I'm seizing a vehicle, and I run over the neighbor's dog as I'm backing out of the driveway, whose fault is it? When you stop to think about it, that animal's life would never have been placed in jeopardy if the guy had been paying his bills on time."

Beyond animal rights, the Repo Men also opined on matters of gender equality.

"Only a coward initiates an attack on a woman," one of them posited. They were, unquestionably, the noblest words I ever heard come out of his mouth.

"Now, on the other hand," he continued, "If she's man enough to hit you, then she's man enough to get hit right back."

So much for chivalry.

When not considering life's weightier questions, the Repo Men directed their energy towards the grill operator and wait staff. Innuendo and verbal sexual harassment were hurled at everyone with no provocation. I recall a much higher level of decorum in my high school locker room after lacrosse practices.

For whatever reason, I was the lone exemption from the Repo Men's taunts. Some perceivable element of indignation in my countenance may have convinced them I wasn't worth the effort, or maybe they just felt bad for me because they knew about my previous career track. Of course, I should appreciate the uncharacteristic benevolence that they extended, but all I can do is lament that they never gave me a chance to use any of my premeditated comebacks.

One of my would-be retorts involved pointing out that when one has been in the repo game for more than a decade, the corporate advertisement on his truck should reflect a capacity to correctly spell "repossession." But somehow, calling their attention to the fact that their vehicle needed another "s" painted on it didn't seem sufficiently denigrating.

Though I never exchanged any antagonistic remarks with them, every conversation with the Repo Men was painfully awkward. No matter how hard I tried, I simply couldn't relate to them.

"Hey, Repo Man. How's your night been treating you?"

"Oh, it's been a great one so far. This girl came out of her house while we were taking her Corvette and . . ." he stopped, bursting into laughter.

"And what?"

"It was great, Man. We made her cry *and* throw up."

"That's terrific," I said flatly. "That must have been really neat to see firsthand."

Apparently the Repo Man construed my tone as some sort of chastisement.

"You misunderstood me. It wasn't like she was doing both at the same time. She cried first, *then* after she collected herself for a minute, she puked all over the car."

"Oh," I said, forcing a smile. "That makes all the difference."

"Of course it does. Don't get me wrong, I'm in this for the money, but it's the little perks like that that really make the job so worthwhile."

He left the store a half hour later to chase down a wayward Chevrolet, offering Edward a cautionary word on the perils of Chlamydia on his way out. As I cleaned up the sugar granules and empty creamer cups the Repo Man left behind, I wondered if he had refrained from mocking me precisely because his livelihood depended on people like me. After all, Repo Men spend their time cleaning up the messes left by financiers who make loans to people that have no business receiving them. By cleaning up after a Repo Man, I had just completed the circle of economic justice.

$$$$$

When they weren't belittling the Waffle House employees, the Repo Men spent much of their time deriding a 48-year-old regular customer named Kathy, whose orange hair, large blue eyes, broad face, and constant requests for free drinks brought to mind a feral tabby cat soliciting a saucer of milk. At 10 P.M. every night (and I do mean every night), Kathy entered the store and seated herself at the end of the low bar. You could set your watch to it.

Kathy didn't consume anything other than Diet Coke on most nights. On the rare occasion when she did eat dinner at the store, she usually ordered a double plate of plain hashbrowns, always paying in cash. Apparently observing the cooks and servers was entertainment enough for her, because she never read, listened to music, or initiated conversations with the other patrons. She was perfectly content to stare at us as she smoked cigarettes and bounced her leg.

Kathy was consistently polite and patient throughout the early morning rush hours, prefacing all of her requests with, "Whenever you get a chance, Jimmy, would you please . . ." The calmness and civility were welcome a relief amidst the din of the nighttime revelers, creating a soft spot in my heart for her.

After seven hours of watching "Waffle House Follies," Kathy spent her last hour at the store providing comedic fodder for a cadre of morning coffee drinkers. After an hour of enduring their barbs, she promptly retired at 6 A.M., always donning a pair of earmuffs before departing. (To my mild surprise, the earmuffs were still being worn on June mornings.)

My interaction with Kathy took an unexpected turn on an early Sunday morning when she came up two dollars short on her dinner tab and asked me if I would be willing to lend her the cash she needed to make up the difference. I gave her two bills without thinking much of it. Kathy patronized the store every night, so I doubted that she would skip out of town. And even if she did neglect to repay, my wallet could withstand the loss of principal. If nothing else, it was a small token of appreciation for a customer that never harassed me about anything.

I didn't give any thought to the loan until the following week, when Kathy approached me again to solicit a five-dollar borrowing. I reminded her that she still owed me two dollars and that additional lending wouldn't be prudent for either one of us until the first debt was settled. Still, I didn't want to appear callous to my favorite customer, and I had always enjoyed loan underwriting during my insurance company years. Before I knew it, Kathy and I had signed an agreement establishing a revolving credit facility.

Admittedly, most loan agreements are not signed on the back of a Waffle House order ticket, but my rudimentary document covered the loan conditions nearly as well as some of the 200-page corporate bond indentures that I've read. Under the terms of our contract, Kathy could borrow—at any time, for any reason—up to five dollars from the Bank of Jimmy. Not one additional cent of credit would be extended beyond that mark. After signing the contract, Kathy immediately drew down an additional three dollars, with a promise to repay me during the following week.

$$$$$

In 1912, J.P. Morgan expressed his views on loan underwriting in testimony before the House Committee on Banking and Currency:

Committee Counsel: Is not commercial credit based primarily upon money or property?

J.P. Morgan: No, sir; the first thing is *character* (emphasis added).

Committee Counsel: Before money or property?

J.P. Morgan: Before money or anything else. Money cannot buy it.

Committee Counsel: So that a man with character, without anything at all behind it, can get all the credit he wants, and a man with the property cannot get it?

J.P. Morgan: That is very often the case.

Committee Counsel: But that is the rule of business?

J.P. Morgan: That is the rule of business, sir.

As the country's preeminent banker, Morgan knew whereof he spoke. In a financial context, **character** refers to a borrower's trustworthiness. The term "credit" derives from the Latin *credere*, which means "to believe" or "to trust." A creditor's belief in a borrower's ability and intention to repay his debts provides the foundation for finance. In the absence of trust, borrowers and lenders will not get together.

In addition to character, three other factors are considered in the process of underwriting a loan: capacity, collateral, and covenants.

Capacity refers to a borrower's ability to service and repay his debt obligations. Bankers use several metrics to gauge this ability.

Collateral represents the assets pledged by the borrower to the lender. Should the borrower default on the loan, the lender can seize the collateral and sell it to a third party.

Covenants are the terms under which the loan is extended. For example, a borrower may promise not to incur any additional debt without first obtaining permission from his current lenders.

Together, these factors constitute "the Four C's of credit." A potential borrower that can satisfy these criteria is considered "creditworthy."

When I first studied the Four C's as part of the CFA curriculum, I read that "character" and "capacity" were the most important aspects of credit analysis. Intuitively, that seemed right. You need to know a man's intentions and his ability to execute on them. Covenants are merely a check to keep him honest, and collateral serves as an airbag to cushion the blow should the borrower prove unable or unwilling to make his payments.

While assessing character is admittedly a somewhat nuanced and subjective process, assessing a borrower's capacity to repay debt is a fairly prosaic endeavor. If you can bear with me for a few minutes, I'll show you how.

$$$$

Corporate lenders are primarily focused on three questions: (1) How does the company's operating income compare to its debt service costs? (2) How long would it take the company to completely pay off its debts? (3) What is the value of the company's assets relative to its debts?

Of course, there are infinite variations on these metrics, but these represent the major components. The loan officer (or credit analyst) begins by examining the company's balance sheet, which is a snapshot of its assets and liabilities (debts) *at one point in time.*

Acme Co. Balance Sheet, 12/31/2009

Assets	Liabilities (Debts)	Equity (Capital)
Property, Plant, & Equipment $2,000,000	Bank Loan at 5% Interest $1,000,000	Common Stock $1,000,000

The lender will also examine the company's income statement, which depicts its financial performance *over a period of time* (in this case, one year).

Acme Co. Income Statement, 12/31/2009

Sales	$1,000,000
Cost of Sales	($500,000)
Selling, General, and Administrative Costs	($200,000)
Operating Income	$300,000
Interest Expense	($50,000)
Income Before Taxes	$250,000
Income Tax Expense	($100,000)
Net Income	$150,000

Given this information, we can get a good feel for the company's credit risk:

1. Debt service coverage. Operating income reflects the amount of money earned from running the business before any interest or tax payments are made. In 2009, Acme generated $300,000 in operating income but paid only $50,000 in interest, meaning that it covered its interest expense six times over ($300,000 divided by $50,000). That's a pretty good margin of safety for a lender.

2. Time needed to repay debts. The company's net income roughly captures the amount of cash that it generates in a year—in this case, $150,000. Assuming the company can continue to earn this much income, Acme would need 6.7 years to repay its entire bank loan (liabilities of $1 million divided by $150,000 of income). Not bad.

3. Value of debts vs. assets. Assuming the reported asset values are a fair gauge of their market values (this is not always the case but suffices for this illustration), then liabilities of $1 million divided by assets of $2 million = 50%. Again, a fair number.

All in all, Acme looks like a decent credit risk. We don't know what widgets they sell, and frankly, we don't need to care unless their sales are declining dramatically. If they've sold a lot of widgets in the past, they'll probably keep selling a fair amount of them in the future. The main things we should worry about are rising expenses and increasing debt.

While the particulars vary somewhat, mortgage candidates can be evaluated using a similar array of credit metrics. Assume a prospective homebuyer has a gross salary of $100,000 and brings home $70,000 after taxes. She has saved $60,000 for a down payment on a $300,000 home and would like borrow the remaining $240,000. The total annual payments on a 30-year mortgage at a 6% interest rate are $17,270.

Again, we start with some financial statements (although these are pro forma because the loan has not yet been approved):

Homebuyer's Balance Sheet, 12/31/2009

Assets	Liabilities (Debts)	Equity (Capital)
House	Mortgage at 6% Interest	Down Payment
$300,000	$240,000	$60,000

Homebuyer's Income Statement (Expected for 2010)

After-tax income	$70,000
Living expenses, ex-housing costs	($36,000)
Discretionary income before housing costs	$106,000
Mortgage payments (annual)	($17,270)
Discretionary income	$123,270

Now, let's ask the same series of questions that we asked the corporation: can the borrower service the debt? How long will it take the buyer to repay the debt? How large is the borrower's debt relative to her assets?

1. Debt service coverage. The homebuyer will be paying her mortgage using the income that she retains after paying taxes and other living expenses. Therefore, we compare her "discretionary income before housing costs" relative to the size of her estimated mortgage payment. The homebuyer is expected to have $34,000 in income before housing costs, nearly two times the size of the mortgage payment. ($34,000/$17,270 = 1.97). Should she experience a decline in discretionary income due to a pay cut or an unforeseen expense, the debt service coverage ratio would fall but probably still remain high enough for the borrower to continue to pay her mortgage.

2. Time needed to repay debts. Should the borrower apply all of her discretionary income to prepaying her mortgage, she could fully repay the loan in roughly fourteen years. Loan balance of $240,000/$16,730 per year in discretionary income equals 14.3 years. (This calculation assumes that the borrower's income does not decline and/or her expenses do not rise.)

3. Value of debts vs. assets. If the borrower defaults on the mortgage, the bank will foreclose on the house and sell it for cash. The larger the borrower's down payment, the greater the bank's recovery in the event that the home is placed in foreclosure. Assuming that the house was appraised at its selling price ($300,000), the mortgage loan-to-value is 83% ($240,000 loan divided by a $300,000 asset). If the borrower immediately goes into default, the bank will not lose money on the loan as long as the value of the house does not decline by more than $60,000.

In recent years, most mortgage bankers became less disciplined in applying these time-tested underwriting criteria, relying instead on sophisticated computer models that could (ostensibly) project loan default rates better than the three aforementioned ratios. Rather than focusing on debt service coverage ratios and borrowers' repayment ability, the new models were heavily reliant on accurate estimates of home price appreciation rates.

Until 2007, these models appeared to work very well because American home prices had experienced a steady upward climb. Even though many homeowners lacked the ability to service their debts, mortgage default rates remained low because the rising housing prices enabled the borrowers to readily refinance their mortgages. When housing prices began their precipitous decline, the lenders that had taken a corner-cutting approach to underwriting were hung out to dry.

I had no intention of making the same underwriting mistakes with my loan to Kathy. Even though the only collateral she could offer was a half-eaten plate of hashbrowns, I could take great comfort in the knowledge that she had the capacity to repay me. After all, I had personally verified her income stream.

Every morning between 5:30 and 5:45 A.M., I swept the store, gathering a considerable amount of dust, napkins, and change (usually north of 70 cents) during the process. When I had completed sweeping all of the debris into the center of the floor, I would retrieve the dustpan from the corner. In the five seconds that I needed to grab it, Kathy would bolt from the end of the low bar, snatch all of the coins from the trash pile, and scurry back to the bar. I was considerably impressed by the speed of her movement, although her attempts at subtlety during the process left much room for improvement.

By consistently garnering the 70 additional cents of daily income, I knew that Kathy could repay her five-dollar loan after a week of scavenging the fruits of my dust pile. Clearly, the *ability* to repay was not in question. Kathy's *willingness* to honor her debts was a more complicated matter, however.

As I was drafting the loan agreement, Kathy had informed me that she had been struggling with some mental health issues for the past few years. I can't say I was terribly surprised by the revelation. Anyone whose primary source of weekend entertainment consists of people watching at Waffle House is probably due for a clinical evaluation. I wondered if too many nights spent in the store were the cause (or result) of her breakdown.

I didn't hold Kathy's illness against her, as I had felt my own sanity slipping away in recent weeks. Hearing the juke box play "Raisin Toast" and "Why Would You Eat Your Grits Anywhere Else?" for the thousandth time is enough to make anyone long for the comfort of a padded room at the psych ward.

It wasn't until a discussion with the Repo Man two weeks later that I became aware of the severity of Kathy's condition. Her appearance was two hours overdue, so I asked the Repo Man if he knew anything about her whereabouts.

"What day of the week is it?" he asked.

"Wednesday. Why?"

"Oh, that explains it. Every other Wednesday afternoon, Kathy surfs the electric wave. She's probably still recuperating." Failing to grasp the metaphor, I pressed him for details. Kathy, he informed me, regularly received electroshock therapy.

While her eccentricity was undeniable, I assumed that the Repo Man was pulling my leg. But just to be on the safe side, I asked Edward if he knew anything about her treatments.

"You heard right, Jimmy. They've had that broad in an electric helmet for the past eighteen years," he said.

After corroborating the Repo Man's claim, Edward went on to tell me that Kathy had recently been employed by a Target store. Her employment had been abruptly terminated for stealing from the cash register. When I informed him that I had extended her five dollars of credit, he simply shook his head. Before approaching me, she had already hit up nearly every employee in the restaurant. In all, Edward estimated, she probably owed the cooks and wait staff in excess of a hundred dollars.

So I had just loaned money to a woman with acute mental illness, who also happened to be a thief. Beyond that, I already had a line of other creditors in front of me.

"If everything you said is correct, Edward, I don't suppose this contract is worth the paper it's written on," I said, producing the revolving credit agreement from my pocket.

After a few seconds of perusing the document, he broke into hysterical laughter.

"And you . . . you . . . used to . . . invest money . . . for a living?!" He was laughing so hard that he had to force out the words in staccato. He announced my financial arrangement to Tim and another server, who found it similarly hilarious.

"Hey, I got a similar document in my back pocket!" Edward continued. "A man sold it to me for ten dollars. It says I get a cut anytime somebody pays the toll to cross the Brooklyn Bridge. But I'm still waitin' on that first royalty check . . . must a got lost in da mail."

He smacked me on the shoulder and leaned into my face. "Jimmy, if that's how you been investin' money all of these years, maybe you better off at the Waffle House after all."

$$\$\$\$\$\$$$

I finally saw Kathy again the following Saturday night. She tapped her fingers nervously on the bar top as I delivered her obligatory Diet Coke.

"Good evening, Kathy. How have you been?"

"Not so good. My head's really been out of sorts lately," she said.

"Didn't you tell me that 'out of sorts' was the status quo?"

"No, it's been worse the past couple of days. I've been doing a lot of sleepwalking."

I didn't consider sleepwalking particularly abnormal behavior, but I had to admit that Kathy's condition seemed a bit acute.

She had awakened that morning to discover that her bathroom doorknob had been forcibly detached and that a pair of jeans had been deposited inside the bowl of her commode.

Kathy spent several minutes trying to unravel the enigma of how she had managed to remove the doorknob given that she kept no tools whatsoever in her apartment. I nodded politely as she continued her speculations, but all I could think about was the imminent write-off of a certain five-dollar loan. Although I already had testimony from two credible witnesses, I couldn't help but ask her to verify the accounts of electroshock therapy. I normally didn't ask my customers such blunt personal questions, but given that my economic interests were at stake, an exception was clearly warranted.

I only had to provide the subtle hint of missing her presence on Wednesday night to cajole Kathy into providing an enthusiastic description of her shock therapy regimen. It was clearly the highlight of her week. The electric currents, she explained, produced a calming effect that assuaged her severe anxiety. She spoke with the same passion that most women use in championing the restorative effects of a body wrap treatment at a day spa. She was such a convincing advocate for the procedure that I was half inclined to ask her who I needed to speak with to receive a few volts myself.

"Oh, before I forget, Jimmy, here's your five dollars." She reached into her pocket and presented me with a handful of coins. I could scarcely believe my eyes. I thanked Kathy for her prompt repayment, desperately trying not to think about where the coins might have recently been.

Reaching into her other pocket, Kathy produced her copy of our loan contract and held it up proudly. She explained that, beyond their palliative effects, the shock treatments also sharpened her short-term memory.

"You didn't think you were going to get your money back, did you?" she teased playfully.

"The thought never crossed my mind, Kathy," I said. I tried to imagine what J.P. Morgan would make of this whole situation.

"Jimmy, I've got one more question for you."

I braced myself for another drawdown on the revolving credit facility, but she took the conversation in an unexpected direction.

"I was on a walk last night and I heard a bird chirping. I'm trying to figure out what kind it was. Do you know what bird makes the sound 'whoo, whoo, woooo'?"

I studied her face for a minute, trying to ascertain if this was some kind of trick question.

"I believe that an owl makes that sound, Kathy."

A look of absolute shock overcame her. "Are you sure? I could have sworn that it was a cardinal or a blue jay."

$$$$$

As our sales volume declined after the school year ended, we were increasingly able to handle all of our patrons with just three servers. Occasionally, a superfluous fourth server would be reassigned to work his/her shift at our airport location a few exits down the interstate. It was a newer, cleaner store whose management team had been in place for several years. To say that they did things more professionally would be a gross understatement.

While my regular store kept an inventory of six or eight prepared salads in the refrigerator, the airport store maintained a stock of fourteen. I can barely express how inexcusable I find this practice. In my opinion, Waffle House shouldn't even serve salads. They are horribly incongruous with everything else on the menu, an effete touch which detracts from the experience of capriciously gorging on breakfast food in the middle of the night. Driving to a Waffle House to order a salad is every bit as lame as flying to Paris only to consume a Big Mac and Coke once you reach the Champs-Elysees.

Instead of taking a free-for-all approach to the cash register, airport management limited its operation to two persons in an effort to keep drawer shortages down. They mandated that we verify the numbers of all customers phoning in an order prior to cooking any food. Servers did pretentious things like garnishing bowls of chili with complimentary saltines packets. The wait staff didn't bicker with the grill operators, patrons, or even with each other. The sanitation score was a nosebleed-inducing 97.5. In short, the store was a model of customer service, efficiency and attention to detail. I found it all somewhat nauseating. The place just felt too sterile to be considered a bona fide Waffle House.

It wouldn't be fair to dismiss the location as hopelessly bland, however. It was in close proximity not only to the airport, but also to three different night clubs which provided the majority of its early morning customers. Recently, two young men had gotten into a row over a female's affections which culminated in one of them brandishing a firearm in the parking lot. Perhaps the store had some redeeming value after all.

In addition to the occasional gunplay, the airport Waffle House had one other entertaining feature—the Linebacker, a six-foot, broad-shouldered, fourteen-year company veteran (by far the longest tenure of anyone I had met personally). The Linebacker took no crap from anyone. Surly customers were shown to a booth, then deliberately ignored for the next twenty minutes. A playful remark from another server was immediately met with a crass comeback. Even the grill operators, who normally call the shots on the restaurant floor, gave the Linebacker a considerable berth. Incidentally, the Linebacker was also female.

The Linebacker and another waitress were assigned to the cash register while I was given charge of maintaining the dish pit when not tending to customers or taking call-in orders. It was amazing how much the client demography differed from eight miles down the road. On the two occasions that I did work at the airport, I was struck by the number of New Yorkers patronizing our establishment. There are just a handful of Waffle Houses north of the Mason-Dixon Line, and none in New York or New Jersey. As far as the meatheads from Long Island were concerned, we were a major tourist attraction. Many of them had never consumed grits, let alone had a woman threaten them with a hot bowlful.

I was glad to have their patronage for two reasons. Firstly, they tended to be very good tippers—it's much cheaper to eat in

Raleigh than in New York City. Secondly, they served as a powerful reminder that I hadn't missed much by not pursuing my financial career in that part of the country.

On my first night at the airport, I was bantering with one Empire State resident about the cost of a Bloomberg terminal when I had to excuse myself to answer the store telephone.

"I need an order o' hashbrowns." the voice said. "I also need to speak with a good server. I doubt you have anyone good in the store right now, but I suppose I'll ask anyway."

It took me about two seconds to identify the caller. It was Edward. He was terribly curious to know how I was faring without his supervision. I assured him that for the time being, all was well. He congratulated me, expressed his skepticism about my prospects, and hung up.

The rest of the evening passed without much incident. The airport store didn't have a regular cohort of early morning coffee drinkers, enabling us to clean up with little interruption before first shift arrived. After cashing out one of the last customers, the Linebacker surveyed the store, then turned her gaze towards me.

"You know, I'm tired of watching you wash dishes," she sighed.

"Well, what would you rather watch me do?" I asked innocently.

"Do you *really* want an honest answer to that?" she asked, poking me in the ribs.

I put down a dish and turned towards her. With a large grin on her face, she bounced her eyebrows several times. I was pretty certain I knew what she was intimating.

I had to tread lightly here. On one hand, I thought the excuse of being happily married could quickly get me off the hook. On the other hand, recent experience had taught me how volatile some women were and how quickly situations could escalate. I couldn't afford to reject her too forcefully. If push came to shove, I would be giving up at least forty pounds of muscle mass to this dame, so an altercation was out of the question.

I decided to steer the conversation towards economic matters. In college, I had found this to be an effective method for quickly dispatching aggressive coeds. I could only hope that I hadn't lost my touch.

Fortunately, my ploy worked beautifully. To my great surprise (and relief), the Linebacker proved unexpectedly eager to wax philosophical on banking. Her mother had opened a savings account for her as a child, which she promptly closed at age eighteen. Since that time, she had kept every cent she owned on her body at all times. She had several reasons for this practice, chief among them a belief that banks had been designed for the sole benefit of Semitic peoples. I assured the Linebacker that the greatest banker in American history, J.P. Morgan, had been a consummate WASP. She had never heard of him.

The Linebacker's biggest reservation, though, lay in her resentment of financial intermediaries. Granted, she didn't use the term "financial intermediation," but that is exactly what she described.

"What is the point of me putting my money in the bank so that they can pay me one percent on my money and turn around and lend it to someone else at five percent? They're gonna use my money to make all that money for themselves just for sitting on their butts? I don't think so. If I'm gonna lend anyone money, I'll do it myself."

I explained to the Linebacker that banks added value to their depositors in two ways: 1) Banks can create a diversified loan pool across a broad array of borrowers. This diversification of risks helps to protect the lenders' principal. 2) The bank absorbs the first 10% (or so) of credit losses on the loan pool, providing yet another means of defense. She already knew this but remained unsold on the idea.

"If nothing else," I said, "your money is safer in a vault than it is at your house or on your person."

"I doubt that," she asserted.

"Look," I said, "if the bank gets robbed, your deposits are insured by the FDIC, which is effectively backstopped by the federal government. What happens if you keep all of your cash in your shirt pocket and then you end up getting mugged?"

"Would *you* mug me?" she asked soberly. I had to concede that she had a real point. Had Jack the Ripper made a move on her, this woman would have easily stomped his face in.

We conversed for a few minutes before our conversation was interrupted by a ringing cell phone. The Linebacker, it turned out, had a boyfriend. While we had spent the night waiting tables, the LBBF (Linebacker's Boyfriend) had been out clubbing. He had spurned the advances of an admiring female, much to her chagrin. No sooner had the LBBF turned his back than the scorned woman commenced bludgeoning him with a beer bottle. The police were summoned after he retaliated with fisticuffs.

After a few hours in jail, the LBBF bailed himself out— presumably by using a chunk of the life savings which he kept on his person at all times. He was very constructive on his prospects for acquittal on grounds of self-defense. I never found out whether he was exonerated, but I'm confident that the whole incident could have been avoided by diverting his admirer into a dialogue on the banking system.

$$\$\$\$\$\$$

"Neither a borrower nor a lender be," Polonius tells his son Laertes in Act I, Scene III of Shakespeare's *Hamlet*. Anyone that has ever loaned money directly to another person will immediately recognize the wisdom in this timeless piece of advice.

A lender does not stand to materially benefit from making a single loan. In exchange for a fixed (and usually modest) rate of return, he risks losing his entire investment. For a lender, the best possible outcome is simply getting all of his money back from the borrower. An investment that contains a large amount of downside relative to a small amount of upside is said to have an **asymmetric payoff**; the risks and/or aggravation substantially outweigh any possible benefits.

Romancing your boss's daughter is the classic example of an asymmetric payoff. You don't have to ponder the matter too long before you realize that the prospective benefits fall far short of the potential headaches involved. Potential upside: minimal; potential downside: considerable.

The best way to mitigate the asymmetric payoff inherent to lending money is by pooling lending activities. When an investor lends money to a large number of borrowers (rather than a mere handful of them) the riskiness of his investment declines dramatically. Assuming the money is generally loaned in a prudent manner, the number and diversity of the loans will alleviate the effects of a few defaults.

The pooling of credit risk borrowers benefits borrowers as well as lenders. Because the loan diversification will cushion the impact of individual defaults, lenders are willing to charge a lower average interest rate to each borrower.

Investors can lend out their money to a pool of borrowers by purchasing shares in a mutual fund that purchases loans or bonds issued by corporations, municipalities, or governments. The mutual fund manager acts as the investor's agent as he selects the securities for purchase on his behalf. However, the fund manager is not liable for the performance of those investments; the saver bears all of the risk. Effectively, the saver is lending directly to the pool of borrowers.

Saver ▶ Borrower

Rather than lending directly to borrowers via mutual funds, savers can place their money with a **financial intermediary**, who in turn lends it out across a pool of borrowers. A **commercial bank** is the most common type of financial intermediary. When you deposit your money in a bank, you are lending money directly to the bank, who in turn lends to the ultimate borrower. That is, the bank simultaneously borrows AND lends, thus forging a **chain of debts.** (Incidentally, this practice flouts both sides of Polonius' dictum).

Owe money to　　　　　*who owe money to*
Bank borrowers　▶　Commercial Banks　▶　Depositors

Before they got into the money lending business, early banks were in the business of providing physical security for precious metals. Depositors placed gold (or silver) in the bank vault, where the bullion could be better protected than at their own homes. In exchange for the gold, bankers gave their depositors a receipt which was redeemable for the exact number of ounces placed in the bank's care. The gold receipts issued by banks were known as "banknotes." A liability of the bank, they represented a claim on its assets—gold. Far less cumbersome and less prone to theft, banknotes began to supplant gold and silver coin in commercial transactions. *Banknotes had become money.* Banknotes which are backed entirely by precious metals stored in a vault are sometimes referred to as **warehouse money**.

Because the public was content to use banknotes as money, only a small number of depositors exchanged their notes for gold on any given day. Observing this phenomenon, the bankers soon conceived a better use for the gold which had been sitting idly in their vaults. They would lend it out and earn interest on their depositors' funds.

Of course, the banks had to maintain at least some gold on hand to return to depositors that wished to redeem their banknotes. The amount of gold in the bank vaults earmarked for redeeming depositors is called the bank's **reserve**. As long as the depositors never redeemed their banknotes en masse, the scheme could work. **Fractional reserve banking** was born.

As its name implies, a fractional reserve bank does not maintain a 100% gold reserve against the value of the banknotes

NEWTOWN BANK
Balance Sheet - October 30, 2010

Assets		Liabilities	
Gold	$1,000,000	Banknotes	$10,000,000
Loans	$9,000,000	(11% Warehouse Money)	
	$10,000,000	(89% Fractional Money)	

that it has issued. Instead of completely backing its liabilities with gold, a portion is instead backed with loans. Depositors, aware that some of their money was being loaned out, demanded that their banks should keep the "fractional reserve" of gold above a specified level, measured by a **reserve ratio**.

The reserve ratio is the proportion of reserves relative to the bank's liabilities. This ratio dictates how much of the depositors' savings can be invested into loans. The remainder, or **required reserves**, must be kept in the vault.

NEWTOWN BANK
Balance Sheet - October 30, 2010

Assets		Liabilities	
Gold	$1,000,000	Banknotes	$10,000,000
Loans	$9,000,000	(11% Warehouse Money)	
	$10,000,000	(89% Fractional Money)	

The balance sheet indicates that Newtown Bank maintains only 1 million in gold to support the 9 million dollars of banknotes that it has issued. The gold reserves are just a "fraction" of the bank's liabilities: 1 million/ 10 million, or 10%. While reserve ratios have changed over time, they have historically varied between ten and twenty percent of deposits.

A bank with very high reserve levels is said to be liquid. If the bank did not maintain adequate reserves, it faced the problem of **liquidity risk** if a large number of depositors simultaneously demanded their gold back.

Besides ensuring that the banks had enough gold to satisfy banknote redemptions, depositors had another concern: **credit risk**. Credit risk (also known as default risk) is the potential that a bank's borrowers will fail to repay their loans. If enough loans started to go bad, a bank's assets would soon be worth less than its liabilities. The face value of the banknotes would exceed the value of the loans and gold backing them. The banknotes would begin to trade below their face value, thereby destroying the depositors' wealth.

In order to insulate themselves against loan defaults, the depositors required that the bank owners contribute their own gold to the bank vault. The bank owners' capital would serve as a buffer to absorb any losses from souring loans.

Leverage measures the ratio of a bank's liabilities to its stockholder capital. Newtown Bank's **leverage ratio** is 10.0 (10 million in banknotes divided by 1 million in capital).

NEWTOWN BANK
Balance Sheet - November 30, 2010

Assets	Liabilities	Stockholder Capital
Gold $2,000,000 Loans $9,000,000 $11,000,000	Banknotes $10,000,000	Stock $1,000,000

If loan defaults rose to a level exceeding the stockholders' capital, the stockholders would lose their entire investment and the remaining losses would be absorbed by the depositors. The bank would go bankrupt, a condition known as insolvency.

Liquidity and credit risks were the two primary problems facing banks. They could fail for either reason: 1) inadequate reserves, or 2) insufficient capital to absorb loan defaults. But as long as a large share of the banknotes weren't being redeemed and the vast majority of its loans were being paid on time, the banks remained solvent and liquid. *Banknotes could continue to function as money.*

Of Newtown's *original* $10 million in depositor gold, only $1 million remained in the vault. (The other $1 million in gold was contributed by the bank stockholders.) The other $9 million in gold was loaned out. As Newtown's borrowers redeposited their gold at other banks, those banks in turn issued their own banknotes. Newtown Bank's depositors' gold was not only supporting its *own* banknotes, it began supporting *other banks'* banknotes, as well. As the scheme continued, a large quantity of banknotes was soon pyramided on a relatively small base of gold.

Banks Really Do <u>Make</u> Money

<table>
<tr><td align="center"><u>Banknotes</u>

$10 million</td></tr>
</table>

<table>
<tr><td align="center"><u>GOLD</u>
$1 million</td></tr>
</table>

By fractional reserving, banks can transform $1 million in gold into
$10 million in banknotes (the gold reserve requirement is 10%).

Through the magic of fractional reserve banking, *banks were creating money on their own.* Savings were being recycled into investment [the bank loans]; new money [the banknotes] was the byproduct. Money was now inextricably intertwined with credit, and the fate of both rested entirely in the hands of commercial banks. Economic life was about to get a lot more interesting.

Chapter 4

YOU CAN'T BANK ON ANYTHING

"All money is a matter of belief." —Adam Smith

The great thing about cooking is that it is more or less a **natural science**, like chemistry, biology, or physics. That isn't to say there isn't an art to it—of course there is. But cooking is a talent that can be imparted. If a culinary numbskull like me can learn to prepare an edible plate of hashbrowns, the skill can be obtained by anyone with sufficient determination. (On the other hand, I suspect that Edward's conversational flair can only be obtained through a genetic endowment.)

Unlike cooking, economics and investing are **social sciences**, along with psychology, anthropology, and political science. While natural sciences are focused on the physical world, social sciences are devoted to understanding human behavior. For many reasons, the conclusions drawn by natural scientists are far more dependable than those made by social scientists.

In the first place, natural science experiments generally transpire in laboratory environments in which all pertinent variables can be perfectly controlled. If you mix a given set of ingredients in their correct proportions and heat them for an appropriate length of time at the specified temperature, you will generate a consistent outcome. Consequently, a patron can enjoy the same fare in a

Pittsburgh Waffle House in 2010 that he did in Atlanta fifty years ago.

Given the myriad of physical and psychological nuances of every human being, social scientists have a much more difficult time designing genuinely controlled experiments. In the human laboratory, no two situations are ever perfectly identical. Further, the variables (i.e., people) are constantly changing, and so is each person's relative significance in the system.

Secondly, the results of a natural science experiment can be evaluated fairly quickly. Eating a T-bone dinner is a discrete, one-time event. The steak's taste will immediately apprise the customer whether or not the grill operator has botched the order. In contrast, investing is an ongoing endeavor, so assessing the merits of a particular investment strategy will greatly depend on the time period being evaluated. The genius hedge fund manager who doubles his money in a year is likely to be the complete moron who loses 60% of his portfolio's value over the next six months.

Most importantly, natural scientists' expectations cannot influence the outcome of any experiment. Regardless of what a grill operator *thinks* will happen if he sets the grill at an excessive temperature and does not adjust his cooking time accordingly, he will end up burning the food. Conversely, human experiences are constantly affected by the beliefs of social scientists; outcomes are largely dependent on reactions to past events. Human expectations for the future, based on past experiences, affect the future itself. This phenomenon of feedback loops between cause and effect is often called "reflexivity."

A perfect illustration of reflexivity in action is the film, *Back to the Future*. Marty McFly (brilliantly played by Michael J. Fox) is a harried adolescent who inadvertently travels back in time from 1985 to 1955. He spends several weeks with his then high-school-aged parents, trying to prevent their actions—as well as his own—from compromising their future marriage.

Marty carries with him a 1984 family photo, which enables him to determine how his maneuvers are paying off. As a result of his miscalculated actions, Marty's brother and sister soon disappear from the picture and his own body begins to fade. After another maneuver, Marty's parents finally kiss at the "Enchantment Under the Sea" dance, and he and his siblings are restored in the photograph.

A theme emerges during the film: however benign his intentions, Marty can never be sure how his slightest move in 1955 will end up affecting the lives of many people thirty years later. Such is the nature of life. Each change of our tack forces a subsequent reevaluation of the course upon which we're headed.

Societies, as well as individuals, experience the reflexivity phenomenon in their collective psychology. Since the dawn of mankind, material success and prosperity has fostered pride. As the arrogance increases, conventional wisdoms are disregarded in favor of tenuous theories propounded by social scientists. The longer the prosperity continues, the more outlandish the philosophies become. "We are wiser than our forebears, hence we are no longer plagued by their problems" is a common refrain during these periods.

Of course, the day of reckoning eventually arrives in the form of war, famine, plague, or economic calamity. Chastened, the populace begins to substitute humility for hubris and reevaluates its thinking. In due time, prosperity returns and sentiments of pride begin to creep back in.

This **pride cycle** of affluence, followed by foolish excess, then decline and humility, is endemic to all civilizations. 3,500 years ago, in consequence of their pride and iniquities, Israelite settlers in Canaan were conquered by Philistine armies, losing the Ark of the Covenant in the process. Centuries of military and economic hegemony in Europe cultivated a similar spirit of hubris in the late Roman Empire. The egocentrism led Rome to betray her Visigoth allies, who eventually responded by sacking the city in A.D. 410.

Because of its propensity to undermine national and individual prosperity, a sentiment of pride should always be checked. Inasmuch as we curb our prideful feelings, we become wiser creatures. Inasmuch as we don't, we condemn ourselves to repeating the cycle indefinitely.

$$\$\$\$\$\$$

The most recent nadir in my personal pride cycle arrived on an April Friday morning. The grill operator and I had been hit with an aberrantly high volume of customers immediately after the other server had left at 1 A.M. Consequently, I couldn't begin cleaning the store until ninety minutes after my usual start time. When Debbie arrived at 7 o'clock, I was still laboring in the dish pit. My salutation had been met with a grumbled "morning" in response. She had been in a consistently foul mood for the entire week.

"Why are you still washing dishes?" she snarled.

"I wrote 53 tickets last night. Mary didn't do any side work or dishes before she left, so I got stuck with all of them."

"I see," she said flatly. She headed to the back room, where I overheard Matthew ask her about several cash register shortages that had occurred over the past few weeks. After a few minutes of conversation, I heard my name.

"Jimmy's the common denominator," she said.

I was attempting to get some hardened chili to part from a steel pot when she returned to the floor and hurled the accusation at me directly.

"Do you know how to count?"

"What?"

"Do you know how to count? And subtract? And make change?"

"I think so. That is, I remember doing exercises on making change in Mrs. Diehl's first grade glass. But that was back in '83, so in all candor, I may be a little rusty by now. Why?"

"We've had six drawer shortages over twenty dollars in the past two weeks, and you were working on four of those shifts."

"Am I being indicted for theft?"

"Theft, no. But I think you may have some difficulty counting change."

That was the last straw. My MBA and CFA charter did not give me omniscience in the capital markets, that I would allow. But the inability to make change? Was she kidding?

Edward could label me "stupid" when it came to calling orders; that didn't bother me because it was true enough. Impugning my capacity to subtract was where I had to draw a line.

I briefly debated how best to defend my intellect. I could have pointed out that besides the 80% of my coworkers who were convicted felons, one was mildly cross-eyed, and the other (by her own admission) could not subtract without the aid of a calculator. I could have asked a rhetorical question: why would two major life insurance companies permit me to trade 50-million-dollar blocks of corporate bonds if I couldn't perform bond math, which is patently more complicated than making change for a ten-dollar bill?

I elected for a third route. I had paid fifty-one thousand dollars out of my own pocket to acquire an MBA. During orientation, the dean had assured my classmates and I that the skills attained during the pursuit of our degree would be applicable in our vocations. Now was my big chance. I would use principles of quantitative analysis inside the Waffle House. In retrospect, I think Don Quixote had much better odds when he charged the windmills.

"How many drawer shortages did you say there have been?"

"Six in the last two weeks. You were working on four of those shifts."

"Uh-huh. Debbie, are you aware that you need to have thirty observations to make any statistically significant statement about whether my presence is correlated with the shortages?"

"Maybe it's not to *you*, but to Waffle House, twenty dollars is statistically significant."

"That's not what I meant. You need to have at least thirty *incidents* of twenty-dollar-plus drawer shortages before you can legitimately correlate them with my failure to properly subtract."

"Whatever. All I know is the drawer has been short, lately, and you've been working several of those shifts." She returned to the back room and lit a cigarette.

I had heard the term "kangaroo court" before, but I never really appreciated it until just then. I guess my inference that someone using fancy terms like "common denominator" would be well-versed in correlation coefficients. I just couldn't win.

"Y'all looking for help?" I turned to find a young man standing at the cash register.

"Given that we've recently fired three people, I'd presume the answer is an unequivocal 'yes.'"

"Are you the manager?"

"Goodness, no. I'm not even the assistant manager. *She* knows how to count; I'm still learning. But if you complete this form, I'll see that she gets it."

As I watched him fill out the application, a hand patted my back.

"You look tired," Matthew said. "It's obvious you had a rough night, so I went ahead and took care of your meat count tickets for you. Just take care of that last table over there and you can go home and get some sleep." He gestured to a booth where three graduate students had seated themselves.

"And don't worry about Debbie—she's just in a mood this morning. For what it's worth, I think you do know how to subtract."

I thanked him for the vote of confidence and reviewed the young man's application. He had, of course, been convicted of a felony. His explanation: "Guilt by association. At the wrong place, at the wrong time."

Boy, could I relate to that sentiment. I was finally beginning to understand the necessity of the "no firearms on these premises" sign in the break room. I didn't even own a gun, but the idea of firing a few rounds into the lights above the high bar had become an appealing proposition.

The graduate students were excitedly discussing the results of an intramural basketball game when I sauntered over to their table. Their t-shirt logos and cocky demeanor evidenced their status as students in an eminent MBA program. "We are three sharks, ready to conquer an ocean of commerce," their body language said. All I saw was three naive fish in a barrel, ripe for the shooting.

The dean of their business school had cofounded Alpha Managers twenty-five years ago and was known to frequently refer to the firm during his lectures. Students considered it a great honor to land a summer internship, let alone a permanent position, at the firm. I approached the booth with a modest hope, namely, that finding an Alpha Managers alumnus waiting tables at the local Waffle House would summarily destroy their model of the universe. This was going to be a lot of fun.

"Hey, how are you fellahs doing this morning? Any of you taking the investment class that the Dean teaches?" I asked in a ridiculously enthusiastic tone.

"Yeah, I'm taking it now," one said.

"Are you learning a lot?"

"I think so."

"That's good, I'm very happy to hear that."

"Hey, how did you know that the Dean teaches that class?"

"Oh, I used to work for his firm. Until two months ago."

His eyes visibly widened. "You were working at Alpha Managers?"

"Yes, in the Product Management group. Now could I interest you guys in some chocolate waffles? Or perhaps some hashbrowns?"

"Wait a minute. How did you end up working here?"

"That's not so important," I said. "What is important is that you boys start your day with a healthy, balanced meal."

"You *really* worked for Alpha Managers?" he asked incredulously.

This was going even better than planned.

"I'll tell you what, guys. You let me take your orders, and then I'll share a few anecdotes. Is that fair enough?"

They readily consented. I called their orders, brought out their drinks, then ducked into the back room. I sat down on the stool in the office, where I could observe their bantering behind the one-way mirror. Their demeanor was starting to shift from ebullience to confusion. I emerged back onto the floor, trying to maintain as straight a face as I could.

"So what happened?" one asked.

"We're going to have to drop you another waffle because we burned the first one. I'm terribly sorry about that, sir."

"No, I mean with your career."

"Well, I'm only a salesperson now, but with sufficient tenacity, I *could* be promoted to assistant manager in another eighteen months. If you wouldn't mind putting in a good word on my behalf with the manager, I'd sure appreciate it."

"Why aren't you at Alpha Managers, anymore?" The student to my right was getting visibly frustrated, and stifling my laughter was becoming increasingly difficult.

"Simple. As mortgage bond prices collapsed last year, our clients began closing their accounts. Our fees declined, so the firm couldn't support as many personnel. I got hit in the third wave of layoffs."

"But . . . you were at *Alpha Managers*," he protested.

"Yes. And now I'm at Waffle House. What's your point? "

"But that . . ." he shook his head violently. "That doesn't make any sense. You guys were supposed to be super smart. I mean, some of the top academics in the country."

"Have you ever heard of the Black-Scholes option pricing model?"

"Sure, everyone has. The guys that invented it received a Nobel prize in economics."

"That's right," I said. "They won it in 1997. The following year, the hedge fund they founded had the most spectacular collapse in the history of Wall Street."

Founded with a billion in capital in 1994, Long-Term Capital Management (LTCM) posted several years of annual returns in excess of 40%. By early 1998, the intellectual brain trust had grown to nearly $5 billion in capital and $130 billion in assets, creating a leverage ratio of 25-to-1. That summer, LTCM's highly-leveraged bets began to go awry. As its capital declined by more than 80% during the first three weeks of September, the fund's imminent failure threatened to compromise every trading desk on Wall Street. On September 23rd, the Federal Reserve Bank of New York orchestrated a $3.625 billion bailout by LTCM's creditors in order to prevent a total collapse in the financial markets.

"Academic credentials are no guarantee of good investment performance," I concluded. "Similarly, a stellar resume or an MBA degree from a leading institution does not ensure finding a job in a tumultuous economy."

I inquired how long the students had been in their program. The man to my left was in his first year; the two to my right were in their second (and final) year. One of them had secured post-graduate employment. I congratulated him on his good luck and leaned towards his less fortunate companion, framing my nametag between my thumb and index finger. It was within six inches of his eyeglasses when I resumed speaking.

"You see this?"

"Yuh . . . yeah," he stammered.

"Take a long, hard look at it," I admonished him. "In a few more months, it could have your name on it." I leaned back slowly. The first-year student covered his mouth as he chortled. The soon-to-be-employed man sat agape. The third—in whose face I had thrust "JIMMY, Salesperson since 2008"—was visibly shaking.

I wished the men well on the rest of their journey through higher education and excused myself to the break room. A plate of hashbrowns which I had hastily cooked four hours ago sat waiting for me. As the store had no microwave, I had no way of reheating them.

In the course of my career, I have eaten at four- and five-star restaurants in New York, Atlanta, Las Vegas, and Tokyo. No meal served at any of those establishments has been nearly as satisfying as the one I consumed on that Sunday morning. You see, a cold plate doesn't matter when your food has been seasoned with irony, the tastiest condiment of all.

$$\$\$\$\$\$$

"It is pride," C.S. Lewis wrote, "which has been the chief cause of misery in every nation and every family since the world began." As I have come to understand that the abuse of leverage is simply a manifestation of pride, I realize that truer words have never been spoken.

Instead of increasing their leverage solely issuing banknotes, banks began to write other kinds of liabilities. These instruments— checking accounts, savings accounts, and certificates of deposit— enabled depositors to participate in the interest earnings of the bank's loan pool. Broadly speaking, these non-banknote liabilities also functioned as part of the money supply.

The weighted average interest rate that the bank earns on its loan pool is called the **interest yield**. The weighted average interest rate that the bank pays on its deposits is known as its **cost of funds**. The **net interest margin** is the difference between the interest yield and the cost of funds. If the interest yield of the loans is 5% and the cost of funds is 3%, then the net interest margin is 2% (5% minus 3%). Normally, banks typically earn net interest margins between two and four percent.

The net interest margin is the bank's profit earned for 1) the legwork involved in underwriting the loans; 2) using its stockholders' capital to absorb the loan losses; and 3) returning cash to depositors on short (or immediate) notice.

The return on the stockholders capital is: Interest Yield + (Net Interest Margin x Leverage). By borrowing money at 3%, lending it

NEWTOWN BANK
Balance Sheet - Dec 30, 2010

Assets		Liabilities		Equity	
Reserves	$2,000,000	Savings Accts	$10,000,000	Stock	$1,000,000
Loans	$9,000,000				
	$11,000,000				

Interest yield:	5%	Cost of funds:	3%	Return on Equity:	25.0%
→	$550,000	→	$300,000	→	$250,000

at 5%, and leveraging their capital ten times, the bank stockholders earn a 25% return on their money (ignoring overhead expenses). Despite providing nearly 90% of the loanable funds, the depositors earn a paltry 3% return.

If the bankers want to earn even higher rates of return on equity, they have three options:

1. Pay depositors a lower rate of interest

2. Lend money at a higher rate

3. Use more leverage

We'll consider each of these options in turn.

1. Pay depositors a lower rate of interest. Generally speaking, this is the least practical option. Competition for deposits generally keeps banks from dramatically lowering the interest rates on savings accounts. Any large decline in deposit rates will be met with a wave of withdrawals as depositors seek a higher rate of return at another bank.

2. Lend money at a higher rate. In addition to contending for deposits, banks also compete with each other to lend money to creditworthy borrowers. Banks will lend at lower rates to persons that they believe have a high probability of repayment. (Remember the "four C's": character, capacity, collateral, and covenants.) If the bank wants to earn higher interest rates, it must resort to lending money to persons or businesses of increasingly dubious character, limited means of repayment, and little collateral. A good example of indiscriminate lending is granting loans to persons of dubious mental health whose only form of collateral is a plate of half-eaten hashbrowns.

As a concession to the bank for assuming higher default risk, the less creditworthy borrowers will agree to pay higher interest rates. By making these dicey loans, Newtown could raise its interest yield to 1%, thereby boosting its shareholder return to 36%:

NEWTOWN BANK
Balance Sheet - March 30, 2011

Assets		Liabilities		Equity	
Reserves	$2,000,000	Savings Accts	$10,000,000	Stock	$1,000,000
Loans	$9,000,000				
	$11,000,000				

Interest yield:	6.0%	Cost of funds:	3.0%	Return on Equity:	**36.0%**
→	$660,000	→	$300,000	→	$360,000

3. Use more leverage. For every one unit increase in leverage, the stockholders' return increases by the net interest margin. In the example below, Newtown has increased its leverage from 10 to 15, causing its return on equity to climb from 25% to 35%.

NEWTOWN BANK
Balance Sheet - March 30, 2011

Assets		Liabilities		Equity	
Reserves	$2,000,000	Savings Accts	$10,312,500	Stock	$687,500
Loans	$9,000,000				
	$11,000,000				

Interest yield:	5.0%	Cost of funds:	3.0%	Return on Equity:	**35.0%**
→	$550,000	→	$309,375	→	$240,625

All else equal, easier lending standards will increase the demand for land, houses, and other long-term real assets (also known as **capital assets**) on which most individual consumers spend their loan proceeds. The same holds for business assets: factories, warehouses, machinery, timber, equipment, etc. The demand for these capital assets is largely dictated by bankers' ability and willingness to furnish the capital. The other source of demand for capital assets is borrower optimism. If individuals and businesses feel confident that a prospective investment will increase in value, they will be confident to make the purchase. Efficient use of capital assets is the engine of higher productivity and, therefore, greater wealth.

Financial assets such as stocks, bonds, and bank loans are claims on capital assets. Ergo, business optimism and readily available credit drive up the prices of financial assets and capital assets. A rapid rise in the prices of financial assets is known as **asset inflation**.

Asset inflation should not be confused with the consumer price inflation that we have previously discussed. Inflation of consumer products, i.e., those goods which are *immediately* consumed, results from the money supply growing at a faster pace than the volume of consumer goods. (Remember the quantity theory of money? The "P" in the equation primarily consists of consumer prices.)

$$M \blacktriangle \ V = P \blacktriangle \ Y$$

To summarize, the loan growth that occurs in the asset column of a bank's balance sheet is a major driver of asset inflation. The growth in the money supply that occurs on the liability column of its balance sheet (through the fractional process) is the major driver of **consumer price inflation.** Money is backed by bank loans, whose values are tied to the prices of capital assets.

	support		*which support*	
Capital assets	▶	bank loans	▶	money

Bankers, while not renowned for being the life of most parties, are social animals nonetheless. Responding to the behavior of borrowers and other bankers, they are prone to alternating bouts of group optimism and pessimism. In their euphoric periods, bankers lend money on easier terms to increasingly less worthy borrowers, creating credit expansion. In more sober times, bankers are more discriminating in their lending decisions, causing credit contraction. The fluctuation between periods of credit expansion and contraction is known as the **credit cycle.**

Because asset prices are driven by both credit availability and speculator optimism, they are subject to self-reinforcing reflexive actions between speculators and their lenders. A rise in asset prices increases speculative fervor and demand for debt. Bankers, encouraged by the higher prices, lend speculators more money to purchase real estate, stocks, or other assets. The asset prices rise again, and the upward spiral continues.

Often, the asset prices reach a level that far exceeds any fundamental business justification. At this point, a prudent banker would be gravely concerned about borrowers' ability to repay their loans and quit extending credit. Instead, most lenders are content to rely on further asset appreciation. The party mentality has taken over.

It's safe and easy for most bankers to stick together and engage in the same reckless behavior. Of course, there are always a few who choose to remain sober rather than participate in the frenzy of easy credit and asset inflation. As the party continues, these people are often derided for failing to understand the "new paradigm." The sober bankers, while correct in their assessments, often become unpopular with their borrowers and shareholders alike.

In the short term, an illusion can become a temporary reality as long as it has a critical mass of popular acceptance—it doesn't matter if the emperor is really naked as long as everyone is willing to act as though he's actually wearing clothes. But as anyone who has been to high school is well aware, popular opinion and stupidity are frequent bedfellows. There is no long-term safety in numbers when the entire group is acting foolishly.

Sooner or later, reality strikes. The borrowers have insufficient cash flow to service their debts and begin to default on their loans. The rising loan losses deplete the banks' capital, constraining their ability to make new loans. Healthy banks begin to raise borrowing rates and tighten their lending standards. Highly leveraged banks, who had previously enjoyed high returns for their stockholders, suffer the most. They quit making new loans and, in many cases, call in existing loans in an attempt to raise their capital back to healthy levels.

As banks begin to withdraw financing, asset prices begin to decline. Potential borrowers grow pessimistic, resulting in further deterioration of asset prices, causing banks to become even more reticent to lend. The virtuous circle of asset appreciation has turned into a vicious downward spiral. The greater the overpricing in capital assets and the greater the banks' leverage, the more painful the adjustment process becomes.

The lesson is clear. As long as humans inhabit the earth, the pride cycle isn't going anywhere. And as long as humans are running banks, the credit cycle will surely be there as well.

$$\$\$\$\$\$$

I realize some of my culturally deprived readers (namely, those living north of the Mason-Dixon line or west of the Mississippi River) may have never encountered a bowl of grits. Please allow me to educate you on a dietary staple of the God-fearing Red States. Traditional grits is prepared by boiling ground corn kernels into a sticky, viscous porridge and then adding butter and salt. Second only to Nascar, this culinary masterpiece represents the South's greatest cultural achievement.

Waffle House customers consume over three million pounds of grits every year. I have seen them flavor their bowls with cheese, pepper, sugar, jelly, and chopped sausage patties. I have no personal recommendation on how grits is best consumed, because I don't eat the stuff.

My colleagues informed me that grits are also served daily at nearly all North Carolina penitentiaries. Ostensibly, grits are offered because it's a very inexpensive way for the state to keep the prisoners flush with carbohydrates. I'm inclined to think that their motives are far more odious. There's something about a whitish-grey bowl of porridge that smacks of a depressing 19th-century British workhouse (think *Oliver Twist*). Serving plain grits every day must undoubtedly demoralize the prisoners, effectively pre-empting any temptation to riot. I imagine a cruel warden laughing mercilessly as he personally ladles every scoop.

Beyond their dull appearance, grits exhibit an annoying ubiquity. They end up *everywhere* inside the Waffle House—on countertops, in between fork tines, even stuck on the back of order tickets. Even after a cup has been manually sprayed and run through the dishwasher, a grain or two inevitably remains clinging to its inside. Fortunately, the wayward granules can be readily camouflaged from customers by adding sufficient ice to the cups. But ice or no, burnt grits in a glass of water unfailingly draw customer ire, given their strong resemblance to dead gnats.

Because they are extremely adhesive and are always served at very hot temperatures, grits are the culinary equivalent of napalm. A grill operator told me (with a considerable degree of conviction) that the U.S. could completely extirpate Al Qaeda if we could simply manage the logistics of pumping large quantities into every large hole in Afghanistan. I had to concede that the idea had merit. The image of bin Laden drowning in a flood of the stuff is terribly appealing. But as I learned early one Saturday morning, terrorists aren't the only ones that need to fear a hot bowl.

Although the high bar assignment made me accountable for only six seats, I also had the responsibility of covering all to-go orders. Normally, I preferred this job because the automatic ten percent gratuity added to take-out checks meant that at least half of my total customers couldn't stiff me even if they wanted to.

The main drawback to the high-bar gig was trying to assuage the jealousies that inevitably arose from dividing my attention to both dine-in and dine-out patrons. Given the already harried state of the restaurant, it was simply impossible to keep everyone happy.

I was trying to communicate with a mute customer, who I believed was ordering a BLT sandwich, when we were interrupted by a girl to his right.

"Where's my food?" her shrill voice demanded. She had ordered three strips of bacon and a bowl of grits ten minutes ago, but the grill had been so backed up that I hadn't yet been able to call in the bacon order. I advised her of the situation, scooped a bowl of grits, and placed it in front of her.

"I'll bring out the bacon as soon as it's ready. In the meantime, please enjoy your grits."

She looked at my nametag. "Whuh-oah," she said in a confrontational tone, eyeing my nametag.

"Uh, 'Jimmy,' is it?" I nodded.

"Well, Jimmy, this is unacceptable. You need to bring out my bacon at the same time as my grits. I'm not going to put my bacon into a bowl of cold grits."

I assured her that I would bring a fresh bowl when the bacon was ready. At the end of our exchange, the mute man tapped my arm and pointed to his sweet tea. Signaling its bitterness, he puckered his lips and shook his head violently. Before I could offer to bring him more sugar, he gestured for my pen and scrawled out "Coke" on a napkin.

I called in the bacon orders for him and Grits Girl and brought out their beverages. The mute man nodded his head in gratitude; the girl wasn't so thankful.

"I hope you know I ain't payin' for this Sprite, Jimmy."

"Why is that?"

"You took too long getting it to me. You got to be faster if you want to get paid."

I put my hands on the counter and looked her right in the eyes. Eight consecutive weekends of this sort of churlish behavior had worn me thin. It had already been a long night, and I was in no mood to be addressed this way by a girl ten years my junior.

"Ma'am, I desperately want you to enjoy your dinner. But I'm new at this and I need a little information so I can optimize your Waffle House dining experience. Would you kindly tell me if you would prefer me to bring your food promptly or slowly?"

"What kind of a dumb question is that?"

"Well, I'm a little slow on the uptake when it comes to understanding contradictory orders. First, you tell me I was too fast with your grits. Then, I take too long on the Sprite and you start bitching at me."

Her mouth fell open as her two friends gasped simultaneously.

"What did you call me?" she fumed.

"I didn't call you anything. But I did accuse you of bitching at me."

"I'll tell you what's going to happen now," she said coolly as she placed her hand around the bowl. "You're gonna wear these grits, Jim-may!" She began cocking her arm.

I had done a fair amount of amateur boxing off and on over the past eight years. I wasn't the most aggressive fighter, but I had become extremely adept at slipping punches. Dodging a bowl of grits wouldn't be any more difficult, particularly having been given advance notice of its arrival.

"You know, I brought those grits out so long ago that they're probably cold by now," I said flatly. "If you really want to scald me, let me get you a hot bowl first."

Before she could offer a rejoinder to my salvo of trash talk, a coworker threw his body in front of me, spreading his arms across my chest in the manner of a bodyguard shielding a VIP from an assassin's bullet. After making a few conciliatory remarks to her, he put his hand on my shoulder and walked me into the break room.

"You can't talk to the customers like that!" Tommy exclaimed.

I spent the next ten minutes receiving an impromptu lecture on appropriate customer interaction from a twice-convicted felon. My words had inarguably been inappropriate, but the infraction seemed minor given that my coworkers frequently used the f-bomb, n-bomb, and all the other bombs in front of customers with total impunity. It was a tough pill to swallow.

I returned to the floor and found my dissatisfied customer still sitting at the high bar. She was visibly surprised by my approach.

"I'm sorry for what I said earlier," I began. "Things get a little hectic in here on weekends and I can get impatient. My outburst was inexcusable, and I hope you'll forgive me. I'm still fairly new at this." She gave me a deliberate nod.

"As a waiter, I'm not authorized to give you a free meal. But I would like to pay for yours," I said, placing a five-dollar bill on the counter. "I hope you'll visit us again soon."

"Well, Jimmy, I'll have to think about it."

A young man seated at the end of the bar overheard the conversation and decided to test the limits of my goodwill. "Hey man, I think you mighta been looking at me cross-eyed when you brought out my T-bone. How about covering my tab while you're at it?"

$$\$\$\$\$\$$$

When the crowd subsided at 4:30, I rolled the mop bucket outside the store and began to replenish it with hot water from an exterior spigot. It was halfway full when Tommy caught up with me. I expected him to continue his sermon where he had left off, and I wasn't looking forward to it. Instead, I received an outpouring of empathy.

"I've had some customers say some awful stuff to me. But no one had ever threatened to algreen me like that girl did to you. She left me no choice but to throw myself in there."

"She threatened to do what to me?"

"The grits. She was fixin' to go algreen on you."

Tommy then explained to me the origin of the term "algreen." In the mid-1970s, soul legend Al Green was assaulted by his girlfriend as he was climbing into the shower in his Memphis home. The deranged paramour heaved a pot of scalding hot grits on poor Al's back, causing third-degree burns on his back, stomach and arms. As Green was writhing in pain on the floor, she fled the bathroom and shot herself with his pistol.

Al was rushed to the hospital and emerged from his convalescence several months later with a decidedly religious mindset. He forsook R&B, began recording gospel music, and became an ordained minister. So, to "algreen" someone meant that you were going to douse them with hot grits in hopes of burning them so badly that they would emerge from the experience with a newfound fear of the Almighty.

"Your problem is that you're trying to do too much," Tommy explained. You need to focus on keeping a small number of customers happy instead o' trying to please everybody. It's better to let an impatient customer leave before they can place an order. Instead, if you start waitin' on 'em and they get frustrated, they'll probably walk out without paying."

"Or throw their food at you," I interjected.

"True 'nuff," Tommy said. "But whatever else happens, you gotta keep your cool. It's never worth lettin' folks get you so worked up you end up tellin' 'em off, no matter how much they deserve it."

He had a point. It's useless to tell someone to go to hell when they're already headed in that general direction.

I pulled my mop bucket back into the store and began mopping the floor. I had only been at it for a minute when Edward decided to interrogate me about the night's events.

"I saw you had a little trouble with the customahs last night, Jimmy."

"Edward, I can't take much more of this. These college girls are going to kill me."

"I don't blame 'em. I feel like killing you myself half the time when you mess up your calls."

"Yes, Edward, but at least you're reasonably polite about it. I mean, I used to work my butt off for Japanese clients, but they never got so nasty with me. And I lost them a few billion dollars. These girls freak out if their grits are lukewarm."

"Has any customers been speaking to you in Japanese?"

"No, Edward."

"And do you see anyone come in here wearing a kimono or carrying a samurai sword on their belt?"

"No, I haven't, Edward."

"And do you see any signs that say 'Tokyo' anywhere 'round here?"

"I can't say that I have, Edward."

"Then why would you expect to get treated like you was serving waffles in Japan? What was it Dorothy done said in that *Wizard of Oz* movie: 'Toto, we ain't in Kansas no mo.'"

"I believe that's what she said, yes."

"Well, you ain't in Kansas. And you ain't in Japan neither, so you'd better get used to it. Look, if you are accustomed to riding in a Cadillac," he said, turning an imaginary steering wheel, "and then you go mountain biking," he continued, moving his fists in small circular motions, "you should anticipate a bumpier ride. Ya see, a mountain bike don't have as good a suspension as a Coup de Ville."

In this case, Edward's logic was undeniably cogent. My new vocation had taken me pretty far through the looking glass. I had to be more conscious of the cultural nuances of my customers.

"You're right, Edward. I just don't understand why some people have to be so rude."

"Well, when the first Waffle House opens in Tokyo, you can apply for a transfer. I'll even put in a good word for you with the corporate office. Then you'll be able to wait on all them polite Japanese folks."

"You'd do that for me?"

"Yeaauuuh," he said with a confirming nod. "It can be a little rough with those girls sometimes. But you'll be alright. Just be glad you don't have to fight off a pack of monkeys like the ones that ripped that scarecrow to pieces." He turned back to the grill and diced a cheesesteak patty with his spatula. "Flyin' monkeys. I hate those thangs."

$$$$

For as much time as he spent upbraiding me, Edward appeared to genuinely enjoy guiding my transformation (however gradual) from hapless financier to server extraordinaire. The week after my run-in with Grits Girl, I overheard him enumerating my new talents in the sort of boastful tone that a master uses when cataloguing the tricks he has imparted to his new puppy.

"You ought to see him now," he said proudly to two young men at the high bar. "The man can wash dishes, set up the tables, wipe down the tables, serve the food, and even cook some of the food. Hashbrowns, waffles, burgers, eggs, he do that okay. Obviously, there's some things that still elude him. For example, omelets are still way over his head." The boys gave an understanding nod. "But he knows the price of almost everything on the menu. And the man does real good arithmetic—he can add with the best of them. He was a financial man in his past life, so he's got a knack with numbers, which serves to offset his weakness elsewhere. And there *are* still a few chinks floating around in his armor. Ain't that right, Jimmy Jam?"

As I started to respond, Edward advised me that his question had been purely rhetorical. He was merely using me as an illustration for an economics lecture.

"Take this man here," he said, pointing at me. "There's always work to be done, somewhere. The only question is what kind of job it is, where the job is, and if you're willing to accept the wage. As long as you're willing to adapt yourself to different kinds of work, then there really ain't no such thing as a recession," he posited.

$$\$\$\$\$\$$

The **business cycle** refers to economy-wide changes in production over a number of months (or years). During the upswing of the cycle, total output increases at a relatively fast pace, worker productivity increases, and unemployment generally declines. During a downswing, production declines as factory capacity and labor go unused. Companies shutter plants and lay off workers. A **recession** occurs when a deterioration in the economy's output lasts for two consecutive three-month periods.

During the late 19ᵗʰ and early 20ᵗʰ centuries, there was widespread agreement among economists as to the causes of the business cycle. Recessions and unemployment were the result of changes in the structure of production (i.e., the type, location, and labor composition of output)—exactly as Edward had posited. This is known as the **Classical theory of the business cycle**. It is the most lucid explanation for why recessions occur, which makes you wonder why it hasn't been taught in university classrooms for the past seven decades. I myself hadn't encountered it in any form until I eavesdropped on Edward's lecture.

Prior to Adam Smith's writings, economic slowdowns were generally attributed to a scarcity of money and/or a general overproduction of goods. Smith had exploded the first myth in *The Wealth of Nations*. (Remember, producing more money only results in higher prices, not more production.) Jean-Baptiste Say developed his "Law" as a means of repudiating the "overproduction" fallacy. There could never be excessive production of all goods, Say claimed, only of particular goods.

Although Say didn't write extensively about the business cycle, Say's Law provided the foundation by which later economists understood it. As economies developed, production became increasingly specialized. Greater division of labor (and capital) enabled quantum leaps in productivity. Consequently, standards of living dramatically improved. People were able to consume more goods simply because they were producing more of them. However, the division of labor and capital that Adam Smith heralded as the great driver of economic productivity had an unfortunate downside.

In a developed economy, people do not consume most of their own production but rely extensively on trade. The welfare of individual businesses and workers depends heavily on their ability to find willing buyers for the goods which they produce. Therefore, each economic actor must forecast what sort of goods that others desire for months (or even years) before he actually produces it.

For example, a woman who attends medical school and studies oncology is making a prediction that chemotherapy will be needed after she finishes her residency. Effectively, she is wagering that cancer will not be cured until many years after she begins to practice medicine. Of course, if a bona fide cure for cancer is discovered, she will find that the demand for her services will quickly evaporate.

Now imagine how the doctor's spending habits will change when the market no longer has a need for her specialty. Because she is no longer producing a valuable good, she will lose her ability to purchase the goods and services of others. The medical service that she had been supplying may have constituted a demand for a luxury automobile. If the doctor can no longer sell her services, the car dealer will soon find his own sales declining. As the car dealer sells fewer automobiles, the demand for steel and rubber will decline in turn.

The principle here is simple, yet profound: if one person fails to produce a desired good, she loses the capacity to purchase someone else's production. That is, *one person's supply constitutes another person's demand.* If one set of producers cannot buy, then another set cannot sell. So a disruption of supply in one market affects the supply in another market, and so on. Economically speaking, John Milton was absolutely right in stating that "no man is an island."

As the doctor's situation illustrates, production miscalculations are quickly transmitted from one individual or business to another. Because one person's production is another's consumption, a reduction of output in one industry reverberates throughout other sectors of the economy in a chain reaction. That is, declining supply in one sector reduces the demand for products in other sectors.

Production miscalculations can occur as the result of a sudden "disruptive" technological breakthrough, as in the case of the hypothetical cancer cure. But in most cases, the errors usually occur as a result of the pride/credit cycle. Rising asset prices cause too much capital and labor to be allocated to a "hot" industry (such as the housing market in recent years). *The greater the misallocation of capital and the more leverage employed, the greater the adverse repercussions in the broad economy.*

While *relative* overproduction of undesirable (or unprofitable) goods may temporarily occur, a *general* overproduction of goods is not possible. Economic downturns do not occur because an economy has produced too much of everything. Resources become idle only because they have been producing *certain* goods that are no longer in demand.

A general "demand failure" is never the cause of recession, because supply is always the basis for demand. The problem of recession is that supply exceeds demand in particular segments of the economy. Companies that fail to supply the correct type of goods, at a market-clearing prices, will be left with unsold inventories or unused labor. Consequently, the "unused" laborers soon receive layoff notices.

It's easy to deride the market as a callous, faceless institution that cares only about profit and nothing for an individual's job security. But that attitude betrays a misunderstanding about what the market really is. "The market" is really just another name for "the people," and it is the most purely democratic institution on earth. You can think of each dollar as a vote. The number of votes you receive is a function of how much worthwhile stuff you produce for other voters. If you are making a product that is in high demand, but is in short supply, you will garner a lot of votes in the form of dollars.

By equating "the market" with "the people," recessions can be understood as a referendum on the economy. The question being decided is how society will allocate its resources. The electorate casts its votes for businesses that generate value in the form of high-quality products and/or competitive prices. Those companies that produce undesirable products or whose sales cannot cover their production costs are voted out of office.

Some 19th-century economists believed that recessions and unemployment resulted from overproduction of all goods. Recessions, they claimed, resulted from being too productive! Of course, this notion is a total canard. Think about it: if recessions were caused by making too much of everything, then society would be in a constant state of depression and our standards of living would not have improved exponentially over the past two centuries.

Say's *Treatise* provides the key to surmounting recession and unemployment: "when a nation has too large a quantity of one particular type of product, the means of disposing of them is to create goods of another variety." *The appropriate response to recession isn't to quit producing; it is simply to begin producing different items.* Economic recovery arrives as businesses rationalize their costs, re-price existing products, and offer new products that are in demand.

Recessions, while uncomfortable for those adversely affected, are a necessary adjustment process. Capital and labor are redeployed from industries where there is too little demand into areas where there will be demand (at cost-covering prices) for the goods produced. In the oncologist's case, she might find gainful employment by working in another branch of medicine (or, in a worst-case scenario, by waiting tables at a 24-hour dining establishment).

Economies consist of millions of products and countless types of labor. Some of these products will be demanded at certain prices, others will not. It is just that simple. The key to maintaining output and employment at high levels is to produce goods and services in correct proportions to each other. If these ratios of various types of production are correct, then all products will be sold at prices that cover their costs of production.

Recessions force companies to use their resources—namely, labor and capital—more efficiently. As these resources are reallocated to the changes in market demand, output increases and employment conditions alleviate. However, if potential workers are not offering the types of skills desired by employers, or if their wage and salary requirements are excessive, they will remain unemployed. Naturally, no one wants to admit that the labor skills they are offering are 1) undesirable or 2) priced too high. But if we truly believe Say and the Classical economists, then the onus lies with the unemployed man to restructure his production, just as Edward asserted.

Forty years ago, financial services comprised only 3% of total U.S. output. By 2007, the sector mushroomed to 7.5% of the nation's economy. Instead of building bridges or designing more fuel-efficient vehicles, mathematicians and engineers had been recruited to Wall Street, where they designed financial schemes to put people in homes that they simply couldn't afford. The reckoning of an untenable situation was at hand. The economy was enduring a massive restructuring of its production, and the adjustment process had robbed millions of other Americans of their livelihood. The type and cost of production that they had been supplying was considerably mismatched with the demand for that same output.

As far as my own job loss was concerned, the market clearly no longer demanded another PR man to furnish an optimistic assessment of the mortgage market. Accordingly, if I wanted to retain some capacity to consume, I was forced to produce a commodity for which a healthy market still remained: namely, cheap, quality breakfast food. Undoubtedly, the shift had been for the greater good of society.

A dramatic change in the field of your production can be a traumatic thing. When you have been engaged in one line of work for the best part of a decade, it's difficult to imagine yourself doing anything else. I tried to think of my new job as a career "restructuring," but after a few weeks, the word began to sound awfully euphemistic. After all, a root canal "restructures" your tooth. But for both recessions and root canals, the long-run benefits are well worth the temporary discomfort involved. Regrettably, economists have forgotten this truth for the past seven decades.

The primary responsibility of economists is to forecast and interpret recessions. They are particularly bad at it. To accurately prognosticate a nation's output involves a solid understanding of each of its industries and the dynamic interaction between each of them. Considering these innumerable idiosyncrasies across thousands of industries and millions of firms, you begin to understand why projecting the precise path of the economy is truly a fool's errand.

How economists view the world:

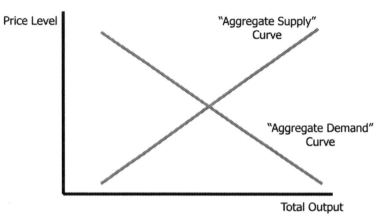

To create a patina of sophistication to hide their theoretical shortcomings, modern economists employ intricate mathematical models and fancy graphs to represent the aggregate economy. Lost in the math and the charts, however, is an appreciation for the diversity of goods and services produced, as well as their individual prices. Economists pay minor lip service to this "aggregation problem," and then proceed with their modeling just as though it never existed.

Above is a graphic representation of the broad economy taught in all macroeconomic textbooks. "Total output" represents the myriad goods and services in an economy which sell at a weighted-average "price level." Early in the term, college economic students are taught how to draw this "X," then spend the rest of their semester being inundated with bogus theories about business cycle fluctuations resulting from the movements of these two lines.

The graph is a very convenient way to look at the world. Unfortunately, it wholly ignores all of the subtle but important nuances of economic reality—namely, the structure of production. In this model, there is no diversity of industries, products, or labor. As far as the graph is concerned, a waffle and a BMW are the same product, sold at the same price. What a tremendously accurate depiction of the way things really work.

In the world of the graph, the movements of the aggregate supply and the aggregate demand curves are considered independently of each other. Regrettably, most contemporary economists have long since forgotten that economic demand is, has always been, and will always be determined by supply. Were they to reconsider the graph's value in the context of Say's Law, they would realize that only a fool would take it seriously.

Because economists value elegant mathematics more than common sense, Say's Law and the Classical theory of the business cycle have been completely omitted from contemporary textbooks. My first exposure to these principles came from Edward, who had no formal training in economics. It's amazing how perceptive a man can really be when his mind hasn't been compromised by college professors. Then again, nobody understands the "no free lunch" principle of Say's Law better than the man who has just cooked three chicken sandwiches.

Chapter 5

CRIME AND PUNISHMENT

"No man for debt shall go to jail from Garryowen in glory."
—Irish drinking song

In celebration of its fiftieth anniversary in 2005, Waffle House commissioned its own version of Monopoly. "WAFFLE-OPOLY" was produced exclusively for company employees and has become a collector's item amongst die-hard fans of the restaurant. Game pieces include eggs in a skillet, cheeseburger, T-bone, pie slice, coffee mug, and iced tea. Waffle slices and company stores substitute for houses and hotels. A Waffle House sales associate adorns the one-dollar bill. Higher denominations feature company executives.

Waffle House store locations serve as property spaces. In lieu of Pennsylvania, Reading, B&O, and Short Line railroads are four company principals appearing in caricature. Each is accompanied by an eponymous menu item: Alice's Iced Tea, Bert's Chili, Lib's Patty Melt, and Walt's Soup. The "Go" and "Free Parking" corner spaces have been renamed "Grand Opening" and "Free Refills," respectively. The other two corner spaces of WAFFLE-OPOLY are marked "Corporate Office" and "Go to Corporate Office."

While I appreciate the mandate to Waffle-ize the board, the game designers might have left the original "JAIL" and "Go to Jail" designations in place. At my store, every male employee except the manager and yours truly had spent time in a state or federal correctional facility.

My colleagues spoke of their prison time in the same manner that middle-aged suburbanites might reminisce about their high school football injuries. Tommy lifted his shirt to display two bullet wounds which he had obtained in separate gunfights, one of which had led to a conviction. As a rejoinder, Edward brandished a knife wound on his forearm and related an account of the prison yard brawl wherein he obtained it. After exhibiting their battle scars, they each went on to describe those that they had inflicted on their adversaries.

I briefly considered relating the time that I had incurred a severe bruise while making a game-winning save as the lacrosse goalie of my prep school team, but soon thought better of it. However dramatic my adversity may have seemed during high school, it paled in comparison to being kissed by a .38 slug.

Where ex-jocks might boast of passionate escapades with cheerleaders, Edward related several accounts of romancing female prison guards. After months of speculation as to why a female would seek employment at a male correctional facility, he had received an epiphany. No woman, he realized, would ever pursue that vocation unless she was absolutely desperate for attention. The romantic liaisons weren't exactly the stuff of Walt Disney films. Snow White doesn't share her first kiss with Prince Charming when she confronts him about the contraband she's just discovered in his foot locker.

Edward had briefly labored as a custodian and in the prison laundry before finally obtaining a kitchen job. He became head chef in short order, overseeing six other cooks as they served breakfast and lunch to eleven-hundred inmates. (And, yes, they did serve vast quantities of grits.) The job only paid a dollar for a day's labor, but Edward soon discovered a way to augment his income by fermenting orange and tomato juice mixes in the kitchen heating ducts. Within 24 hours, he could manufacture a four-ounce drink that would set even the largest convict with three sheets firmly to the wind.

While I was quite certain that Edward's distillery was in violation of prison rules, I couldn't help but admire his entrepreneurial spirit. Most of his beverage sales were dollar-denominated, but transactions were also frequently paid for in cigarettes, which were broadly accepted as currency. Although Edward wasn't in the habit of extending any form of credit, many inmates frequently loaned cigarettes to each other. In the penitentiary, however, tardy debt repayments were not met with the same level of clemency that they might have been on the outside.

Lenders taught borrowers a visceral lesson in the importance of honoring their debts by sabotaging a cigarette with a small ball of aluminum foil stuffed with shaved match heads. Halfway through such a custom-manufactured Newport, the deadbeat debtor's cigarette would explode in flames to tremendous comedic effect. The gag didn't always precipitate swift debt repayment, but at least the creditor could get a measure of justice.

Of course, Edward explained, this trick could be played on relatives as well as derelict borrowers. He had recently offered a modified cigarette to his sister-in-law, whose hair almost caught on fire as a result. Edward had nearly fallen off his chair convulsing in laughter; she found the prank considerably less amusing than he did.

"Some people just can't appreciate a practical joke," I offered.

"Well, that's women for you," Edward said.

In prison, Edward had taken a variety of vocational training courses that had enabled him to perform a wide array of tasks subsequent to his parole. Over the past four years, he had worked in construction, painted houses, and done a number of odd jobs which allowed him to showcase his new skills in plumbing and small-engine repair. When money became really tight, he took his pool cue to the local billiard hall and earned a few dollars playing eight ball. I don't know whether his wide array of talents would technically classify him as a "Renaissance Man," but he certainly had an unimpeachable work ethic.

Incidentally, Edward loathed the idea of anyone going on the dole, although not for reasons common to middle- and upper-class Americans. While most people have an aversion to public welfare schemes on the grounds that government redistribution of wealth is tantamount to theft by the state, Edward's justification was much more primal. In his mind, any man who accepted a handout despite being able to find work (albeit not in the field of his choice) was compromising his masculinity. Any self-respecting man, he asserted, should at least have the initiative to take on some part-time work as a gigolo. I can't (or rather, shouldn't) weigh in on whether he had done so himself.

$$\$\$\$\$\$$$

If Edward epitomized the criminal justice system's ability to transform a shiftless man into a hard-working one, the store also had a case study in recidivism. On the weeknights when I wasn't working with Edward, I was paired with a thirty-five-year-old parolee named Maurice. While deviousness, infidelity, and penchant for larceny are not uncommon traits, very few people exhibit all of them. Maurice did. In spades.

Taken individually, each of these attributes was obnoxious. But aggregated behind an unapologetic Cheshire cat grin, Maurice's personality defects proved unexpectedly entertaining. He was the man you loved to hate—a ghetto version of J.R. Ewing.

In lieu of the double-breasted suits worn by Larry Hagman, Maurice sported flannel shirts and low-riding blue jeans that exposed six inches of his plaid boxer shorts. J.R. emerged from his Mercedes wearing a ten-gallon hat; Maurice rolled up to the Waffle House in a Cadillac Escalade and adorned himself with a black do-rag.

Maurice's favorite scam was giving free T-bone and sirloin steaks to his friends, who then paid a token amount of hush money to keep the servers quiet about the inventory theft. I regret to admit my inadvertent complicity in one of these transactions. I should have known that a game was afoot when Maurice magnanimously volunteered to wait on their table for me, but I had accepted his offer. Since I had seen him purloin my gratuities on two occasions, I figured that at least this time he would have to work for the money that he would have stolen, anyway.

When he wasn't engaging in unethical business practices or planning a tryst on his cell phone, Maurice spent his discretionary time sleeping in booths whenever the store was vacant. I didn't go out of my way to banter with him, but sometimes the dialogue found its way to me.

"People around here have been talking about you," he said. "They say you was a banker or somethin'."

"Well, the people have their facts wrong," I said.

"So what was it that you did, Man?"

I didn't feel like telling Maurice that I had spent the last two years writing condolence letters to institutional investors. A little creativity was in order.

"I used to blow up banks," I said coolly.

"No kiddin'. I had a cousin that used to rob banks. Like they say, it's a small world after all."

"I never said I robbed them. I said I blew them up."

"So what, did you use like dynamite or something?"

"Vault jobs are for rank amateurs," I asserted.

"So how did you blow them up then?"

"Well," I said in the most casual tone I could muster, "my crew and I convinced the bank officers to give us the money. Then we turned around and used that money to buy a lot of mortgage bonds. Then those bonds tanked, leaving the banks with no capital. So now the U.S. Treasury Department, and in some cases a foreign government, has to rebuild them. That's what it means to blow up a bank."

My claim was 90% true. A number of our Japanese bank clients had taken substantial write-downs on mortgage-backed bonds that we had purchased for them. I couldn't help but wince as I read their press releases, knowing that we were to blame for their atrocious quarterly earnings. None of the banks had actually folded as a consequence, but the results were still bad enough that I had to seriously consider that I might have been partially responsible for at least one incident of boardroom seppuku.

Maurice eyed me as he stroked his goatee. After a few seconds of contemplation, he finally broke his silence.

"You're one bad mofo," he said, offering me a fist bump.

"True dat," I said, punching his knuckles.

He headed back to the grill, shaking his head and repeating the phrase "blowing up banks." The large grin on his face and zealous tone in his voice led me to believe that he wished he had conceived the scheme himself. After all, bank demolition was more lucrative than accepting small cash kickbacks in exchange for furnishing your buddies with free sirloin dinners.

I smiled. With just a modicum of hyperbole, I had firmly established my street cred.

$$\$\$\$\$\$$

There are, broadly speaking, two ways to get rich in business: 1) start your own small business and expand it; or 2) work for a corporation and ascend the ladder over the course of your career. The first course necessitates a lot of creativity, managerial skills, long hours, and tenacity. The corporate route primarily requires the ability to politick, endure endless conference meetings with a straight face, and write needless memoranda.

But there's yet another route to a pot of gold without the nuisance of attending medical school. It requires little intelligence, formal education or political acumen. And here's the best part: its potential for generating wealth is virtually unlimited.

The model is simple: a speculator borrows a lot of money, uses the cash to purchase real estate, maintains or makes improvements to his lot, and waits for the value of the property to appreciate. If the bet pays off, the speculator keeps the profits. If the bet sours, any losses exceeding his investment cost are transferred to a third party.

Real estate is the most common type of capital asset financed by the banking system. In most cases, the borrower puts down a fraction of the purchase price of the land and buildings—typically, between 10 and 25% of the property's value. The remainder is furnished by the bank.

In the example below, an investor purchases a small shopping center for $10 million. He invests $2 million of his own capital and borrows the remaining $8 million. A $10 million capital asset— the shopping center—supports $10 million in financial assets, which represent claims on that property. (Remember, stocks, bonds, and bank loans are just stakes in capital assets.)

A Typical Real Estate Transaction

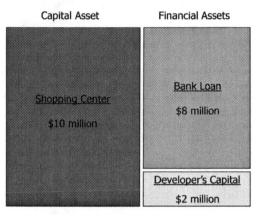

Here's where the story gets interesting. Not only has the developer borrowed money to finance the building purchase, but the bank has also borrowed money to finance its lending.

While the real estate speculator has a legal obligation to repay his debt to the bank, the bank has a concurrent legal obligation to repay its depositors. The bank is lending its money on a principal basis, i.e., on its own behalf. It is *not* an agent investing the money on behalf of its depositors. This point cannot be overemphasized.

On average, banks borrow roughly ninety dollars for every one dollar of their own capital that they lend. In this case, the bank borrows $7.2 million from its depositors (90% x $8 million). These borrowings could be in the form of banknotes, checking accounts, or savings accounts. Each of these accounts is also a type of financial asset, and all of them constitute the money supply.

The developer financed a $10 million capital asset (the shopping center) with $8 million in bank debt. But the bank has financed the $8 million loan with $7.2 million of financial assets. Because a chain of debts has been created, a $10 million capital asset is now supporting $15.2 million dollars in total debt.

When Real Estate Gets Scary

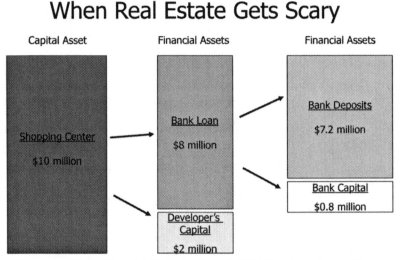

There are $15.2 million of debts backed by only $10 million in capital assets.

If the developer can earn sufficient rental income from the shopping center to service his debts, he stands to earn a nice rate of return on his $2 million investment, particularly if the property climbs in price. If he sells the property for $13 million, he would earn a 150% rate of return ($3 million gain divided by his $2 million in capital). But regardless of how much the property's value rises, the bank will not see an extra nickel of interest income, and neither will the bank depositors. Despite financing only 20% of the investment's total cost, the developer retains all of the upside benefit.

During the expansion phase of the credit cycle, real estate buyers are incentivized to employ as much leverage as possible. In the example above, a buyer that puts down only $1 million and subsequently sells the property for $13 million will earn a 300% return on his capital.

During asset booms, holders of both capital assets (e.g., real estate buyers) and financial assets (e.g., banks) will be strongly tempted to increase their returns by maximizing their leverage. As long as the boom continues, both levered real asset buyers and levered financial asset buyers will reap large economic rewards.

As the downturn in the business cycle unfolds, our shopping center begins to lose tenants. (Some of them may have gone out of business; others may have found cheaper rent elsewhere due to recent overbuilding.) The diminished rent fails to provide adequate cash flow to service the bank loan. The bank forecloses on the property and sells it at auction. As long as the bank can dispose of the shopping center at a price above $8 million, its capital will not be threatened. If the bank sells at any level below $8 million, however, the losses begin to drain its capital.

In the down phase of a normal credit cycle, banks slow their lending and/or call in loans in an effort to replenish their capital. Because of bankers' rising cash preference (i.e., liquidity preference), depositor savings are no longer quickly recycled into investment, and economic uncertainty rises. In turn, businesses and consumers also become more judicious in their spending decisions, increasing their cash preference. As more cash sits idle in bank vaults and consumer pockets, money travels through the economy at a slower pace of circulation, or velocity.

The primary effect of the declining velocity is to place downward pressure on capital asset prices. Additionally, some consumer prices may experience moderate price declines as people scale back on discretionary purchases ($MV\blacktriangledown = P\blacktriangledown Y$). But in general, the prices of consumer sundries will not fall off a cliff. Even in a recession, most people aren't willing to hoard their cash to the point where it means foregoing purchases of toilet paper (although there may be noteworthy exceptions in some parts of West Virginia).

Here's where the story can get really ugly. As depositors learn that a large number of their bank's loans have started to go bad, they begin to get nervous. They know that as the bank's capital cushion is eroded by the loan losses, their deposits become increasingly unsafe. Accordingly, they begin to withdraw their money en masse in a **bank run**. Because most of the bank's assets consist of loans (rather than cash), it is unable to satisfy all of the redemption requests. The bank is now simultaneously experiencing acute severe credit problems (from the defaulting loans) and liquidity problems (as depositors redeem their checking and savings accounts for cash). In many cases, the contagion of fear spreads as a run on one bank sparks a run on several others.

There is something very unique and strange about money. It is created gradually in commercial banks through the fractional reserving process but can be rapidly destroyed through an erosion of confidence. During bank runs, bank liabilities cease to function as money. Businesses quit honoring checks written against the accounts of less reputable banks. Depositors redeem their accounts for cash, and the fractional reserving process is thrown into reverse, causing the money supply to shrink.

Just as blood transmits the output from one organ to another, so money enables the exchange of economic production. When the body hemorrhages large amounts of blood, the blood pressure drops, and organs begin to shut down. The economy exhibits similar effects when the public severs the "monetary arteries" in bank runs. When money is being destroyed, it becomes nearly impossible to exchange real production because money itself becomes the primary commodity in demand. Economic actors have little incentive to produce because they know that their potential customers will be hoarding their cash rather than exchanging it for production. As a consequence of the "blood loss," the real economy shrinks rapidly in a pernicious downward spiral known as **debt deflation**. ($M\blacktriangledown V\blacktriangledown = P\blacktriangledown Y\blacktriangledown$)

As both the money supply and the real economy shrink, wages and consumer prices begin to drop precipitously. The decline in consumer prices puts another round of pressure on asset prices. For example, if bread prices keep falling due to money destruction, then the value of the bakery (the capital asset which produces the bread) must soon follow. So a drop in the money supply lowers the prices of capital assets.

supports

Money ▸ Capital asset prices

Capital assets only have value to the extent that they represent a claim on money (in the form of rent or profits from production). But remember, in a fractional reserve banking system, the money supply is almost entirely supported by bank loans. And bank loans, in turn, are supported by capital asset prices.

support   *which support*   *which supports*

Capital asset prices ▸ Bank loans ▸ Money supply ▸ Capital asset prices

Money is the link which forges the chain of debts into a triangle of interdependent liabilities.

The triangle is the strongest shape….

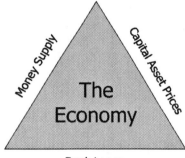

But each of the sides must be firm!

Once a triangle is constructed, the angles between the sides are permanently fixed, making it the strongest geometric shape. Unlike a rectangle, whose sides will bend or totally collapse under stress, the triangle responds to pressure by either contracting or expanding. Its resiliency makes the triangle indispensible in architectural applications when strong supports are needed—e.g., bridge trusses. Of course, these benefits are entirely contingent on the resiliency of each of the triangle's sides. If one of them is fragile, the weakness spreads, splintering the shape into pieces. So it is with the economy: the money supply, asset prices, and bank lending must all be sound, or the entire system can collapse.

The commercial banking system creates two layers of debt behind one capital asset. During periods of asset inflation, this arrangement enables a cohort of bankers and speculators to become fantastically wealthy through the magic of leverage. During the reckoning of debt deflation, however, the correction in asset prices compromises the entire economy as the medium of exchange is destroyed.

Here, then, is capitalism's dirty little secret: Creating multiple layers of debt enables immense private profits, while creating the potential for large losses that are socialized throughout the entire economic system. In an immoral arrangement, the sins of a minority are involuntarily borne by the masses.

Adam Smith is not pleased.

$$\$\$\$\$\$$

Just as much as nationalism or religious zeal, money has been a primary driver of history. And yet, monetary events get tragically short shrift in history curriculums. I suspect that historians deemphasize the role of banking and money in their analyses primarily because they don't understand how it actually works (putting them in the same league as most economists).

The United States suffered through numerous bouts of debt deflation during the 19th century. These episodes are generally referred to as financial "panics" or "depressions." The labels are apt: if you wake up one day to find your entire life savings destroyed when your bank collapses, the natural reaction is indeed panic and depression.

Each of the "panics" —1819, 1837, 1857, 1873, and 1893— had the hallmarks of any credit cycle: prosperity and aggressive lending practices followed by souring loans and bank runs. I find the first two incidents particularly intriguing, because they are linked to America's seventh President.

In late 1818, the U.S. Government was obligated to deliver $4 million in either gold or silver to European investors in payment of debts incurred for the Louisiana Purchase fifteen years before. The Second Bank of the United States, a precursor to our modern Federal Reserve, was required to make this payment on the government's behalf. Effectively, the United States Treasury needed to withdraw its money (i.e., gold) from the bank in order to repay its debts to the European creditors.

In order to meet this obligation, the bank was forced to demand repayment (in the form of gold) of loans that it previously made to commercial banks. In turn, the commercial banks had to demand repayment of loans which they had extended. As the Second Bank of the United States called in its loans, a shockwave went throughout the entire economy. The flow of gold went as follows:

U.S. commercial bank customers ▸ U.S. commercial banks ▸ Bank of the United States ▸ U.S. Gov't ▸ European lenders

The ensuing "Panic of 1819" caused a severe contraction in bank credit. As the banks erased their liabilities (banknotes & deposits), money was destroyed, and prices fell. This was a tolerable situation if you held most of your wealth in the form of gold or you were a European who owned U.S. Treasury bonds. It was a bad situation if you had borrowed money from a commercial bank and had to pay it back in a hurry. Unfortunately, Andrew Jackson was one of those borrowers. Hard-pressed to repay his real estate debts during this period, Jackson developed a lifelong hostility to all fractional-reserve banks.

General Jackson, wildly popular for killing hundreds of British soldiers during the War of 1812 (and thousands of American Indians in subsequent years), was elected President of the United States in 1828. Jackson spent most of his first term coercing Indians into relocating west of the Mississippi River. He was also successful in coercing South Carolina to accept a punitive tariff by threatening to close its ports. Jackson's only political failure was one he couldn't settle at the point of a gun: despite his cajoling, the wives of his cabinet members refused to socialize with each other.

In 1832, Jackson was elected for a second Presidential term. Having subdued the British, the Indians, and the South Carolinians, but still unable to resolve the "Petticoat Affair," Jackson opted for another target. He decided to settle an old score with the Second Bank of the United States. His primary opponent was the president of the bank, Nicholas Biddle.

A Philadelphia native, Biddle was an intellectual prodigy. He graduated from Princeton University at age 15 as the class valedictorian. A trained attorney, he spoke fluent French and prepared the majority of the report for the Lewis and Clark expedition. In the Pennsylvania legislature, he had campaigned heavily for public education. It's safe to describe Biddle as a "Renaissance Man." It's also safe to say that his bank never had any real chance of survival once Jackson trained his guns on it.

In early 1833, Jackson decided to withdraw all of the federal treasury's deposits from the bank. Knowing that economic chaos would surely result, Treasury Secretary Louis McLane refused. Jackson replaced McLane, but his successor also refused to make the move. Finally, a third appointee, Roger B. Taney, complied with the President's request. Having lost its largest depositor, the Bank of the United States was forced to call in its loans in order to accommodate the treasury's demand for gold and silver specie. The resulting credit contraction threw the country into a recession.

The U.S. Senate censured Jackson on March 28, 1834, for his action in removing the deposits from the bank. The President defended his decision on the grounds that the national banking system was unconstitutional. He ascribed the economic malaise to the actions of Biddle, who he believed was "out to get him." Not everyone agreed with this explanation for the recession, which was more or less analogous to shooting a houseguest and then blaming him for bleeding all over your living room carpet.

The following January, an unemployed housepainter named Richard Lawrence attempted to shoot the President as he emerged from the Capitol Building. Both of the would-be assassin's pistols misfired, and Jackson promptly began bludgeoning the assailant with his cane. After being apprehended, Lawrence explained that after the President's death, "money would be more plenty" —meaning that credit conditions would ease absent Jackson's meddling with the Bank of the United States. Lawrence's trenchant economic analysis was spot on. Unfortunately, his credibility was summarily compromised when he claimed to be Richard the Third, an English king who had died three-and-a-half centuries before. The paint fumes, it seemed, had gotten the best of him.

Lawrence needed only to wait a few more months to see the reexpansion of lending. After the treasury withdrew its specie from the national bank, the money was deposited into a number of state-chartered banks managed by Jackson's political supporters. The "pet banks" wasted no time in issuing massive amounts of banknotes against their new gold and silver reserves. Much of the new bank credit was lent to speculators for the purchase of public lands, many of which Jackson had appropriated from the Indians.

The sale of public lands increased five times between 1834 and 1836, as a large portion of speculators purchased land from the government with paper money issued by the pet banks. Ironically, Jackson, who hated fractional-reserve banking, had provided the means of encouraging its widespread abuse.

	owed paper money to		*who owed gold and silver to*
Speculators	▶	Banks ▶	Bank depositors

Unnerved by widespread reckless lending practices, Jackson decided to again clean house. On July 11, 1836, he ordered his Treasury Secretary (his fifth) to issue the "Specie Circular." The mandate declared that beginning in mid-August, the federal government would refuse to accept anything but gold and silver specie in payment for sale of public lands. Effectively, the federal government was declaring that it would no longer recognize private banknotes as money.

You can imagine what happened next. Following the government's lead, speculators began to redeem their banknotes for gold and silver. The banks called in their loans in a desperate scramble to meet a wave of depositor withdrawals. Capital asset values plummeted, bank runs ensued, and consumer prices collapsed as the money supply was destroyed. By the time the smoke cleared, over a third of the nation's banks had failed. A five-year depression—surpassed in severity only by the 1930s Great Depression— soon followed.

The depression had only begun to unfold when Jackson left office in March of 1837. In his farewell address, he railed against "indiscreet extensions of credit" which "engender a spirit of speculation injurious to the habits and character of the people." He lamented the "wild spirit of speculation in the public lands," noting that speculators tended to "withdraw their attention from the sober pursuits of honest industry."

Curiously, Old Hickory neglected to mention that much of the "indiscreet extensions of credit" were made by banks which Jackson had provided with gold reserves only a few years before. Another omission: Jackson had devoted much of the past eight years to confiscating lands from the Indians—the same lands, in many cases, favored by the speculators that he inveighed upon.

Asked what his most important accomplishment had been, Jackson replied, "I killed the bank." His two regrets? "I didn't shoot Henry Clay, and I didn't hang John C. Calhoun" (the Speaker of the House and Jackson's Vice President, respectively). To be fair, Jackson had dueled at least thirteen times in his life, so from his perspective, shooting someone was just another day at the office.

In recognition of his unmatched prowess at killing British, Indians, and the U.S. economy, the U.S. Treasury placed Andrew Jackson's portrait on the twenty dollar bill in 1928. The Federal Reserve banknote was redeemable in gold or silver at the bearer's discretion. By 1971, the note was not redeemable for either. It was primarily backed by federal debt, which Jackson had fought so hard to eradicate. The man who despised fractional reserving and central banks now had his mug on a paper note issued by a central bank. What goes around really does come around.

[An interesting aside: Jackson's triggerman at the Treasury, Roger B. Taney, played an instrumental role in fomenting another financial crisis twenty years later. As chief justice of the U.S. Supreme Court, he delivered the majority opinion in the 1857 case of *Dred Scott v. Sandford*. The ruling threatened to open up all western territories to slavery, causing the bonds of east-west running railroads to plummet in value. Many of those railroad bonds were held by large New York banks. Depositors became nervous and bank runs ensued, resulting in a financial collapse known as the Panic of 1857. Incidentally, the case also expedited the Civil War.]

$$$$$

The Waffle House Way outlined a specified order for attending to customer needs. No matter how busy we were, all patrons needed to be acknowledged immediately upon entering the store. Customers waiting to pay at the register were given the second highest priority. Delivering orders was third, and taking new customer orders was last. And of course, all customers were to be served in the same order in which they arrived at the restaurant.

This system is perfectly viable for four servers attending to fifty civil customers late on a Sunday morning. But going strictly by the book at 3 A.M. on a Saturday morning is downright naive. Waiting on fifty inebriated future convicts, you adhere to the dictum, "the customer is always right," at your own peril. As far as I was concerned, the tenets of *The Waffle House Way* went out the door as soon as the local bars made their last call.

The company manual stated that customers appreciate hearing "Welcome to Waffle House!" as soon as they cross the store threshold. I had used the phrase consistently during my training on the first shift. Sure enough, customers usually waved or smiled when you greeted them. However, it's much harder to deliver the salutation with a straight face when your words are drowned out by four miniskirt-clad female diners hurling epithets at each other.

There was no standard operating procedure for dealing with this sort of behavior. Should you try to stifle the girls' animus by soliciting their orders? Their truculence might be quelled with a few waffles, although the issue of who will order first might fan the flames. You could simply wait for the fur to fly and then notify the police. But if you summon law enforcement every time someone gets really out of line, your customer base will be summarily halved. On some occasions, I flouted company policy by attending to my customers based on their physical condition rather than their order of arrival. When a girl entered the store bearing a bruised cheek from an altercation at a club, I immediately brought her a cup of ice and took her order in front of several patrons who had already been waiting more than ten minutes. While they might have been offended, none of them expressed any indignation at my decision to triage.

"I woulda taken that other gal if it hadn't been for these," the girl said, pointing to a pair of zebra-print stilettos that she had placed on the low bar counter. "They threw off my balance."

"You'll get her next time," I said cheerfully.

There were other late-night contingencies that the manual utterly failed to address. What if the servers have been so occupied with taking and distributing orders for the past three hours that there has been no time to wash silverware? When you run out of forks, do you catch up with the dishwashing, running the risk that the food on the grill might go cold? Or should you deliver the ham and cheese omelet with a spoon, as I did at 3:45 A.M. on a Sunday morning? I had hoped that my delirious chuckle would garner a little sympathy as I explained the predicament to the customer. My apology didn't win me enough sympathy to garner a tip, but under the circumstances, I was grateful enough not to have been algreened.

Four A.M. quickly became my favorite time of day. Typically, its arrival signified that the last of the barflies had entered our doors. Once they had been served, I had a full hour to devote to my side work. However mind-numbing sweeping and mopping the floor might have been, I found it a delightful reprieve from customer interaction. No tip, however large, would have been adequate compensation for those coveted moments of tranquility. At 5 A.M. every morning, the first of the Coffee Drinkers saluted the staff and took his seat at the low bar. Clad in a flannel shirt, B.D. was in his late sixties and had recently retired from a career consisting of a series of odd jobs. He was soon joined by two affluent, albeit casually dressed businessmen, Mark and Wallace. Lawrence, the only decaf drinker of the bunch, was generally quiet, although he occasionally favored the rest of the group with anecdotes from Vietnam. The youngest man in the group was forty-five-year-old Joey, who ran a heating and air conditioning service. Anticipating their arrival, I always brewed a fresh pot of coffee at 4:55, and poured each of their individual cups by the time they opened the restaurant door. Except for B.D., all of them smoked. None of them ever ordered breakfast.

The Coffee Drinkers harassed the employees, albeit in a far more benign manner than the Repo Men. Most of their conversation was focused on local politics and sports, particularly UNC basketball. For the most part I just listened quietly, though I was occasionally called upon as an expert witness when economic subjects were introduced. While not always Sunday school appropriate, the Coffee Drinkers' banter was a welcome change of pace from the barflies' dialogues. Decorum was always maintained, and most diatribes were thankfully brief.

The only genuinely surly member of the group was Joey, whose visage evidenced at least ten more years of life mileage than he claimed to have. He was horribly finicky about the freshness of his coffee and became incredibly indignant at the smallest triviality. When John cited a newspaper report on the county's low level of cumulative rainfall, Joey spent the next ten minutes profanely inveighing on the matter. I was willing to forgive the college-aged barflies for this sort of churlish demeanor, but I found it repugnant coming from a man twice their age. His crassness was particularly inexcusable given that he couldn't assign blame to a high blood alcohol level.

After downing three cups of coffee, Joey habitually retreated to the men's room for a full ten minutes before finally leaving the store at 6 A.M. His timing in this endeavor was particularly uncanny. Typically, the only available time that I had to clean the restroom was immediately after he had vacated it. I was left to bask in an aroma only slightly less offensive than his disposition.

While I finished cleaning the store, Edward lit a cigarette and seated himself next to the coffee drinkers at the low bar. He usually engaged in their playful banter, but every few days he would ask if they knew of any part-time employment opportunities. As he explained it, networking was crucial to finding gainful employment if you had spent any time in prison. In the absence of someone willing to vouch for the current state of your character, you would be summarily written off as a good-for-nothing ex-con.

"The Waffle House is one of the few institutions that believe in giving a man a second chance in life," Edward said. "Most other places don't want anything to do with you once they know about your past mistakes."

I could empathize with him. I had spent several weeks trying to get McDonald's to take me seriously, but I couldn't even land a face-to-face interview with the manager. Waffle House, on the other hand, didn't care that I had been a white-collar guy. My total lack of experience hadn't been an impediment, either. All they cared about was whether I was doing a good job for them today. It was wonderfully egalitarian.

In Edward's theology, the worst imaginable sin was wasting one's potential. While he was grateful to be out of prison and to be earning a real wage, he still had reason to be frustrated. It wasn't just the lower wage that he had to accept; circumstances prohibited him from applying his full array of culinary skills. He simply wanted to share the scope of his talents with his customers.

Perhaps his career frustration was the reason that Edward had been riding me so much. When I had tired of serving grits, he knew that I could readily switch gears and resume the easy gig of office life. Edward, on the other hand, had few viable alternatives.

The district manager had approached Edward about pursuing the management training program. After some investigation, Edward had declined the offer. He had done the math and realized that despite any tenacity that he might bring to the job, the probability of meeting the stipulated hurdles for performance-based compensation was simply too low. After factoring in the increased aggravation of supervising temperamental employees, it was a no-brainer. For the time being, he was perfectly content to remain a Master Grill Operator.

$$\$\$\$\$\$$

After bussing the Coffee Drinkers' cups, I generally left the store around 7:15 and arrived home ten minutes later. I spent the next three hours checking email, playing Tetris, and reading *The Wall Street Journal* online before finally retiring around 11 A.M. Nearly every one of my shifts concluded with tension in my lower back. Working three of them consecutively was unbelievably physically, mentally, and emotionally taxing. It took two full days for my mind and body to fully recover.

Russian psychologist Ivan Pavlov famously demonstrated the power of behavioral conditioning by using a bell to call his dog to his food. After a few repetitions, the dog started to salivate in response to the bell, even when the food was not present. Now imagine an interesting twist on Pavlov's experiment: ring the bell, show the dog a fresh can of Alpo, then beat him with the Sunday newspaper a few seconds after he makes it to the dish. Repeat ten times. On the eleventh occurrence, note whether the "ding" induces salivation or simply causes the poor mutt to mess in his pen.

I don't think anyone has done this research, but they need not bother. I can tell you exactly what the hapless canine will do when that bell rings: he will nervously look in all directions, frozen to inaction out of fear of offending his master. I know this because that was my reaction to a very similar set of circumstances.

During my first two months on third shift, I had developed an incessant nervous feeling which I could only shake for a few hours a day. The sensation was so intense that I could barely discern normal hunger pangs when they struck. Consequently, I had lost nearly ten pounds, a considerable amount of weight for my frame. Eventually, I came to understand that the bugaboo I was dreading was simply the early morning bar crowd rush.

In this life, there are things to act, and things to be acted upon. I had to decide which camp I was going to be in. Was I condemned to spend my days as a Pavlovian dog whose behavior was solely dictated by external stimuli? Or was I a free agent with the capacity to choose my own reaction to adverse circumstances?

Several employees took the edge off of third shift by using recreational drugs or alcohol before they showed up for work. Our store hadn't mandated a drug test in several years, so there was little risk of being caught. I had initially frowned on the unprofessional behavior, but at this point I could empathize with the inclination to self-medicate. There's only so much abuse a man can take before his sanity expires. I didn't entertain the idea myself, though—I've always been averse to chemical intervention in the brain. Drugs— legal and illegal—are a poor coping mechanism for life's problems. A real man, I decided, doesn't flee from reality: he confronts it head-on with snarky remarks. The best way to survive in hell is to poke fun at the devil whenever you can.

I have always been a terrible liar when my motive is covering my sins; I simply cannot do it with a straight face. When my intent is purely sarcastic, however, I can deadpan with the best of them. I perfected this trait during my college years by making the most outlandish claims possible to female guests at fraternity parties. A standard act was to relate gruesome personal anecdotes from my Marine Corps service during the U.S. invasion of Grenada. I'm proud to report that most of the coeds bought my story, if only because they didn't realize that the invasion transpired when I was six years old. But whatever my listener's reaction, I always felt better for having spun the yarn. When you don't take yourself too seriously, you're much less likely to be offended by anything anyone else has to say.

The first opportunity to employ my new strategy presented itself the following Thursday. Three women sat at a booth, flanked by a three-year-old boy in a high chair. After the ladies ordered, I inquired if the child was going to require any food.

"Nah, Jimmy. He's just going to share with me. Didn't your mama ever feed you off her plate when you was his age?"

"No, ma'am, I'm afraid she didn't."

"Aaaw, that's too bad. Your mama loved you, didn't she?"

Her tone of voice was irritating in and of itself, but dragging my mother into the dialogue was totally uncalled for. The gloves promptly came off.

"She loved me enough to breastfeed me until I was ten years old. That's the hallmark of *real* maternal love, you know."

"No, she didn't do that, Jimmy. You just playin' with me."

"I wish that were the case, Ma'am," I said, lowering my head. "It's so difficult to afford these frequent visits to the psychiatrist on my salary."

Later that evening, a customer insisted that we remove all traces of pork from the grill before cooking his T-bone. As he scraped the grill for the third time in an effort to satisfy the request, I suggested to Edward that we secure a rabbinical blessing before finally pronouncing it kosher. The insulted customer refused to let me wait on him any further. I excused myself to the office, where I watched him eat his steak with his bare hands through the one-way mirror.

Edward advised me to use more discretion when making editorial remarks. I reminded him that I had suggested that the rabbi only bless the grill, not circumcise the customer.

"I was just having a little fun. It seems to me that the man overreacted."

He admitted that he had been amused by my remark but abstained from smiling, given the customer's temperament.

"If you're gonna make comments like that, you better grow eyes in the back of yo' head. You never know who's got a gun in their car."

Prison life had dramatically heightened Edward's consciousness of his surroundings. He knew exactly what was transpiring in every corner of the restaurant at all times. With the exception of the bar rush hours, he could always recite the make and color of every car in the parking lot at any given moment.

"Ya see, both of us can't afford to be playin' with the customers like that," he continued. "It would be bad enough if you got shot, but at least we could still keep the sto' open when the ambulance came. On the other hand, suppose I laugh and he comes back and blasts both of us. Now we got two men down and we'd have to close the store for at least three or fo' hours. That wouldn't be acceptable to management."

"What, having two chalk outlines on the floor?"

"Well, that too. But they really hate to close the sto' on account of anything."

As far as I know, a gunshot wound on the premises is the only legitimate justification for halting service at a Waffle House. If you are inclined to test this theory, may I offer one piece of advice: to ensure store closure, the victim should receive at least two slugs. Management will likely interpret a single bullet as simply being the punch line of a practical joke.

The Waffle House never, and I mean never, closes. Every location in the country remains open 24 hours a day, 365 days a year. Christmas is one of the company's highest-grossing days of the year; servers and grill operators working the yuletide shift often receive $100 tips from regular customers. And while the bond market's pace unfailingly slows during most Jewish holidays, any given Waffle House can be found celebrating Passover by grilling ten pounds of bacon.

I'm quite certain that Waffle House will be the last remaining testament to Western Civilization after the rest of it has collapsed under its own weight. Say what you will about its food, servers, or ambiance, but the Waffle House's tenacity is unimpeachable. Our restaurant hadn't been closed for so much as an hour in more than five years. You probably think I'm speaking in exaggerated terms. I'm not. The year before I began my employment, a hurricane caused a twelve-hour power outage at our store. The generator kicked in, candles were lit, and hashbrowns were cooked. At another nearby location, an inebriated customer drove his vehicle right through the wall. Distracting though the spectacle was, service was never interrupted.

Although it may have eventually culminated in a bullet wound as Edward suggested, my facetious attitude proved quite therapeutic in the interim. Within two weekends of my decision to become the Teflon Server, I was wholly impervious to all complaints during the bar rush. I matched every ounce of customer impertinence with an increased measure of sarcastic indifference. It was incredibly empowering.

A middle-aged man, observing my poise (and probably the dumb grin on my face) as I tended the register amidst the early morning din, wondered at me.

"It's amazing how you do that. What's your secret?" he asked.

"What's that?"

"How do you stay so calm when all these people are yelling at you all the time?"

"It's simple," I said. "After 2 A.M. I just think of them as animals."

Recent experience had taught me that it does not pay to conduct yourself as a tuxedo-clad English butler when you are outnumbered ten to one by a group of surly inebriants. On the contrary, you must act like a farmer dressed in bibbed overalls. Your job is to slop the pigs, and there can be no question about who rules the barnyard.

The following week, my equanimity won me another compliment with a monetary reward to boot. I had been waiting on a couple at the high bar when twelve boisterous high school seniors had materialized in three booths. Two of the boys were too restless to sit anywhere and spent an hour just running back and forth between their friends' tables. I coolly explained my rules of engagement to the kids and attended to them at an unhurried pace.

After the students left, I retrieved a credit card receipt from the couple at the high bar. They had given me a forty-dollar gratuity.

"What's this for?" I asked incredulously.

"I've been a cook at an upscale restaurant for the past two years," the man said. "None of our servers could handle three tables like that without completely freaking out. You, on the other hand, were as cool as Clint Eastwood in a gunfight. Those kids weren't going to leave you a hefty tip, but you certainly deserve one."

I performed less admirably the following week as I waited on a group of four middle-school-aged kids. After ordering a hamburger and hashbrowns, one of them made an innocent request for Parmesan cheese.

"Did you see anything on our menu that would necessitate us keeping Parmesan cheese on hand?" I asked.

"I just thought it might go well on my burger."

"Well, we do keep a small supply in the commissary but we serve it exclusively with Oysters Rockefeller. Could I interest you in a plate?"

His friends laughed at my suggestion, and the kid shrank back into his seat. I felt bad. He was just trying to spread his wings by having a late-night dinner with his buddies, and here I was taunting him. Five minutes later, I delivered his food, along with an apology for my sarcasm. Standing up for myself was one thing; striking preemptively was another.

Even when I wasn't being particularly antagonistic, my fatigue and exasperation were getting the best of me. I was becoming impatient with Spanish-speaking customers who had difficulty ordering in English. A simple requested for hashbrowns from a middle-aged construction worker threw me into a rage.

"Potatoes," he said, pointing to its menu picture.

"Hashbrowns!" I corrected him in a resentful voice. "These are called *hashbrowns!*"

My indignation wasn't justified in the least. My Latino customers were unfailingly courteous. They always thanked me for the smallest effort I made on their behalf and never neglected to tip. Penalizing them for any linguistic deficiency was simply callous. A cool demeanor may have been a prerequisite for waiting on the bar crowd, but referring to my customers as livestock was probably crossing the line.

A dose of charity was clearly in order. I decided to treat my customers they way I would want to be treated, giving them the benefit of the doubt until they broke my trust. Further, I vowed to take better care of my stomach in hopes of improving my disposition. Regardless of how crowded the restaurant became, I wasn't going to let my table-waiting responsibilities preclude me from eating for more than six hours.

From then on, whenever hunger struck, I simply called in an extra side plate of hashbrowns along with the customer order. After delivering the food, I retreated to the back room with the plate and a bottle of ketchup. Thirty seconds later, I was back on the floor with renewed gusto. Hashbrowns, like Popeye's spinach, have a tremendous capacity to reinvigorate the constitution in short order.

$$\$\$\$\$\$$

Despite my resolution to choose my words more judiciously, I couldn't help but indulge in occasional moments of unrestrained candor. After I finished calling in an order for two young women and their Japanese grandmother, Debbie informed me that it was my turn to clean the store lavatories. In particular, a toilet paper roll lodged in the base of a urinal required my attention.

After receiving my instructions, I filled three glasses of orange juice and placed them in front of the women at the low bar counter. "Here are your drinks, ladies. Now if you would excuse me for several minutes, I need to fish something out of the urinal, and then I'll bring your food right out."

In retrospect, it wasn't the most decorous exit line I could have chosen. I entered the men's room and verified the problem. Unfortunately, the store was still short of toilet wands, and I had no intention of manually removing the obstruction. I asked a colleague, Lamarr, to cover the table while I devised a solution to my problem.

I exited the store through the back room and emerged into the cool morning dawn. I stood still for a minute, reveling in the fresh air and the hum of the highway traffic, which produced an unexpectedly soothing rhythm. The sun had broken through the clouds, illuminating the forested ravine which sat between our restaurant and the interstate. The idyllic scene was marred only by a large pile of hashbrown cartons, syrup jugs, and other miscellaneous refuse in the valley below. I ripped a three-foot branch from a nearby bush and began stripping most of its leaves. Within a few minutes, I had manufactured a passable toilet brush.

After I retrieved the toilet paper roll, I gave the commode bowl a thorough scrubbing. The handcrafted brush worked surprisingly well—despite applying a considerable amount of pressure to the porcelain, only a few leaves separated from the branch. Thoroughly pleased with myself, I proudly leaned the instrument in the corner of the restroom alcove. In my estimation, it added some much-needed ornamentation.

No sooner had I begun admiring my handiwork than Lamarr confronted me about his recently departed customers.

"What's the deal with that old Japanese lady?" he asked.

"What do you mean?'

"Her granddaughters tried to leave a tip, but she yanked their hands back just as they were about to set the money down. What gives? Did you offend her or something?"

"I can't imagine I said anything offensive," I said. "Hey, what do you think of this?" I said, pointing to my brush. "It only took me five minutes to make, but it cleans the toilets really well."

"That's great," he said. "Are you sure you didn't say the wrong thing before you gave me that table?"

"I might have. Are you sure their waffles weren't too crisp?"

"There was nothing wrong with the food. I just can't believe a classy woman like that would stiff us unless the service was bad." His face made it clear that he held me accountable for their parsimony. Undoubtedly, he would not be pleased to learn that I had announced my intention to intersperse restroom cleaning with serving their food. Just as I was about to confess, I remembered an important element of Japanese culture that I had learned during a business trip to Tokyo the previous year.

"The Japanese never pay gratuities," I said. "Not to waiters, hotel bellboys, cab drivers, anyone. If a foreigner even attempts to tip, a waiter will refuse."

"I wouldn't refuse," Lamarr said. "They're not in Japan now, they're in America."

"Yeeeaaauuuh, " I said in agreement. It was the only comment that came to mind.

$$$$$

I had another small victory the following Friday morning when Matthew, the store manager, counted the drawer at the end of the shift. As the only server working that night, I had full discretion over the cash register. Instead of coming up short, the drawer's cash balance exceeded the sales by three cents.

"I've never had a drawer come out that close," Matthew said. "You know what that means?"

"It means that I probably don't need the remedial arithmetic class that Debbie suggested I take at Community Tech."

"That's right, pal," he said.

Vindicated, I skipped to the store exit with more spring in my step than a young man in love. Nine years of post-secondary education hadn't been such a waste after all. My mirth was suddenly preempted by a shout from the office.

"Hey, Jimmy, before you leave, I need you to do the bathrooms again this morning."

"Oh . . . right," I said plaintively. I trudged back inside and began donning a pair of latex gloves.

The despondency must have been written all over my face. Ever the consummate manager, Matthew decided to provide some much-needed comfort.

"Hey, Man, it'll only take a minute."

"Yeah, it's not a big deal."

"And besides," he continued, "you can use your stick again," he said, pointing to the alcove where my toilet wand was propped up against the wall. "That makes the job a little easier, right?" He gave me a smug grin.

I had to smile. For once, I had left a private possession on Waffle House premises for 48 hours and no one had stolen it. Providence had finally begun to smile on me.

"Indeed it does, Matthew. Indeed it does."

That was the last conversation I ever had with Matthew. The following Tuesday night, his wife showed up at the restaurant to inform him that she was moving out. Their marriage had been under tremendous strain ever since he had lost his lucrative construction job, a fact he had freely shared with most of the cooks and wait staff. After she left, Matthew fled the store in a fit of despondency. No one has heard from him since.

Edward derided the departure as consummately amateur conduct. Matthew, he argued, should have completed his shift and submitted a two-week notice. Admittedly, the exit had been unprofessional, but I felt the situation. There simply can't be many things in life more depressing than being dumped by your wife of six years in the back room of a Waffle House at two in the morning. Receiving a Dear John letter written on your (former) best friend's monogrammed stationary seems downright humane by comparison.

Debbie's attitude changed dramatically after she began serving as interim store manager, following Matthew's departure. Her incessant criticism was replaced with a spirit of optimism and gratitude. She thanked me for my willingness to work extra shifts and clean the store in preparation for an inspection by representatives from corporate headquarters. In a separate conversation, she lavishly praised my honesty and apologized for having intimated that any previous drawer shortages had been my fault. It was a nice change of pace to hear her applaud my character and exonerate my math skills from all previous charges.

Within 48 hours of commending me for my integrity, Debbie was terminated from employment at Waffle House for an ethical shortcoming of her own. As assistant manager, she had the responsibility of delivering weekly cash profits to the bank every Sunday afternoon. Shortly after the bank opened one Monday morning, the district manager was advised that the money had been deposited. She inspected the store's safe to discover that in addition to several hundred dollars in profits, the $300 petty cash fund had also disappeared.

Scuttlebutt had it that Debbie had used the money for a drug purchase. Her indiscretion had not been a premeditated act of malice, but a momentary weakness due to a tragic addiction. I felt bad genuinely bad for her. She had frequently complained of the struggle to pay for her daughter's tuition and could have used the higher income resulting from the official promotion to store manager.

After Debbie's abrupt dismissal, the district manager assumed the reins of the store. Previously, I had only had brief interactions with her during shift changes when she was filling in for absent employees. A fifteen-year Waffle House veteran, Sharon had a reputation as being a skilled grill operator and a tough but fair boss. She had been gracious enough to not press charges against Debbie on the condition that the store was remunerated for the stolen cash; Debbie's mother obliged on her behalf.

Sharon was willing to accommodate vacation requests given sufficient notice but had absolutely no patience for absenteeism. The first time I called out of work, I gave her six hours notice, citing a rib that had been badly bruised during a sparring session.

Sharon was not pleased but accepted my excuse and wished me an expedient recovery.

My second call-out, also a boxing-related injury, evoked less sympathy. I knew the physical requirements of this job when I had taken it, Sharon said. If I chose to jeopardize my ability to work with my avocation, then I needed to seriously reevaluate whether I really wanted to stay on as a server.

The thinly veiled threat caught me completely off guard. Although I had lost my job on two prior occasions, I had taken cold comfort in hearing that my work had been par excellence. In all of my performance reviews, I had always been lauded as a thorough and dedicated employee. For the first time in my working life, I was being threatened with termination on the grounds of negligence.

Managing restaurant employees for a decade and a half, Sharon had undoubtedly heard every imaginable excuse for truancy. I couldn't fault her for being skeptical about my claim; sustaining two severe injuries over the course of three weeks probably sounded like a stretch of the truth. Eventually, she backed down after I offered to submit X-rays and hospital paperwork for her perusal.

Sharon's chastisement was a difficult thing to bear, if only because I couldn't argue with her sentiments on personal responsibility. The minute an employee started to complain about a problem, she immediately urged him to take a proactive approach to remedying the situation, himself, and intervened only after he had exhausted all other alternatives.

Whatever else could be said about her, Sharon knew how to handle people and run a business. She had no tolerance for b.s. and accomplished tasks with a considerable economy of effort. If she gave any of her employees legitimate cause for complaint, I never heard any voiced. I often pondered how much her managerial acumen would have been compromised by attending an MBA program.

In business school, Sharon would have been taught to manage employees using information gleaned from employee personality assessments. Once the data had been translated into color-coded pie charts and bar graphs, Sharon would have learned to convene two-hour committee meetings with fellow executives to discuss how the charts could be used to resolve personnel issues. It was a much more sophisticated approach to managing people than her archaic method of holding employees personally accountable for their actions.

Since my argument with Debbie on statistical sampling, I had only conceived of one other application of material I had learned in business school—namely, the revenue potential of shared marketing arrangements. The classic example of this strategy is promoting Disney film franchises with plastic toys included in McDonald's Happy Meals. Because school-age kids are huge consumers of both fast food and animated media, the marriage works beautifully. Similarly, I envisioned Waffle House teaming with the County Board of Health in offering a discounted cervical cancer vaccine with every All-Star Special ordered between 2 and 4 A.M.

Whereas Sharon had greeted my second boxing injury with a stern reprimand, physical injury and illness had been met with sympathy from my former supervisors—with one notable exception. While I was working for Alpha Managers, I once showed up to work with a black eye garnered from an opponent's uppercut. I thought it gave me a certain element of cachet relative to most of my colleagues. The greatest weekend adversity that they could boast of on a Monday morning was posting a double-bogey on a par three at the local country club.

My boss gently reprimanded me for my recklessness. I was a professional, he declared, and needed to act accordingly. I assured him that despite the bruise, there had been no cognitive impairment, but that wasn't the source of his concern. In less than a week, our firm would be hosting a contingent of Japanese bankers. Our clients, he explained, would not be particularly pleased to discover that one of the men responsible for supervising their portfolios spent his discretionary time receiving repeated blows to the head.

There are exceptions, of course, but generally speaking, boxing is not a white-collar pastime. There were a few white-collar guys at each of the three gyms I've trained at, but they were decidedly in the minority. Wall Street types are much more inclined to boast about their golf game than their ability to deliver a powerful overhand right. Although I enjoy golf as much as the next fellow, I don't take the game seriously on the grounds that a man's handicap is a sorry proxy for his masculinity. You can discern a lot more about a man's character by how he responds to a barrage of punches than how he reacts to a ball landing in a sand trap.

Besides me, the store had two other servers that had been amateur pugilists. Tyrell had fought several bouts in Police Athletic League events, while Mike had been a very competitive Golden Gloves fighter in his youth. Both of them hailed from New York City and had been paroled after serving time in federal prison for drug offenses.

A 36-year-old of medium build, Tyrell was the only child of a very devoted mother. In his own words, he grew up to become "the stereotypical young, drug-slinging, gun-toting black man feared by suburbanites." While he didn't make excuses for his past behavior, Tyrell did lament the absence of a positive male role model during his adolescence—he had known his father only by reputation.

After working eight months on first shift as one of the store's highest-grossing salespersons, Tyrell switched to third shift in order to pursue continuing education at Community Tech. He expected to begin work as a fiber optics technician as soon as his parole was finalized. Besides being articulate and highly motivated, he always maintained an admirable degree of composure. I first became aware of the latter attribute when a young black girl, claiming (erroneously) that she had been shortchanged an egg, hurled an n-bomb at him. In a manner worthy of Atticus Finch, he coolly reproved her for using the epithet and arranged for another egg to be added to her plate.

Of anyone I worked with, Tyrell's disposition seemed the least conducive to the life of a felon. After I shared this observation with him, he explained that he had always committed crimes methodically, rather than with the reckless abandon of his peers.

"That why I went so long without getting caught," he added.

He had dealt drugs and committed other felonies for the best part of a decade without receiving a single charge. When he was finally convicted, it was by virtue of guilt by association with the actual perpetrator. The irony of serving time on account of someone else's offense—which had been less heinous than so many of his own—compelled him to become very religious. Upon his parole, he began playing the drums for worship services at a local church.

Mike was a six-foot-three, 240-pound, jovial man who was finishing his parole at a halfway house when I first met him. He had assembled an impressive 14–1 record as an amateur boxer and served as a frequent sparring partner of another amateur named Riddick Bowe. Only weeks before he would have turned pro, Mike was arrested for cocaine trafficking and sentenced to twenty years in federal prison. Riddick Bowe turned pro and went on to become the world heavyweight champion.

Although he was clearly remorseful for the sins of his past life, Mike didn't dwell on them. Indeed, he had the most consistently upbeat attitude of anyone in the store. When he wasn't serving All-Star Specials, he spent his discretionary time developing his nascent record label. He had only been at it for a few months, but he already had two acts signed. I had to appreciate his attitude and tenacity.

While he was serving his sentence at a Federal Correctional Institution in Fairton, NJ, Mike made the acquaintance of an incarcerated former bank executive. His company, Silverado Savings & Loan, had been the poster child for a banking debacle popularly known as the "Savings and Loan (S&L) Crisis."

In the wake of substantial deregulation in the early 1980s, many S&Ls (a type of bank that specializes in residential mortgages) had made a series of imprudent loans, particularly in commercial real estate. Over the next ten years, 745 of the S&Ls went bankrupt as the souring investments burned through their stockholders' capital. Their depositors, however, were made whole by the American taxpayer.

Since 1934, the federal government had been insuring S&L deposits through an entity known as the Federal Savings and Loan Insurance Corporation (FSLIC). Similar to the FDIC, the FSLIC charged a fee to member banks to insure against the risk of bankruptcy. As the crisis grew, the FSLIC quickly depleted its own reserves, leaving taxpayers to make up the difference. The final price of the tab ran in excess of $120 billion, $1.2 billion of which was accounted for by Silverado. The S&L bailout substantially contributed to the large federal budget deficits in the early 1990s, marring the last years of George H.W. Bush's presidency (along with an economic slowdown exacerbated by the deteriorating credit conditions).

Incidentally, then-President Bush's son, Neil, had been a Silverado director. While serving on the board, Neil Bush had neglected to notify the board that a business partner was contemplating a $3 million investment in Bush's oil exploration company at the same time that Silverado was forgiving the man $8.5 million of his debts—on the grounds that he was approaching insolvency!

As a result of this and other incidents, an S&L regulator determined that Neil Bush had engaged in numerous "breaches of his fiduciary duties involving multiple conflicts of interest." He was not indicted on criminal charges, although Bush did settle a civil suit out of court with the FDIC for $50,000. The Resolution Trust Corporation Suit (a government entity that liquidated the failed S&Ls) brought a separate suit against Bush and other Silverado officers, which was ultimately settled for $26.5 million. Not all of Silverado's officers were so fortunate. For his role in the failed institution, Mike's cellmate received ten years in federal prison.

I don't know enough about the case to say whether other people were more deserving of a conviction. What I do know is that when someone's abuse of debt inflicts $1.2 billion of costs on hapless taxpayers, it stands to reason that someone should end up doing time. What I can't figure out, however, is why Mike should have served twice as many years for distributing drugs. The social costs of illicit drug abuse are high, but the social costs of debt abuse are downright astronomical.

Drugs, per se, are not intrinsically evil. Nearly every drug has a legitimate medical usage. Opium derivatives like morphine are essential to alleviating extreme pain; cocaine is used as a topical anesthetic in nasal surgeries. However, both of the aforementioned substances are ripe for misuse, and it's probably fair to assume that most of Mike's customers were not outpatient surgical centers.

Everyone recognizes that drug abuse generates social costs to innocent victims. In addition to adverse health effects on the user, drug abuse weighs on families, workplaces, and communities. Fathers neglect their children, employees become lethargic and dishonest, and theft and violent crime escalate as a consequence.

As a nurse, my wife has administered drugs to the relief of many suffering patients. Conversely, she has also attended to countless victims of substance abuse. As she has explained to me, drugs are only appropriately employed if three conditions are met:

1. They are used for the right reasons

2. In appropriate dosages

3. Administered by a responsible professional

Just as doctors and nurses are charged with the prudent administration of drugs, financiers are charged to lend carefully. In its proper usage, debt finances what Jean-Baptiste Say called "reproductive investments," which raise productivity and enable a sustainable rise in living standards. This responsible application of debt benefits business owners, employees, creditors, and consumers alike.

Over the past decade, bankers have neglected to follow Say's advice in their debt prescriptions. For the ten years ended in September 2009, banks increased commercial and industrial lending to business by 34%. Loans secured by real estate, on the other hand, grew by nearly 215%. As a share of total bank assets, commercial and industrial loans declined from 17% to 10%, while the share of real estate loans increased by a comparable amount—from 26% to 34%.

While some of the real estate lending may have financed business investment, a large share of it was used to finance speculation in the residential housing market. By allocating an increasing share of capital to fund real estate speculation, bankers created a large increase in housing prices. Thanks to speculative fever and easy credit, Americans watched their home values appreciate and assumed they were becoming wealthier.

Unfortunately, housing does not represent the ideal sort of "reproductive investment" envisioned by J.-B. Say. A house is simply a durable good that is consumed over an extended period of time. *Rather than funneling capital to producers, bankers had been using savings to finance consumption.*

In the long run, the power to consume derives from one, and only one, source: increased productivity. Unfortunately, houses are nonproductive assets. No one has ever increased his capacity to produce more goods and services by purchasing a 5,000 square foot monument to conspicuous consumption.

Labor followed the increasing amounts of capital channeled into the housing sector. A large segment of the economy was soon providing large-ticket consumer goods to persons whose demand was supported not by their own production, but by a misallocation of credit. In simplest terms, the housing bubble was simply a large-scale attempt to cheat Say's Law by abusing debt. The result: a reincarnation of the Savings and Loan Crisis on a much broader scale. And just like the last time, almost none of the perpetrators would go to prison.

As I talked with Mike about his experiences selling cocaine, I began to realize how much we had in common. As with most narcotics, debt is easily and frequently mishandled. Time and again, experience has demonstrated that its abuse can destroy individuals, communities, and entire economies. And that's exactly what I had done for the past three years as part of the Consumer Debt Cartel. I had helped to destabilize the American economy by wantonly distributing our drug to the wrong patients, for the wrong reasons, and often in lethal dosages. To be fair, I hadn't been a dealer myself. But I had been one of their public relations men.

Alpha Managers was just a small part of the Cartel. Broker/dealers like Bear Stearns and Lehman Brothers; mortgage banks like Washington Mutual and Golden West Financial; and insurance companies like AIG were all major distributors. And the kingpins? None other than two agents of Uncle Sam, himself: Freddie Mac and Fannie Mae. The growth in the "retained portfolios" of these government-sponsored enterprises accounted for 40% of all new subprime mortgage securities in both 2003 and 2004—a veritable Mr. and Mrs. Escobar.

The Consumer Debt Cartel had enjoyed tremendous profits over the past three decades. As a percentage of total corporate profits, financial services climbed from a 10% share in the early 1980s to a 40% share by 2007. In the process, we facilitated an extraordinary increase in consumer debt levels. In 1980, the average U.S. household had 65 cents of debt for every dollar it earned. By 2007, the ratio had doubled: Americans had accumulated more than $1.30 in debt for every dollar of income. America had become a nation of financial drug addicts.

The recession, I realized, was simply the inevitable overdose after 30 years of building an increased tolerance to consumer debt. Sustainable recovery would only arrive after Americans had checked themselves into rehab and the structure of production adjusted accordingly. Too much labor and capital had been devoted to providing goods to people whose consumption was driven not by their own production, but by imprudent lending. Given the large misallocation of resources, and the tremendous amount of leverage used to finance them, the adjustment process was going to be very unpleasant. The era of the capricious American consumer was about to end.

As Mike's case illustrates, convicted drug dealers often spend decades in prison, even for a first-time offense. Given cocaine's propensity to destroy lives, perhaps the sentences are warranted. But if sentences are truly commensurate with social costs, where does that leave irresponsible bankers? When high-profile financiers misallocate capital and blow up a large bank or brokerage, they don't end up in prison unless there has been a blatant case of fraud. More often than not, they usually land another seven-figure gig at a different Wall Street firm within a matter of months.

By threatening drug dealers with incarceration, the government dissuades a number of would-be distributors. However, those that are willing to flout the law can earn tremendous profits by selling into a market with an artificially limited supply. Like so many other young men in their demographic, Mike and Tyrell had started selling drugs because of this powerful economic incentive. I couldn't think much less of them for having done so. Had they been raised in an affluent Long Island suburb, they might have pursued an even more lucrative career in debt trafficking, done more damage to society, and never run the risk of imprisonment.

Over the course of my life, numerous people have told me that I would have made an excellent attorney. "You have a keen analytical mind," they said. "Why not practice law?"

My typical rejoinder was that I had a much greater interest in seeing justice served than the law enforced. Recent experience has been a vivid reminder of the distinction. For the life of me, I can't make sense of it all.

Chapter 6

THE RESTAURANT OF LAST RESORT

"Give me control over a nation's currency,
and I care not who makes its laws."
—attributed to Mayer Amschel Rothschild

I never saw anyone order three waffles until my fourth month at the store. The twenty-something bartender explained that he wasn't normally so ravenous, but extenuating circumstances had forced his hand. While he was pouring drinks the night before, his girlfriend had called to advise him that she was going into labor with their first child. To celebrate the good news, he spent the next six hours inundating his blood stream with alcohol.

After the first hour of heavy drinking, he had had second thoughts about the prudence of his actions. "I figured the doctors and nurses might get irritated if I showed up drunk to the delivery room. And besides, I probably should be sober when I meet my daughter for the first time."

Before common sense had gotten the best of him, the bartender reasoned that he could continue imbibing as long as he consumed a few waffles afterwards. Their spongy texture, he claimed, made them particularly effective at absorbing liquor from the stomach.

I commended the bartender for his sense of paternal responsibility and delivered him a fourth cup of coffee. He thanked me profusely for being "an angel of mercy" and began reciting an extemporaneous paean to our establishment. Waffle House, he sang, was the only place at 3 A.M. where a man could not only detoxify his system, but enjoy doing so.

Although the vast majority of the 2:30 A.M. crowd had clearly tied a few on before visiting us, most of our customers didn't come with the express intent of sobering up. On occasion, however, the store could function as a surrogate emergency room. A week after my encounter with the bartender, two young men literally dragged an inebriated companion though the front door. They planted his backside on a chair at the low bar and carefully removed his arms from their necks. The drunk wobbled for a second, then promptly collapsed belly first onto the counter. We stared at him for a few seconds before one of his friends finally broke the silence.

"Hey, Jimmy. What should we do for him?"

Once again, I had been presented with a scenario for which *The Waffle House Way* had failed to prepare me. I was barely competent as a server, let alone an emergency room nurse. All I could do was hazard my best guess.

"We'll let him sleep for five or ten minutes. After that, we'll check his vital signs to ensure he's still breathing. If so, we'll start him off with a glass of water," I said in a very professional tone of voice. "If he can handle that without incident, I'd like to administer a cup of coffee, with a little cream and lots of sugar. If he rallies within the hour, we'll give him a small plate of plain hashbrowns. Then we can discharge him."

The patient's friends nodded in agreement.

"And *you* wanted to take him to the hospital to get his stomach pumped," one of them said condescendingly to the other.

His friend conceded the error in judgment. It would have been foolhardy to pay for an ER visit when he could receive comparable quality care at our establishment.

"Uhhll," the drunk suddenly mumbled, straining to clutch a fistful of air.

"Listen. He's trying to tell us something," I said. I bent down and placed my ear next to his head.

"Efful," he groaned louder.

"What's he saying?" his friends asked.

There was a time when I too would have been puzzled by the cryptic sounds. During my first week on the job, I delivered a glass of water in a response to a young customer's request. As I placed it on the table, he glared at me.

"Ah sed ah nade uh . . . foke."

I leaned forward, hoping he'd take my cue to enunciate. "Uh foke!" he repeated. Ten seconds later, I returned with his fork. I entertained the idea of responding in kind by soliciting his order in a thick Scottish brogue but thought better of it. After all, he was the customer. If I was going to work in sales, the onus lay with me to gain fluency in his language (whatever it may have been).

Following the "foke" encounter, I made a concerted effort to listen more closely to my customers and the break room banter. In a few weeks, I could readily interpret various guttural tones for the sundry menu items that they represented. For example, "fru pun" was a common request for fruit punch. By the time the drunk's cry of "efful" reached my trained ear, its meaning was as plain as day.

"Do you want a waffle?" I asked.

That was the magic word. He raised himself up on his elbows and gave a slow nod. I looked into his eyes, trying to gauge the severity of his condition by the glaze on his irises. Regrettably, he performed a face plant onto the counter before I could complete my assessment.

The act was reminiscent of an old Western film. The dying man, having crawled through the desert for days, uses his last breath to beseech a passerby for water before collapsing into the sand.

I delivered the waffle five minutes later, although the man slept at the bar for another hour before he finally consumed it. Within another hour, I had the profuse thanks of his companions for providing him with the energy he needed to leave the store on his own two feet.

Although most inebriated customers were sincerely appreciative of my early morning service, others had markedly less gratitude.

"The gova mint should shut y'all down!" an indignant patron exclaimed, when I advised him that we had just exhausted our inventory of chicken breasts.

Customers were always incredulous when we ran out of chicken, pork chops, or take-out trays. Most of the time, they demanded free meals as compensation for the inconvenience. This was the first time anyone had suggested a store closure. Typically, I responded by offering my sympathies and tried to call their attention to another item on the menu. But this time, I didn't feel like backing down.

"If you really feel that way, why do you keep coming back so often?" I had seen him on the past three Saturday nights.

"Because y'all are the only place that's open at three in the mornin'."

He was right. I couldn't think of any other local restaurants that were open all night. And I couldn't imagine another establishment that would be so tolerant of obnoxious patrons, whatever the hour. Waffle House the only place where churlish barflies could procure hot food at 3 A.M. They simply couldn't get it anywhere else.

Most regulars knew what to anticipate after the bars closed. If they wanted quick service, they would address their servers by name and offer a fat tip out of the gate. The uninitiated were much less sympathetic. In their minds' eye, being forced to wait longer than ten minutes for their food was an all-out assault on their civil liberties.

I knew where this sense of entitlement originated. It's three A.M. and you're famished. Suddenly, it hits you like a bolt of lightning—Waffle House is still open. Your brilliant epiphany deserves to be rewarded with expedient service. Unfortunately, half the town has had the same stroke of genius, so you have to wait your turn.

While the morning shift contributed the largest portion of the store's revenue, the graveyard shift wasn't too far beyond. The late-night crowd generated almost three-quarters as much sales as the breakfast crowd. Between 1 and 4 A.M., we had a monopoly on the restaurant business. Indeed, a large part of our profitability was predicated on our willingness to do what no one else would. We were the Restaurant of Last Resort.

$$\$\$\$\$\$$

In 1873, Mark Twain published his only coauthored novel. *The Gilded Age: A Tale of Today* satirized the greed, political corruption, and real estate speculation which characterized late 19th-century America. Although it was met with less critical success than Twain's other oeuvres, the term "Gilded Age" became synonymous with contemporary economic and social conditions. Incidentally, its publication coincided with the onset of a long depression.

Earlier that year, President Ulysses S. Grant signed a Coinage Act which changed the nation's **monetary policy**. ("Monetary policy" refers to a government's management of the money supply and credit conditions.) Under the new law, the United States would back its currency only by gold reserves. Previously, paper money had been backed by both gold and silver specie. Overnight, silver lost its status as a reserve metal. Banks that had been using silver now found themselves underreserved and were forced to call in their loans. A major financial firm named Jay Cooke & Company failed, and the money supply soon collapsed in a series of bank runs.

The country would endure another severe financial crisis in 1893 as a debt-financed bubble in railroad construction imploded. Fourteen years later, another large-scale panic broke after a group of stock market speculators defaulted on a sizeable loan to a large trust company (a type of lightly-regulated bank). The collapse of the Knickerbocker Trust sent shockwaves throughout Wall Street. Runs on several large banks and trust companies ensued, quickly engulfing the New York financial district in chaos.

The country's most prominent banker, J.P. Morgan, coordinated a desperate effort to provide reserves to faltering banks and trust companies. If the weaker financial institutions should collapse, he asserted, the stronger ones would soon follow suit. In his view, the only alternative to a bailout was a total meltdown of the banking system.

Morgan wasn't bluffing. A veteran of the Panic of 1893, he knew how quickly a single calamity could metastasize across many institutions. Not only had the banks, trust companies, and brokerage houses borrowed heavily from depositors, they also owed considerable sums *to each other*. The financial system, which was charged with recycling savings into reproductive investments, had become a tenuous chain of dominoes.

had borrowed from   *who owed money to*
Speculators ▸ Trust companies & brokers ▸

who in turn owed
Banks ▸ Bank Depositors

At one point, Morgan convened over a hundred bankers and trust company officials to a 3 A.M. summit at his private library to design a $25 million relief program for the imperiled banks and trusts. They weren't going home until a resolution was reached— Morgan, they soon realized, had locked them inside. After ninety minutes of cajoling, the other financiers acquiesced and the reserves were provided. Through the sheer force of his will, J.P. Morgan had succeeded in preventing what would have been the largest implosion of money and credit since Andrew Jackson issued his Specie Circular seven decades before.

While the fallout from "The Panic of 1907" would have undoubtedly been much worse devoid of Morgan's efforts, it was bad enough for the government to take notice. The following year, Congress established the National Monetary Commission to investigate the causes of the crisis and propose an overhaul of the banking system.

After surveying the banking operations of several European countries, Commission head Senator Nelson Aldrich became convinced that the United States needed her own central bank. Working with several prominent bankers and economists, he submitted a proposal to Congress in 1911. The "Aldrich Plan" provided the basis for the Federal Reserve Act, signed into law by President Woodrow Wilson on December 23, 1913. The national bank, that "monster" which Andrew Jackson had so vigorously campaigned to destroy, had been resurrected.

Rather than concentrate power entirely in one entity (as the Second Bank of the United States had done), the new Federal Reserve System had its power diffused across twelve regional banks. The act required all nationally chartered commercial banks to purchase stock in their regional Federal Reserve bank, which would be managed by a board of directors. In turn, a seven-member Board of Governors would supervise the entire Federal Reserve System. Although the Board of Governors was comprised of Presidential appointees, the system was designed to be an independent entity that could act without prior approval from Congress or the White House.

Through the Federal Reserve Act, Congress delegated control of the money supply to the Federal Reserve System ("The Fed"). While many of the Fed's critics argue that its existence is unconstitutional, Article One, Section 8 of the Constitution grants the Congress "Power . . . to coin Money, regulate the Value thereof." The Constitution never explicitly defines money, although Article One, Section 10 forbids States from coining money or making "any Thing but gold and silver Coin a Tender in Payment of Debts."

The Federal Reserve banks would be entirely owned by private commercial banks, although their banknotes (Federal Reserve Notes) would serve as the official U.S. currency. Each Federal Reserve bank would maintain a gold reserve ratio of 40% of the value of its Notes and deposits. The Federal Reserve Notes could be redeemed for gold bullion at the U.S. Treasury Department in Washington, D.C. or at any regional Federal Reserve bank at the rate of $20.67 per troy ounce.

In the new banking regime, the Federal Reserve banks' notes and deposits constituted the nation's **monetary base**. Commercial bank deposits were backed by a fractional reserve of the monetary base, which was in turn backed by a fractional reserve of gold bullion. The monetary base accounted for roughly 20% of the U.S. money supply; commercial bank deposits comprised the remaining 80%. As long as the Federal Reserve was never faced with the threat of a run on its own gold reserves, the system was tenable.

The Federal Reserve Act of 1913:
A "New & Improved" Money Supply

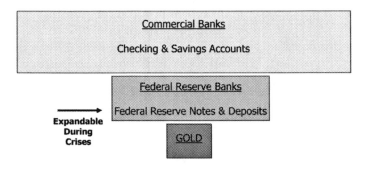

The Federal Reserve Act granted the Fed four important powers: First, it provided an **elastic currency**, meaning that the Federal Reserve banks could issue an increased volume of banknotes in time of crisis. Should nervous depositors begin to withdraw their money en masse, the Fed would step in as **Lender of Last Resort** and lend cash directly to the banks. By providing the commercial banks with reserves, the Fed would sharply reduce the risk of widespread bank runs and destruction of the money supply. When the panic subsided, depositors would resume lending money to the commercial banks, which would then use the deposit proceeds to repay their loans to the Fed. In theory, the downward spiral of debt deflation would never gain sufficient momentum to do serious damage.

Second, in addition to providing reserves to the banking system, the Fed also had power to set reserve requirements for the commercial banks. By managing these two factors, the Fed could manage the creation of money through the fractional reserve process. By limiting money supply growth to a modest pace, consumer price inflation would be contained.

Third, the Fed could set short-term interest rates by buying and selling U.S. government bonds and fixing the rate at which banks borrowed from its "discount window." (This power was later broadened in the 1930s to include managing the rates at which banks loaned their excess reserves on deposit at the Fed to each other.) As short-term rates fell, the cheaper borrowing costs tended to increase capital asset prices. Admittedly, the Fed couldn't exercise direct control over asset prices, although it could certainly affect them.

Fourth, the Act granted the Fed authority to supervise bank lending and establish capital requirements. The regional Fed banks were to ensure that each private commercial bank was following sound lending practices and maintaining adequate capital to absorb any potential losses. If capital buffers were not threatened by imprudent lending and/or excessive leverage, banks would be seldom forced to call in their loans. The magnitude of the upswings and downturns in the credit cycle would be severely curtailed.

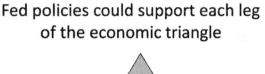

Fed policies could support each leg of the economic triangle

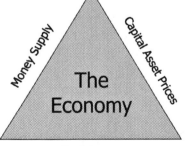

(**Money supply:** Serving as Lender of Last Resort prevents money supply contraction. Setting reserve requirements limits money supply expansion. **Capital Asset Prices:** Lower short-term interest rates support capital asset prices. Higher short-term interest rates help prevent asset price bubbles. **Bank Loans:** Lending Supervision & Capital Requirements reduce probability of a crisis that would force banks to call in their loans.)

In this latter respect—smoothing extreme undulations in the credit cycle—the Federal Reserve would play the same role that the Old Testament prophets played in mitigating the pride cycle. Moses, Isaiah, and Elijah each preached humility and repentance in the midst of pride and debauchery. To the extent the people were humbled by their words and forsook their sins, they were spared from God's wrath.

So too would the Federal Reserve exhort the commercial banks to repent of reckless lending and overleveraged balance sheets. Their calls to repentance could take several forms: higher reserve and capital requirements, higher short-term interest rates, and tougher lending restrictions. During the downturns, the banks would receive clemency as these policies were reversed.

Of course, the efficacy of the Federal Reserve System was predicated on competent and courageous leadership at the Board of Governors. But since the time of Noah, calling bankers (or anyone else) to repentance has never been a fast track to popularity. However foreboding the weather forecast may be, very few people will readily board an ark while there's a good party going.

$$\$\$\$\$\$$

A few minutes after we passed the baton to the first shift on Sunday morning, the third-shift crew formed a break room queue to receive our weekly pay. In lieu of paychecks, the manager paid us cash money straight from the register. The going wage for servers was $2.13 an hour, and the tax withholding rate assumed that gratuities put our income at minimum wage level. The ten percent surcharge added to all take-out orders added a few more bucks, but I was still only netting about fifty dollars.

Not since I had picked strawberries and mowed lawns as a teenager had I felt such a visceral connection to every dollar in my wallet. Each one of them represented the fruit of recent production, and I became very finicky about parting with any of them. The great thing about paying with cash, rather than credit cards, is that removing the bills from your wallet encourages you to ponder whether you are exchanging your production for something of real value.

My unspent currency accumulated on my kitchen bar top for several weeks before I finally bothered to deposit it, along with several pounds of change, at the bank. I always enjoyed drawing a few stares as I pushed several hundred dollars in unsorted small bills across the teller counter. But the best part of the experience was my interaction with the hapless tellers.

"Welcome to Wachovia. How are you this morning, sir?" the young woman asked.

"Well, that depends. Is the bank still solvent?"

"As far as I know."

"Good." I wrote my cell phone number on a deposit slip and slid it across the counter. "Please call me if that situation changes before four o'clock today. I know how tenuous these things can be."

"You've got a lot of cash sitting in your account," she observed.

"That's very reassuring," I said. "I was afraid the bank might have managed to lose it."

"Perhaps you'd like to meet with one of our financial specialists who could help you put that money to work for you."

"You mean to tell me this bank offers investment advice?" I asked in feigned disbelief.

"Yes, we do," she said enthusiastically.

"And how long have you been doing that?"

"Oh, for at least the past ten years."

"I see you're now advertising yourselves as 'A Wells Fargo Company.'" I said, pointing to a poster behind the teller windows. "Correct me if I'm wrong, but didn't that merger occur just a few months ago?"

"Yes, we officially merged in April."

"I thought so. If I recall correctly, it was right after you tried to sell yourselves to Morgan Stanley and Citigroup. Your bank almost collapsed because you purchased a California-based mortgage lending company whose loan portfolio had been poorly underwritten. A large chunk of their option adjustable-rate mortgages went bad, depleting your capital base and triggering intense regulatory scrutiny. If I recall correctly, a few large depositors had even started a run on your bank."

"There were a lot of factors at work," she sighed. "You seem to know a good deal about these events."

"Yeah, that forty-thousand-dollar bath I took on my Wachovia shares kind of seared it into my memory."

"I'm sorry," she said apologetically.

"I'm not mad," I said. "But I am genuinely intrigued that a bank which decimates its own capital base through bad loan underwriting is in a legitimate position to counsel other people on how to invest their money. So I think I'll pass on the advice and just let the cash keep sitting there. What do you think?"

"I understand completely, sir," she said, handing my deposit receipt.

"In fact," I continued, "I'd like your complete assurance that you won't lend my money out at all."

"But then you wouldn't earn any interest."

"But then I wouldn't have to worry about you guys blowing it on bad loans, would I?"

"Will there be anything else, sir?" she asked in an exasperated voice.

"Yeah. Would you mind exchanging these two twenty-dollar bills for four tens? I always get nervous whenever Andrew Jackson is in my wallet. He's in the habit of destroying money too."

$$$$$

I would have been quicker to forgive Wachovia for their underwriting mistakes had it not been for a telephone conversation that I had with a woman in their credit card department the Friday before I started at Waffle House. My card was approaching its expiration date, and the bank was performing its due diligence before issuing me a replacement.

"What is your current income?" the woman asked.

"I don't know. I'm starting a new job waiting tables on Monday, but I forgot to ask about my wage."

"Well, what was your income in 2008?"

"My total compensation was approximately $150,000. But I'm guessing that it will be markedly lower in 2009. To be honest, I have no idea what my new employer is going to pay me. But even in a best case scenario, I doubt that I'll bring home a quarter of what I had earned previously. "

"I'll just go ahead and put down what you made last year," she said. "That way, your credit limit won't be reduced."

I had thought that I knew a thing or two about sloppy underwriting, but this woman was setting the bar lower than I ever would have imagined possible. The banking industry had come a long way since my parents purchased their first home 35 years ago. At the time, my mother's pay stub wasn't even admissible on their mortgage application because the bank considered her income stream too tenuous—i.e., a 27-year-old married woman her age was likely to soon bear children and drop out of the labor force.

Bankers and borrowers both seemed to take money lending more seriously back then. Bank branches were constructed of granite and marble; all of the personnel wore suits. Today, bankers' lackadaisical approach to loan underwriting is reflected in their attire. The khaki pants and polo shirt worn by a Washington Mutual loan officer makes him virtually indistinguishable from a Starbucks barista. (For all of their other deficiencies, at least Wachovia employees still wear neckties.)

$$$$$

If I was indeed going to get my gratuity receipts to a level commensurate with Wachovia's six-figure estimate, I needed a game plan. In markets, you are always looking for patterns that can be

exploited as trading opportunities. So it was with my customers—
if I could gauge a customer's likelihood of leaving a large tip, I
could devote extra effort to his table.

Unfortunately, handicapping a customer's propensity to tip
based on his appearance was an extremely difficult endeavor. A
man dressed like a gangbanger may be just as likely to leave a large
gratuity as a middle-aged man in business casual attire wearing a
Rolex.

There were two demographics, however, that consistently
tipped me well: gay men and obese Caucasian women. I was
heartened by their generosity as it provided me with a career safety
net. If my promised Tokyo transfer fell through, I could still expect
to earn a pretty good living working at a store situated in Greenwich
Village or any town in Wisconsin.

Getting stiffed didn't bother me so much personally. My wife
still had an income and I had saved a lot of money from my prior
career. But seeing my coworkers neglected by ungrateful customers
always aroused my ire.

"I feel like a slave working on third shift," Tyrell said, bussing a
table that had just stiffed him. "You kill yourselves for these people
and get nothing for it. It's like a scene straight out of *Roots*."

I could appreciate his predicament. From what I had observed
during my two-week training period, the breakfast crowd he was
accustomed to waiting on had much looser purse strings than the
barflies. At the end of a typical shift, Tyrell and I were averaging
between 70 and 80 dollars. Lamarr had earned north of 100 bucks,
while Tommy was closer to 200. He attributed his windfall to
having lived in town for thirty years and accumulating a robust
base of devoted fans.

Lamarr's method for success was also straightforward. Because
some customers would stiff the waiters regardless of the quality of
your service, the best bet was to assume way more volume than you
can possibly handle. Instead of following *The Waffle House Way*'s
prescribed method of calling in one table order at a time, Lamarr
took orders from everyone within earshot and then jammed the

grill with a ten-plate call. Unfailingly, the system resulted in a large number of botched orders and a very irritated grill operator.

Lamarr was a short man in his mid-twenties who had spent the previous eight years in the Navy. He claimed that his time in the service had saved him from getting himself "imprisoned or killed." Though his table-waiting skills had ample room for improvement, I couldn't impugn his work ethic. He always completed his side work assignments and offered unsolicited help to other servers with theirs. When I complimented his productivity, he responded by holding his two fists together in front of me. "H-A-R-D" was tattooed on the knuckles of his left hand; "W-O-R-K" was engraved on the right.

"That's what I'm all about," he declared.

"So you like to work hard?" a sultry voice asked. Lamarr and I turned to the high bar where a woman in her late forties was smoking a cigarette.

After Lamarr muttered an affirmation, the woman inquired about his current income level. After conceding that a competent waiter could earn a decent living, she advised him that he could tread a more lucrative path by taking part-time employment as a male escort. Like table waiting, the job required meticulous attention to detail. In addition to the obvious perk of carousing with beautiful women like her, clients paid in cash money, none of which would have to be reported to the IRS.

The invitation had barely escaped her mouth before Lamarr began listing his disqualifications. She continued to pressure him for a few more minutes as he fielded excuses at every turn. Exasperated, he eventually deflected her attention over to me. The woman swiveled around on her barstool and began eyeing me as I swept the floor. I couldn't help looking back at her over my shoulder. She scrutinized me as a cattle rancher at auction might consider placing a throwaway bid on a sickly Angus bull. After a minute, she spoke.

"Well, how 'bout it, Jimmy? Do you know how to meet the needs of a grown woman?" she asked in a skeptical tone.

A classy man would have rebuked her, citing his marriage vows and an unwavering commitment to his wife of eight years. But it was five in the morning, and I was too tired to explain that I had quit wearing my wedding band to the store a few weeks ago—manually unclogging the dish pit drain had been placing it in constant jeopardy. Besides, I doubted that she was the sort of lady to be dissuaded by my marital status. Instead, I simply offered to assemble a list of references from my college days with the caveat that most of the ladies' phone numbers were likely no longer in service.

While my number of local acquaintances couldn't begin to rival that of Tommy, I did receive a fair number of visitors. Church friends usually dropped by early in my shift, often bringing their spouses and children. For many, it was their first Waffle House experience. I thoroughly enjoyed tutoring them on our menu and championing my favorite items. The other servers were intrigued when I waited on a large group of my acquaintances. For some reason, they always assumed that any white customers with whom I had an obvious rapport were my cousins.

Business school classmates and erstwhile colleagues from Alpha Managers also dropped in. Most of them had heard about my new career path through the grapevine and wanted visual confirmation that my employment wasn't some elaborate hoax. For all they knew, the pictures of me in a Waffle House uniform had been Photoshopped before being uploaded to Facebook. While they never failed to tip, my gratitude for their patronage was tempered by the knowledge that they had not been drawn to the store by a passion for hashbrowns. Having fallen a long way from my bond market perch, I had become the Elephant Man.

After devoting a few minutes to satiating their curiosity, everyone voiced support for my new vocation—with one notable exception. An ex-colleague informed me that a few of the younger guys at Alpha Managers bristled at my move. By taking this position, I had preemptively spoiled someone else's chance at finding gainful employment in a weak economy. In their view, a socially conscious person would not have taken the job from someone that needed it more.

It's difficult to fully convey my indignation at this remark. Rather than serving as an additional burden on state taxpayers by collecting unemployment insurance, I was under indictment for performing honest labor, instead. But the sorest spot wasn't that my sense of social justice was being maligned; it was that reasonably well-educated people could have reached such an erroneous conclusion.

If they had any appreciation for free markets or Say's Law, the young men never would have ventured such an ignorant opinion. To the first point, if I was a better employee than other potential candidates, then my absence would have been detrimental to both the store and the customers. To the second, the notion that the economy contains a finite number of jobs is wholly ludicrous. The only impediment to full employment is supplying the correct type of labor, at a clearing price, to markets where it is demanded. If anything, our store needed *more* bodies. Due to a recent spate of firings, employee workload had increased dramatically. For several weeks, we had been running both second and third weekday shifts with only one grill op and one salesperson.

Mary, the waitress with the penchant for Harlequin novels, had been sacked for neglecting her side work. Another waiter, Chris, had been terminated for leaving work midway through his shifts, showing up to work inebriated, and issuing an ultimatum to the manager. Two other servers had been fired for participating in kickback schemes like the one Maurice had going.

I was somewhat surprised to learn that the graft was so common. In the past four months, I had never seen any server steal anyone else's tips, nor had I seen anyone else accused of such a theft. Servers, it seemed, had a double standard when it came to property rights. It was expressly unethical to steal from another employee, but shortchanging your employers was considered fair game. As far as I knew, Maurice hadn't been caught, but his employment had been terminated due to a recent arrest. Apparently, possession of a firearm is apparently a big no-no if you're a convicted felon.

Lois, a waitress who had joined third shift only a few weeks before, had been reported to federal agencies for augmenting her credit card gratuities. By scratching in a "1" in front of single digit numbers, she had transformed a two-dollar tip into a twelve-dollar one. This might have been a tenable scam, except for the fact that she had used the trick on nearly every receipt during her shift. Perhaps if she had previously worked in a restaurant, Lois would have known that eight consecutive customers leaving gratuities exceeding 70% of their tab is more likely to arouse suspicion than accolades for great service.

Then there was Carl, who had been canned for at least three reasons. For starters, he had driven the store's food costs through the roof by furnishing his pals with considerable quantities of free T-bones and personally consuming six to eight cheeseburgers on each shift. I can only suppose that his hunger was primarily driven by his incessant marijuana usage. Granted, a lot of people showed up to work with a buzz, but they were at least fairly inconspicuous about it. Carl, on the other hand, was barely functional. His eyes were constantly glazed, and his hat, apron, and every article of clothing always seemed to be falling off of his body.

The last straw came when Carl took horrible advantage of one of our regular customers. Biggie was a soft-spoken gentleman who dined with us two nights a week, always ordering three pork chops and double hashbrowns. He had earned his sobriquet, as his dimensions and manner of dress were reminiscent of rapper Biggie Smalls.

Several weeks after taking him into his confidence, Carl arranged for a group of his friends (presumably the same ones receiving the free steaks) to mug Biggie at gunpoint in front of his house as Carl watched from his car. After discovering who had orchestrated the attack, Biggie confronted him at Waffle House several days later. Rather than bludgeon Carl in front of an elderly patron at the low bar, Biggie vented his frustration by slamming his fist into the front window of the store. The massive fracture gave the restaurant a terribly ghetto ambiance for the next 72 hours, but I have to admit that the blemish made for an interesting conversation piece.

The melodrama didn't draw much of a reaction from Edward. As far as he was concerned, the personnel turnover merely created an opportunity for him to earn more money. By substituting for the recently-fired employees, he would log more than forty hours a week and increase his marginal wage by fifty percent. The staff shortage had also enabled me to earn some additional cash by picking up extra hours, but my major windfall came in the form of a new recruit who made me look like the world's greatest employee by comparison.

Jennifer had been recently moved into an apartment with a roommate after being discharged from a rehabilitation facility. At one time or another over the past three decades, she had been addicted to every substance known to (and, in fact, including) man. To her credit, the effects of a life hard lived were largely obfuscated by her cheery disposition and a large quantity of makeup.

Jennifer's favorite publication was *The Slammer*, a weekly newspaper that "focuses on local crime in a straightforward, humorous and revealing manner." The publication primarily consists of mug shots of persons "charged with committing Felony and Misdemeanor crimes in the seven days prior to the issue date." You can purchase the North Carolina edition of *The Slammer* for only one dollar. It's a small price to pay to make you feel much better about your own life by comparison.

I had never encountered an issue of *The Slammer* before I met Jennifer. Thumbing through its pages, I found myself reconsidering why I was paying $130 for an annual subscription to *The Economist*. Matters of international political economy, while intriguing, simply cannot compete with your neighbors' dirty laundry when it comes to sheer entertainment value.

"Look at that boy there," Jennifer said, pointing to a booking shot of an unkempt miscreant who had earned the coveted "Mug of the Week" award. The picture was selected for two reasons: 1) although the accused had been charged with domestic battery, the editors noted that he appeared to have been on the receiving end of fisticuffs; and 2) the assailant's middle name was "Demon." "What a hell of a deal," the paper quipped.

For someone so congenial, Jennifer displayed an astounding lack of social intelligence.

Besides calling Sharon at home at 3 A.M. to ask her to adjudicate a personal dispute with another employee, she frequently offered Edward her unsolicited opinion on all sorts of matters. Even when he and another male cook were rating women at the gas station on the other side of our parking lot, Jennifer couldn't resist interjecting. No matter how much disdain Edward showed for her comments, Jennifer never seemed to appreciate how angry she made him. He publicly criticized her every minute, even her failure to stand directly on the designated floor mark when she called in her orders.

"Drop one hashbrown!" she barked, squatting over the mark in a conspicuously wide stance.

"Yes, I believe you may have," he replied. "In your drawers."

"You're crazy, Edward," she said laughing. "Why would you think I did that?"

"Why else would you stand like you were straddling a dirty commode?"

Later that evening, two young men entered the store wearing only boxer shorts and shoes. I recognized them immediately as regular weekend customers. Two of their friends followed behind, laughing and documenting our reactions with their cell phone cameras.

"Are you guys going incognito tonight?" I asked.

"Yeah. If 'incognito' means 'without pants,'" one responded as he high-fived his companion.

Edward let them have their laughs for a minute before finally speaking up.

"Gentlemen, this is a public place. No one wants to see you in your underoos."

"I do," Jennifer contradicted him.

"Big surprise there," Edward muttered.

Although Jennifer had deflected much of Edward's

chastisement away from me, he still found time to put me under the gun. Even arriving five minutes before my shift started would engender a reprimand for tardiness. Edward advised me that, technically speaking, I was supposed to arrive at work ten minutes early. As annoying as the reminder was, I had to admit that Edward certainly practiced what he preached. In our five months together, I never once saw him arrive for work less than fifteen minutes before his shift was due to start.

I took Edward's example to heart and began consistently arriving twenty minutes early, partially in an effort to placate him, but mostly to fill my stomach before the rush started. After weeks of practice, I had finally developed the ability to prepare a respectable double original cheeseburger and an oversized plate of hashbrowns all the way. In my humble opinion, my handiwork was comparable to that of a seasoned grill operator. I was very proud.

Edward had taken notice of my newfound skill set, as well. For several weeks, he had permitted me to cook my own orders whenever he was on a cigarette break. Acting as a surrogate for the great Edward Jarvis (and endorsed by the man, himself) provided a real sense of accomplishment. I didn't have the capacity to prepare anything as fancy as a T-bone or an omelet, but I could ably cook an order of eggs or bacon.

Beyond filling in for him during slow periods, I also tried to help out Edward during the rush hours by dropping my own waffles and marking my plates with the appropriate condiment packets whenever I could. I couldn't properly mark omelet and steak orders, but I was pretty adept when it came to eggs and sandwiches. He even commandeered my bread-buttering services when our traffic got really high. Try as I might, I could never do it fast enough for him.

"Jimmy, you need to butter that toast, not make love to it."

"Well, you know I bring a lot of *passion* to my work," I quipped.

He didn't appreciate the pun.

"You can do it in five seconds, Jimmy Jam. Instead, you puttin' that butter on so delicate I'd think you were smearin' it cross a gal's backside."

I was fairly certain that my new sobriquets—"Jimmy Jam," "Jim-may," "Jimmy John," and on occasion, "Jim Jones"—weren't terms of endearment, but I didn't find them particularly derogatory, either. After all, Edward even scolded employees that procured scratch-off lottery tickets on his behalf for failing to purchase winning cards.

My favorite illustration of Edward's arbitrary chastening occurred over the phone at the start of a weeknight shift. Tyrell, like several other employees, did not own a vehicle and relied on his legs or public transportation to carry him to work. Although he was running late, he had to maintain a slow pace in order to accommodate a large female employee who was walking with him. He advised Edward of the situation, who would have none of it.

"If she's slowing you down that much, you ought to just pick up that big ole football and run it into the end zone . . . the end zone in this case being the store, Ty."

I pointed out to Edward that Emily was two hundred pounds if she was an ounce. "I used to carry cast-iron stoves on my back when I was just a teenager," Edward asserted. "She can't weigh any more than those did."

"What about the weight distribution?" I asked. "I would think that Emily is even more bulky than the stoves would have been."

"Naw, Jim-may. At the end of the day, it don't make no difference if it's a major appliance or just a big gal."

He sat down at the low bar and began eating the take-out sushi he had brought with him. I took the adjacent seat and offered my thoughts on the quality of the sushi I had eaten on business trips to California and Japan. Edward listened politely, asked a few questions about Tokyo, and began ruminating on the subject of kimonos. Specifically, why Japanese men were in the habit of wearing them around the house after work. (This is not

PG material, so I'll leave my readers to speculate as to what his thoughts were.)

In a few more minutes, Edward was imparting a Biblical parable. "So this woman sold her soul to the devil and never aged. But she had a painting of herself that she kept in da attic," he said, gesticulating upward with his finger. "And every time that old broad did somethin' bad, instead of her gettin' a new wrinkle on her own face, the portrait aged instead."

I could only listen to so much of this before calling to Edward's attention that the story's actual protagonist had been a man and that the allegory in question was actually a 19th-century British novel entitled, *The Picture of Dorian Gray*. He continued to protest its Old Testament origin, so I let the claim slide. Whether written by Ezekiel or Oscar Wilde, the point was still valid: Faustian bargains simply aren't worth making.

Halfway through my dinner, Edward's discourse took an unanticipated turn from moral issues to medical ones. While I cleaned the hashbrowns from my plate, he elaborated on his extreme aversion to prostate examinations. He had a real flair for the dramatic, alternating between the roles of physician and patient as he acted out the scenario. His physical comedy was some of the best I'd ever seen, rivaling even John Belushi's finest work.

While few men look forward to said exams, Edward had more reservations than most. In his opinion, submitting oneself to even one doctor's scrutiny would put a man on a slippery slope of perversion. Over a course of months, the patient's deviance would snowball, culminating with his performance in a New Orleans burlesque show.

As I watched Edward's rendition of the can-can, I reflected on how lucky I had been to land a job that offered the amenities of free food and a front-row seat to a world-class comedy show. Generally speaking, I enjoyed Edward's social commentaries more than his personal anecdotes. Each of his tales was a little tall but still marginally credible when considered independently of each other. When I compared the details of the separate accounts, however, matters began to get a little sketchy.

For example, Edward had made these separate claims regarding his father: (1) He had served as a Navy SEAL during the Vietnam War (the first SEAL teams were commissioned by President Kennedy in 1961); (2) he lived to be 88 years old; and (3) he died in 1981.

Any of these three statements, combined with any one of the other two, constitutes an entirely plausible scenario. That is, there are undoubtedly men who (1) died in 1981 at the age of 88; (2) served on SEAL teams during Vietnam, subsequently dying in 1981; and (3) fought in the Vietnam War, then died at age 88 (although this necessitates military service in their early forties during the early years of the war).

Considering all three facts concurrently, a most unlikely situation presented itself: a man born in 1893 begins his SEAL training no sooner than age 68 and finally dies in 1981 (most likely, he unknowingly succumbs to prostate cancer on account of refusing precautionary examinations). As we manned the store by ourselves one Tuesday night, I asked Edward about these discrepancies.

"You ask so many questions, you belong in Hollywood," he curtly replied.

I didn't make the connection between inquisitiveness and motion pictures. But I found it generally best to concede his claims rather than challenge them.

"Well, I don't know about cinema, but I do feel like I'm in a play, Edward."

"Yeah, I wouldn't be surprised to see you come in here one day wearing rouge and eye shadow all over yo' face."

"You've never heard the phrase 'All the world's a stage, and all the men and women merely players'? William Shakespeare wrote that."

"William Shakespeare is under stone."

"What?"

"William is under stone. He's dead."

"And?"

"The man is dead, so it don't really matter what he thought about nothing. Now if Moses had 'all the world's a stage' written on them tablets, then I might give it a second thought. But it ain't."

"Come on, Edward. Shakespeare's the most quoted man in the English language. I mean, don't you ever feel like we're in a play sometimes?"

He shot me a stern glance. I was going to have to build a more robust case.

"Take that guy that came in here last month. He saw his father's ghost, just like Hamlet did. Maybe he was a distraught Danish prince caught in the intrigues of court. I mean, there *are* similarities."

"I'll tell you what I know. That boy's been in here befo', and he ain't no Prince of Denmark. He stocks shelves at the supermarket." He turned to the grill and began scraping charred hashbrown residue from its surface.

"Just 'cause William Shakespeare said something don't make it right, Jimmy. If you spent as much time reading *The Waffle House Way* as you do *Hamlet*, you'd be making two hundred dollars a shift."

When I first read *Hamlet* in high school, I felt a tremendous empathy for the titular character. But now, I had a closer bond with Yorick, the late court jester exhumed by Prince Hamlet in Act V. Closing my eyes, I could envision the shelf stocker sitting at the high bar several years hence.

He has just unearthed my skull from a shallow grave in the ravine behind the store, where I had been hastily buried by three female malefactors who had fatally algreened me three years before. He holds my pallid cranium aloft and begins his monologue: "Alas, poor Jimmy! I knew him, Edward; a fellow of infinite jest, of most excellent fancy; he hath served me a thousand biscuits. And now, how abhorred in my imagination it is! My gorge rises at it . . . I'll have a waffle now."

While I was contemplating the effect of grits on the decomposition process, a rotund patron moseyed up to the bar.

"Did I hear you all say you had a friend named Will that died and you need a headstone for him?"

"Why does it interest you?" I asked.

"I'm a stonemason," the man responded, pointing to his baseball cap. It read, "K & M Memorials: a shrine of memory for those who care."

"Yes, it looks like old Will is going to need one," I said. "Would you mind doing some work on the other side of the Pond?"

"I'll do work as far north as Washington D.C. Cutting stone on the other side of Jordan Lake is no problem."

I should have been more specific in my aquatic references.

"Will was a very important man," I asserted. "How do I know that your work is up to snuff?"

"It just so happens I have some of it with me," the Stonemason responded.

"Let's go outside and have a gander then," I suggested. I had assumed he was hauling a headstone in the bed of his pickup.

"No, it ain't in my truck; it's right here. Look, I carved these myself." He flashed a large grin and pointed to his upper incisors.

I stared at them for longer than a polite person should have. But since he would be immortalizing the greatest writer in the English language, it was imperative that a master craftsman be selected for the job. Also, I had never met a man who manufactured his own teeth before, and the opportunity seemed unlikely to present itself again for at least a few more weeks.

"They're very nice," I said, completing my examination. "I guess that only leaves two unresolved issues—your fee, and what kind of rock we want. Or rather, what Will would prefer, God rest his soul."

While getting the full court press from bond salesmen used to really annoy me, I actually enjoyed the Stonemason's high pressure sales pitch to spring for a granite headstone.

"You really shouldn't even be thinking about marble," he said. "It might look nice at the outset, but it will start cracking after a few years pass."

"Well, this is the Bard we're talking about, so expense really is no obstacle," I said.

The fact that Shakespeare had been dead and buried for nearly 400 years seemed incidental at this point. We were getting down to the specifics of the epitaph when Edward finally interrupted us.

"Jimmy, why are you still bothering this man?"

"We're brainstorming on exit lines for our friend Will. Do you have any suggestions?"

"Yeah, I got an exit line. But it ain't for Will Shakespeare. Bus that table and leave this man alone."

I grabbed a wet towel and began applying some elbow grease to a coffee stain in a corner booth as Edward began to explain my mental shortcomings to the Stonemason.

"You see, that boy's in a parallel universe most of the time. He used to work in an office all day as a finance man, so he's been through that crash which we've all heard about. He's been here several months—which is time enough for most people to adjust—but his brain hasn't finished acclimatin' to Waffle House."

The man nodded.

"He thinks he's in a Shakespearean production," Edward continued. "You see, that's how his brain copes with the big change in his life—he pretends he's an actor."

I thought the Stonemason might be upset that I had deliberately wasted fifteen minutes of his time, but Edward's intercession had its intended effect. He offered Edward his condolences, paid his check, and cast me a pitiful glance as he left the store.

$$\$\$\$\$\$$

Edward busted everyone's chops without much provocation, but his interest in knocking me down a notch had accelerated of late. The criticism reached a crescendo the following week when I responded to his "order up!" bellow at the grill.

"Is this plate mine?" I asked.

"Who else's would it be, Man?" he asked sardonically.

"I don't know. Jennifer's?"

"Have a look around, Jimmy."

Jennifer wasn't waiting on anyone at the moment, and she was the only other server working the shift. Edward was giving me the "what the hell is wrong with you" look. I had been reproved by him so many times that I could accurately predict the length of an impending diatribe by how long he stared at me before he began fulminating.

"You're right, Edward. It looks like Jennifer isn't busy, so by process of elimination, it must be my order."

"Why are you asking me these stupid questions? I know you're a college boy, so you can't be that dumb." The tone was unusually forthright, even for him.

"Maybe I am stupid, Edward. I'm just not as aware of my surroundings as you are, I guess."

"You got eyes, don't you? Do they both work?"

"Yes."

"Then why are you acting like you're retarded? You worked at a bank before."

"No, I worked at two insurance companies. And then at a hedge fund."

I don't know why Edward was so ambivalent about my inquisitiveness. Sometimes, he interpreted my curiosity as a desire to be thorough. At other times, an inquiry drew a stern glance and chastisement for wasting his time.

"So do insurance companies have a 'work for retards' outreach program? What was it they was teachin' you in college? That yo eyes is best used for reading Shakespeare and under no circumstances are they to be put to work spottin' waffles?"

"I admit that I can be a space cadet from time to time. But do you honestly think I've been sandbagging, just playing dumb in order to drive you nuts?"

"Yeaauuuh."

It was time to level with him.

"Edward, you've been at the store for five years. Maybe for you, or some of the other employees, this is a normal gig. But for me, it's brutal. I have to simultaneously be aware of my customers, the grill, the stock of silverware and straws, and a hundred other things. I need to have immediate recall of all the menu prices. I have to know the skill level of each grill operator so I know how fast I can call my orders. Despite a lot of pressure from the customers, and from you, I'm expected to execute all of these tasks perfectly every night.

"At my old job, I used to sit at my desk for three or four straight hours and focus on one task at a time. I could plan out my work flow for days in advance. In my eight years in the bond market, I was given a tight deadline out of the blue on maybe ten different occasions. This is nothing like any of that."

"You mean to tell me you done had the same job for the past eight years?"

"Not at the same company, but I was always working with large institutions in the same industry. I've never dealt with the public before under this kind of constant pressure. *This is the hardest job I've ever had.*"

It was true. My previous years had been spent pouring over company 10-K filings, reading Street research, and writing performance commentaries for clients. I had dwelt exclusively in the ether. The transition from the abstract world to the concrete one had been jarring, to say the least.

Edward stared at me for a few seconds, gauging my sincerity.

"Alright, I can appreciate your situation," he said finally. "You're just a fish that's jumped out of the water onto dry land and you're floppin' around helplessly. Now, from my perspective, I have to think that the fish is a fool for not stayin' in the pond in the first place."

"So if you happened upon a fish like that, would you filet him or throw him back in the water?" I asked.

"I'd teach him to breathe air," Edward said. "But I'd expect that with him being a fish, it would take a while to learn." He clapped his hand on my shoulder. "Don't worry, Jimmy, you'll get it right one of these days."

Edward's temperament became less mercurial in the weeks after our discussion. Not only did the intervals between his reprimands lengthen from fifteen minutes to a full thirty, but the tone of his criticisms softened considerably. However large my mistakes had been, I had finally received a measure of clemency. More deserving people have waited years before they get any.

$$$$$

During twenty-two years in major league baseball, Bill Buckner posted a respectable .289 career batting average and compiled 2,700 hits. The first baseman spent his eighteenth season with the Boston Red Sox, driving in over 100 runs and playing an integral role in his team's march to the 1986 World Series. At the bottom of the tenth inning in game six, the Red Sox led the New York Mets by two runs. Boston was one out away from winning a World Series Championship, their first since 1918.

On the tenth pitch of his at-bat, Mets center fielder Mookie Wilson hit a slow-moving ground ball towards first base. What should have been a routine play quickly turned into a rout. The ball rolled underneath Buckner's glove just as he squatted to intercept it. The Mets scored the winning run on the error, tying the series at 3–3. Two days later, the Mets won game seven, taking the World Series trophy to Queens. For the rest of his career, the untimely mistake would mar Buckner's name. Public forgiveness would not arrive until April 2008, when he threw out the first pitch at the Red Sox season opener. Their hearts having been softened by World Series championships in 2004 and 2007, the Boston fans gave him a four-minute standing ovation.

A similar tragedy to Buckner's befell an American economist named Irving Fisher in 1929. The first man to earn a Ph.D. in Economics from Yale University, Fisher was a pioneer in the field of monetary economics—i.e., studying how changes in the money supply affected production, unemployment, and price levels. (The $MV = PY$ "equation of exchange" was his brainchild.) He also performed seminal academic work regarding the determinants of interest rates.

Beyond his academic life, Fisher was a successful inventor and a renowned advocate for diet, health, and hygiene. He coauthored a book entitled, *How to Live: Rules for Healthful Living Based on Modern Science*, which became a national bestseller. During the roaring bull market of the 1920s, he also enjoyed public notoriety as a stock market commentator.

In late 1929, Fisher famously stated that "Stock prices have reached what looks like a permanently high plateau." Just days after his prediction, the stock market plummeted more than 20%. For months after the crash, he continued to assuage investors with promises of an imminent recovery. In fact, stocks did not bottom until July 1932 and would not retrace their previous high until a quarter century after Fisher made his "plateau" forecast. His reputation never recovered from that singular gaffe.

Like Buckner's mishap during the World Series, one conspicuous public error eclipsed many of Fisher's great accomplishments. One of them, regrettably, was the debt deflation theory of depressions. Fisher had published his theory in a 1933 academic publication in an effort to explain a contemporary depression whose severity and duration hadn't been experienced by Americans in nearly a century. Unfortunately, the public largely ignored the discredited economist and his theory; instead, they heeded a voice across the Atlantic.

No single figure dominates the landscape of 20th-century economics more than John Maynard Keynes. Not only did the six-foot, six-inch Keynes physically tower over his peers, he also cast a formidable intellectual shadow. In the mid- and late 1930s, he propounded a radical theory of the business cycle and depressions which would become economic orthodoxy within a decade. Perhaps no teacher in history, religious or otherwise, has enjoyed such a rapid acceptance of such revolutionary doctrine.

For 80 years, Classical economists understood that recessions were the result of imbalances in the structure of production (i.e., too much of this good, too little of that), exacerbated by the rapid contraction of bank credit. Heretics who claimed that recessions were the result of "insufficient demand" were dismissed as intellectual pygmies unable to wrap their heads around the first, immutable principle of economics: that demand is always derived from production. And that is precisely where Keynes began his attack. He would later describe his magnum opus, *The General Theory of Employment, Interest and Money* (1936), as "a final break-away from the doctrines of J.-B. Say."

In the original version of his *Treatise*, Say had posited that "products are paid for with products." Recessions were born of "too many means of production applied to one kind of product and not enough to another." Several variations of these concepts appeared in 19th-century economic literature as "The Law of Markets" or "Say's Law." However, the explicit definition remained an unsettled matter. Regrettably, this ambiguity made the concept easy prey for a straw man argument.

Keynes defined Say's Law as a "fallacy that demand is created by supply," and elsewhere as "supply creates its own demand." In his interpretation, Say's Law meant that everything produced would automatically be purchased. If this were true, he reasoned, recessions and involuntary unemployment would never occur. Because they are frequent occurrences, Say's Law must be erroneous.

Keynes believed that the Classical economists had over-emphasized the role of production (i.e., supply) in understanding the economy. What was really important was consumption (or demand). When people produced more than they consumed, the Classical economist had assumed that the saved cash would find its way back into the economy in the form of investment. Savers lend money to borrowers, who in turn use the money to purchase investment goods (Savings = Investment).

In the Classical school of thought, a rise in the savings rate should have raised the supply of loanable funds, lowering interest rates and stimulating investment. However, Keynes noted that in a recession, the savings may not be recycled into spending on investment goods because a contagion of fear suddenly increases the demand for cash. That is, Savings = Investment spending + Change in demand for cash. In a deep depression, *money itself* becomes the primary investment of choice. As banks and businesses become increasingly unwilling to part with it, the wheels of commerce grind to an ever-slower pace. The cash hoarding causes the velocity of money to slow; consequently, prices and economic output both decline. (M V ▾ = P ▾ Y ▾)

Keynes attributed the increased demand for cash to "animal spirits," which was his term for describing the alternating phases of humility and arrogance in the pride cycle. He argued that if banks and entrepreneurs were too apprehensive to lend and invest capital, respectively, then a third party needed to remedy the situation. The government should use its **fiscal policy** to pull the economy out of the doldrums. (Fiscal policy pertains to how governments tax their citizens and spend money.)

Specifically, Keynes held that the state should run a **contra-cyclical** fiscal policy, meaning that governments should stimulate the economy against the tide of the business cycle. Taxes should be raised during times of economic strength, creating a budget surplus. When the economy slows, the government should draw down its rainy day fund and spend on public works projects. With proper application of the stimulant, governments could avoid massive economic boom-and-bust cycles that had plagued capitalism since its inception.

Even if the government had not run a budget surplus heading into a downturn, it should go into debt and serve as Consumer of Last Resort. Most traditional economists bristled at Keynes's notion that a government could somehow be doing its citizens a favor by spending money it didn't have. Even if there were some short-term benefit, wouldn't it merely create a debt that would have to be paid for in the long run? His rejoinder: "The long run is a misleading guide to current affairs. In the long run we are all dead."

Keynes maintained that the *type* of spending that government undertook wasn't important so long as the spending took place. In *The General Theory*, Keynes argued that if a government treasury "were to fill old bottles with bank notes, bury them at suitable depths in disused coal mines which are then filled up to the surface with town rubbish, and leave it to private enterprise on well-tried principles of laissez-faire to dig the notes up again . . . there need be no more unemployment and, with the help of repercussions, the real income of the community, and its capital wealth, would probably become a good deal greater than it actually is."

As the government made a purchase, it put cash in the hands of a private individual who would now be empowered to purchase goods himself. To the extent that the recipient of government funds in turn spent (rather than saved) his money, yet another round of spending would occur. The process continued in a virtuous circle which Keynes's acolytes would later dub the "**multiplier effect**." The government's deficit spending would result in a vast increase in economic output, such that the initial round of spending would pay for itself. Whereas Say believed that consumption was constrained by the volume of production, Keynes contended that the only upward limit on consumption was a willingness to part with one's cash.

While Keynes is generally credited with the idea of government contra-cyclical fiscal policy, the concept predates him by several millennia. An Egyptian pharaoh implemented it 4,000 years ago. Genesis 41 tells us that Pharaoh had been harrowed by a dream of seven lean cows devouring seven fat cows and a similar vision involving ears of corn. Frustrated by the inability of his magicians and wise men to interpret his dream, Pharaoh eventually turned to a young foreigner imprisoned in his dungeon. Joseph advised that the dream was a divine vision of Egypt's economic fate. After "seven years of great plenty throughout all the land," Egypt would be overwhelmed with seven years of grievous famine. He told Pharaoh to prepare for the dearth by storing a fifth of the annual grain production during each of the seven plentiful years.

Pharaoh, impressed with the young Hebrew's wisdom, immediately appointed Joseph ruler in Egypt. Joseph spent the next seven years gathering the surplus corn into city granaries. At the appointed time, the prophesied famine arrived—not only in Egypt, but across the face of the earth. The storehouses were opened and the corn was sold to eager crowds. Word spread and Joseph soon found himself distributing corn to hungry foreigners, as well. Egypt's thrift in times of plenty had enabled it to save the world from starvation.

Joseph's story is Keynesian economics at its finest. A prudent ruler stores his country's surplus from the boom years, and then uses the savings to feed his people during a subsequent bust. The policies work pretty well under a very limited set of conditions, namely: a country governed by an all-powerful monarch, who receives divinely inspired dreams on economic matters and has a prophet on hand to interpret them. In a country ruled by a Congress (whose dreams primarily revolve around reelection) and a president advised by less-than-clairvoyant economists, the system doesn't work quite so well.

In a 1934 article for *Redbook* magazine, Keynes wrote, "The very behavior that would make a man poor [deficit spending during a recession] could make a nation wealthy." The words were sweet music to political ears. In the name of "maintaining consumption" and fighting "demand failure," politicians finally had philosophical cover for their profligacy. Washington could justifiably gorge on debt at the slightest sign of economic slowdown. Elected officials and voters alike would soon become debt-addicted prodigals.

The attitude was wholly antithetical to Say's views on the role of government: "The encouragement of mere consumption is no benefit to commerce, for the difficulty lies in supplying the means, not in stimulating the desire of consumption; and we have seen that production alone furnishes those means. *Thus, it is the aim of good government to stimulate production, of bad government to encourage consumption.*"

Within a decade of the publication of *The General Theory*, Keynes had firmly wrested control of macroeconomic thought. The Classical doctrine—that recessions resulted from misalignments of the *structure* of production and the *structure* of demand, exacerbated by the liquidity and capitalization problems inherent to banking—was soon forgotten. Keynesian adherents spent the next forty years building their models of recession around fluctuations in the *level* of demand, rather than in mismatches between the *structure* of supply and demand. The concept of recession as demand deficiency, which Say's Law had been specifically developed to refute, would now become the lynchpin of modern macroeconomic doctrine.

As redefined by Keynes as "supply creates its own demand," Say's Law is clearly an untenable proposition. Everything that is produced does not find a ready buyer, and some goods cannot be sold at prices that cover their costs of production. If these conditions were true, then the noun "artist" wouldn't so often be preceded by the adjective "starving." Every would-be Warhol could find a satisfactory bid for his oil-on-canvas creations.

What Say had actually said was "a product is no sooner created, than it, from that instant, affords a market for other products *to the full extent of its own value*." That is, *desired* goods, which can be sold at prices which cover their costs of production, are the basis of all economic demand. By omitting an essential qualifier, Keynes completely misrepresented the first principle of economics and adopted a consumption- (rather than production-) oriented worldview. In so doing, he opened a floodgate of spurious economic doctrine. And just as importantly, the moral implications of economic activity underwent a subtle, but crucial, shift.

In an economy with large-scale division of labor, a production-oriented person is focused on meeting the needs and wants of others. Those persons and organizations that provide others with goods *of value* earn the right to subsequently consume. A man who is preoccupied with service has little time to cultivate a sense of entitlement. Alternatively, a focus on consumption is an emphasis on immediate self-gratification. It's no wonder Keynes had emphasized the short run to the detriment of the long run. Accordingly, he also spoke derisively of saving and lending: "Interest today rewards no genuine sacrifice, any more than does the rent of land . . . But whilst there may be intrinsic reasons for the scarcity of land, there are no intrinsic reasons for the scarcity of capital." He maintained that market interest rates were "unjust" due to savers' large preference for cash.

Contrary to Keynes's assertion, interest *does* represent a genuine sacrifice: the willingness to temporarily forego consumption and risk one's capital. In order for money to be invested, it must first be saved. Interest is the reward for the delay of consumption and the risk of loss on an unpaid loan. The investment which flows from savings raises productivity, thereby enabling higher levels of future consumption. For this reason, Say had extolled the virtue of saving and subsequent "reproductive" investment spending.

Just like the private sector, government can engage in "reproductive investments" which create higher living standards through prudent allocation of capital. The interstate highway system is a noteworthy example. But in the majority of cases, government deficit spending merely funds current consumption for favored constituencies. In doing so, it saddles posterity with public debt with no prospect for a corresponding increase in living standards. The future generation will not enjoy the fruits of its own production because most of their income has been involuntarily earmarked to pay the tab for their grandparents' bender.

Towards the end of his life, Keynes saw firsthand the abuse of his well-intentioned ideas. After a 1944 meeting with President Roosevelt and White House staffers, he realized that politicians would be strongly tempted to abuse the principle of demand stimulus long after the exigencies of the Depression and World War II had passed. "I was the only non-Keynesian in the room," he lamented. Regrettably, he died in 1946 before he could emphasize the necessary caveats. But it was too late: the Pandora's Box of Keynesian Economics had been opened.

Chapter 7

ROMEO AND JULIET HEDGE THEIR BETS

*"If you have to prove you are worthy of credit,
your credit is already gone."*
—Walter Bagehot, first editor-in-chief of *The Economist*

I had committed most of the menu prices to memory within my first month at the store, although I still had to consult the cheat sheet when a customer ordered an esoteric item. Though customers seldom attempted to order off-menu, we were always willing to oblige inasmuch as the requisite ingredients were found in our kitchen. There was, however, one request which we were unwilling to accommodate: pancakes.

As with waffles, pancakes come in a variety of forms: German pancakes, crepes, Mexican hotcakes. All pancakes, like all waffles, are prepared by heating a batter comprised of flour, eggs, and milk. Essentially, they are both flat cakes prepared without the use of an oven. As far as I can tell, the only real difference between a pancake and a waffle is that the former is cooked on a flat surface, the latter in an iron. Given the similarities between the two, I was surprised by how severely the grill operators bristled at a pancake order.

In their defense, the only frying pans in the Waffle House were six inches in diameter: perfect for cooking two or three eggs, but far too small to quickly prepare a stack of pancakes. On the other hand, the 3-foot by 5-foot grill was unquestionably large enough to handle the order. After some cajoling, the cooks would generally acquiesce, but made their offer in a serious (and hushed) tone: "Okay, I'll make three of them this time, but just for that one table. And you have to swear not to tell anyone about this."

Initially, I couldn't understand why the cooks were more secretive about cooking pancakes than they were about discussing their parole violations and recreational drug habits. I subsequently realized that cooking pancakes is more likely to get you fired at the Waffle House. I'm not really sure why pancakes were such a taboo subject, although I suspect it had to do with our corporate nemesis, another 24-hour establishment that specialized in breakfast food.

The International House of Pancakes (better known as IHOP) was founded in 1958, just three years after Waffle House. In addition to serving the eponymous pancakes, they also offer a few other dishes not served at Waffle House: French toast, crepes, and cheesecake. The rest of their menu offering is quite similar to our own. IHOP has 1,400 locations, only 100 fewer than Waffle House. While our geographic footprint currently encompasses 25 American states, IHOP has locations in the U.S., Canada, and Mexico. I suspect that in the eyes of management, the international presence makes them downright cosmopolitan.

Whereas Waffle House cooks artificial strawberry cubes into our half-inch thick waffles, IHOP serves thick Belgian-style waffles garnished with fresh strawberries. Waffle House offers two varieties of syrup: plain and "warm." IHOP, in all its pomposity, keeps four flavors on each table: blueberry, boysenberry, butter pecan, and strawberry. It's downright obnoxious. And while I don't have any hard data, I'm willing to bet that hiring managers won't even take a second look at your application until you finish serving parole.

While they never conceded that it was a superior restaurant, Waffle House servers would occasionally refer pancake-starved customers to an IHOP location 14 miles away. "But you didn't hear it from me," they added in a whisper. I never made the recommendation but came very close on one occasion when a recalcitrant middle-aged man believed that wearing a sport coat gave him the privilege of ordering off-menu during the three A.M.

rush hour. I had repeatedly advised him that waffles were perfectly viable substitutes, but he refused to bend. Thankfully, his dimwitted girlfriend reproved him on my behalf.

"Honey, you are at *Waffle* House. If you wanted pancakes, then you should have gone to the *Pancake* House. Or House of Pancakes. Whatever they call it."

She was immensely proud of herself for having made the observation. The glare that it drew, however, left no doubt that there would be strong words exchanged when they returned to their car.

$$\$\$\$\$\$$

At first blush, cooking a waffle is a prosaic endeavor. You apply a nonstick spray to a waffle iron, pour a ladle of batter in its center, close the lid, set a timer, and return three minutes later to remove that most sublime arrangement of simple carbohydrates— a golden brown waffle. It sounds so easy. (Then again, so does "buy low, sell high.") The fresh waffle contains a tremendous amount of moisture. Should you need to reheat one, never use a microwave for the job—always use a toaster oven, instead. The former will cause the waffle to emerge hot and soggy; the toaster will produce a much drier result, which is imperative for proper syrup absorption.

Waffle irons can be horribly temperamental. If improperly calibrated, the waffles may cook too quickly, resulting in a burnt shell housing a doughy center. If the iron is not doused with sufficient amounts of nonstick spray before receiving the batter, it will not readily part with a cooked waffle. Additives such as chocolate chips, pecans, and artificial fruit chunks only complicate matters.

An eight-inch steel pick makes prying an obstinate waffle from the iron somewhat easier, but it's still a meticulous task. The tiniest slip frequently results in a second-degree burn, which often remains tender for more than a week. Edward had developed a more effective method for separating waffles from the irons. Delivering a quick palm strike to the tip of its coiled handle, the iron would pop open as the impact of the blow knocked the waffle free.

"Tricks of the trade, Jimmy," he said with a wink.

People were more finicky about their waffle orders than any other item. Our menu advertised "light waffles," which made many customers erroneously assume they had been prepared with buttermilk batter. What it actually meant was that we had left the batter in the iron for thirty seconds less than for regular waffles. A "dark" waffle was simply cooked for an additional minute. There was no "rare" or "medium well" type convention, which would have come in handy one Thursday evening. Instead, the customer resorted to an ad hoc approach.

"Make mine dark—but not too dark," he said.

"Could you be more specific, sir?" I asked. "I want to be sure that we get this right the first time."

"Yeah. I want it a little bit lighter than me." He pointed to his bare forearm. "Make it as dark as . . . Obama. Can you all handle that?"

"I'm not sure that we've ever tried," I said. "We'll do our best."

"I trust you, Jimmy. By the way, my girl also wants a regular waffle."

"She doesn't want it to resemble Bill Clinton in any way, does she?"

During his first two months in the Oval Office, Barack Obama had enjoyed widespread support amongst my customers and co-workers. However, his popularity was summarily undermined when he signed legislation raising federal taxes on cigarettes by 62 cents a pack. It was a pretty expedient way to alienate a demographic that thought of Newport menthols as the fifth food group.

I turned to call the order. "Edward, mark waffle on two, make one . . . like . . . Obama."

"Jimmy, are you placing an order or talking politics?"

I walked over to Edward and whispered the peculiar request in his ear. He nodded, cast a glance at the customer, and poured the batter. In three minutes and forty-five seconds, he peeled the finished product from the iron and set it on a plate. I reached under the counter and produced a recent issue of *The Economist*, whose cover photo featured the President delivering a speech. I discreetly placed the magazine next to the waffle in an attempt to verify that it had been prepared to specification. I glanced quickly at the magazine cover, then at the waffle, and back at the magazine. I knew I didn't have much time before—

"Jimmy, what the hell are you doing reading a magazine when customers are waiting on their food? Take that order out right now!" Edward barked.

I placed the magazine in my apron pocket and set the plate in front of my customer.

"One presidential waffle," I declared proudly. "I hope it's up to par."

For only 45 additional cents, we prepared waffles with chocolate chips, pecans, and berries. All toppings were sprinkled into the iron after the batter was poured, thereby baking them directly into the core. Chocolate waffles enjoyed popularity across a wide array of demographics, while pecan waffles were favored by only a small minority of customers. Strawberry and blueberry waffles, while not an uncommon selection among sober patrons, were incredibly popular with the stoner crowd. I don't know what it is about THC, but apparently the more you have in your system, the more artificial berries your stomach requires.

No matter how liberal I was with a blueberry allocation, it was never sufficient for the always-finicky potheads. Notwithstanding this hang-up, they were much easier to wait on than the drunkards. For one thing, they always came in when the store was less crowded—usually between 1 and 3 A.M. on weeknights. And while they tended to be lousy tippers, the stoners had infinitely more patience than the barflies. Of all of our toking patrons, my personal favorite was the Cookie Monster.

Like his Sesame Street eponym, the Cookie Monster possessed an insatiable appetite and a set of irises that moved at random inside his eye sockets. It was truly a sight to behold. Careful though he was to order only as much food as he thought he could pay for, the

Cookie Monster always came up short. Perhaps I should have been annoyed by his arithmetic ineptitude, but combined with his soft demeanor and general sense of helplessness, I actually found the trait quite endearing.

The Cookie Monster habitually ordered two or three items before asking me to furnish a subtotal. He then proceeded to count his money, and then asked me to repeat the total again. If he had sufficient funds, he would resume ordering until he thought he would break the bank. After he realized that the demands of his stomach exceeded the cash in his pocket, he would spend several minutes trying to decide what items to delete from his order. Naturally, by that point, I had already called it in to the grill operators.

I don't know if Cookie's deficient math skills were a function of poor primary education or the volume of cannabis in his body. During my first few encounters with him, I tried attending to other customers while he fecklessly attempted to reconcile his belly with his wallet. No sooner had the others begun to order than he would interrupt with questions about how canceling particular items would affect his total. Instead of forcing the other patrons to wait indefinitely and losing their business, I simply gave him carte blanche and covered the inevitable shortfall out of my own pocket. During my six months at Waffle House, his was the only customer tab that I ever covered.

All yellow Waffle House tabs have a note on both the front and back asking the customers to pay at the cash register. Most patrons complied with this request. Those that didn't either walked out of the store without paying or left cash on the table. When the Cookie Monster took the latter route, he could always be depended upon to leave an insufficient amount of cash and coin to cover his check. Unfailingly, the difference was less than fifty cents. I was only too happy to pay it for him.

Of the fifty tickets I wrote on most weekend shifts, an average of two of them went unpaid. Given our volume during the bar rush, it was all too easy for dishonest customers to slip out before we could notice. Of course, someone that leaves his check on the table also neglects to tip, but it wasn't the personal economic slight that bothered me. It was what the walk-out represented: theft. The unpaid check might as well have been a shattered window pane that bore testament to a break-in.

Edward taught me that it didn't pay to chase a stingy customer out to his car, because the kind of person that leaves without paying is often the same kind of person that has no compunction instigating violence when he is called out on it. The best way to address the problem was to try to remember the face of an offending party and refuse service if he or she ever returned. As a group of female bandits absconded from the premises, he simply offered the casual observation, "those four hoes just left without paying for their biscuits."

I turned to look at the offending parties to discover that he was actually using the term "hoes" in a descriptive, rather than a pejorative, sense. Their dress, tattoos, and body language fully conveyed the impression that they just finished strutting their wares up and down Hollywood Boulevard.

Although I eventually learned to heed Edward's advice and shrug off the incidents, there was one type of walk-out that always left me incensed. Occasionally, customers would place an order, decide they weren't willing to wait for it, and leave the store while their food was still being prepared. When the unclaimed food came off the grill, it went straight into the garbage.

Not only had the walk-out wasted my time, the cooks' time, and other customers' time, but the food itself had been wasted.

$$\$\$\$\$\$$

As Say explained in his *Treatise*, production represents the creation of utility, or value. By contrast, consumption represents the destruction of value. Any waste of material and labor, however minute, represents a real loss of wealth. A commonly-held economic fallacy maintains that war is an economic boon because a wartime economy usually entails increased utilization of society's labor and capital. Although it is true that heightened military spending by governments may result in a temporary increase in reported economic output, no products of real value to consumers are being produced. Has anyone ever derived any value from "consuming" an artillery shell? Furthermore, the deaths of working-age humans always *subtract* productive capacity from an economy; they never add to it.

World War II has the distinction of generating the greatest manmade decline in living standards in human history. Unprecedented in scale and scope, the war affected every inhabited Continent on earth. Over its six-year course, 100 million troops were mobilized across a comparable number of countries. By its conclusion in August 1945, more than 70 million people had lost their lives. Freedom for the nations of Europe, North Africa, Asia, and the Pacific Islands had come at an inestimable price.

Inasmuch as the Allied victory had been achieved in European and Pacific battlefields, it had been won in American factories. In order to meet the demands of war, the structure of production had undergone an immense shift: a third of the goods and services produced in the United States during 1943 and 1944 were consecrated to the war effort. Government spending, which had accounted for roughly 15% of the economy in 1940, spiked to a nearly 50% share by 1943.

As measured by Gross Domestic Product, total output increased substantially. The economy grew at an average rate of nearly 12% between 1941 and 1945. The large government demand for material ensured that any man who was not serving in the Armed Forces could find ready employment in domestic manufacturing.

The torrid pace of economic growth and attendant decline in unemployment during the war years appeared to be a full-fledged vindication of Keynes's ideas. The Depression, the Keynesian narrative explained, had been caused by a precipitous decline in private spending. The country emerged only as a result of massive government expenditure which had plugged the gap between savings and investment.

Keynesian economic theory quickly gained broad acceptance in both academia and mainstream America in the postwar years. By the mid-1960s, it had become so predominant that the December 31, 1965 issue of *Time* magazine declared, "We are all Keynesians now," in a cover story. In the "New Economics," Say's doctrine was a misguided suggestion rather than a law, and Adam Smith's Invisible Hand suffered from frequent bouts of palsy. Accordingly, the public acquiesced to a larger role for government in managing the business cycle and regulating industry. The only alternative, they understood, was another Depression. But the Keynesian dogma would soon be challenged by a plucky heretic from the University of Chicago.

At barely five feet tall, Milton Friedman stood eighteen inches shorter than the colossal Lord Keynes. The diminutive stature was hardly a reflection of his intellectual power. The volume and scope of Friedman's contributions to economics, statistics, applied game theory, and political thought is truly prodigious and cannot be adequately chronicled in a few paragraphs. But perhaps his greatest achievement was popularizing laissez-faire ideologies of Adam Smith amongst a generation that had come to think of "the free market" as an expletive and of government as a panacea.

Keynes had once written that a master economist "must be a mathematician, historian, statesman, philosopher . . . He must study the present in the light of the past for the purposes of the future." If there was ever a man who met those criteria, Friedman was it. Unlike most economists—who had contended primarily on the basis of theoretical abstractions—Friedman employed a bevy of statistics and historical experience to substantiate his arguments.

In 1963, Friedman and coauthor Anna Schwartz published *A Monetary History of the United States, 1867–1960*, a 900-page tome that surveyed American history through the lens of money and banking. It was a laborious compilation of nearly a century of data on the domestic money supply, inflation rates, gold stock, and bank reserves and deposits. Armed with copious figures and a thoroughly researched historical narrative, Friedman explained the

Depression in much the same terms that Irving Fisher had thirty years before.

According to Keynes, the Great Depression of 1929–33 arose from a global savings glut, particularly in the United States. Falling output, high unemployment, and collapsing asset prices were the symptoms of pessimistic "animal spirits." Skeptical consumers and investors preferred to sit on their cash rather than spend or invest their money, respectively. The increased demand for cash slowed its velocity, or circulation rate. In order to get the monetary bloodstream circulating goods and services again, the economy desperately needed the stimulant of government spending.

Keynes's argument for government intervention rested on the notion that the demand for cash was highly volatile due to the collective mood swings of a fickle public. The economic instability that resulted from these sporadic bouts of money hoarding was the main cause of depressions. Friedman would later describe the theory as "one of those very productive hypotheses—a very ingenious one, a very intelligent one," adding that "it just turned out to be incompatible with the facts when it was put to the test."

The "facts" Friedman was referring to were changes in the money supply. While Keynes had claimed that an increase in demand for money was the *cause* of depression, Friedman demonstrated that it was a *symptom*. As with all depressions, the real culprit in the 1930s was a deflating asset bubble (in this case, the stock market) magnified by the collapse of the banking system. The particulars differed from the 1837 and 1907 panics, but the storyline was clearly the same:

had borrowed from   who owed money to
Stock Market Speculators   ▶   Brokers   ▶   Banks
who in turn owed
▶ Bank Depositors

After the establishment of the Federal Reserve System in 1913, commercial bankers looked to the Fed (rather than private financiers like J.P. Morgan) to provide the banking system with reserves in times of emergency. Most of the cash was furnished by The Federal Reserve Bank of New York under the supervision of its president, Benjamin Strong. Strong had served as Morgan's chief lieutenant during the Panic of 1907 and had ably guided the bank from 1914 until his death in late 1928.

When the stock market crashed the following October, an internecine conflict erupted between the Reserve Bank of New York and the Board of Governors in Washington D.C. Instead of flooding the banking system with cash reserves as Strong surely would had done, the Board allowed the money supply to slowly decline by 3% over the next twelve months.

Friedman believed that the severe, but manageable, recession of 1930 would not have snowballed into a depression had the Federal Reserve provided emergency lending during a spate of bank runs late that year. Between 1930 and 1933, the Fed largely stood by as nearly 40% of America's banks collapsed, taking with them a third of the nation's money supply. At the exact moment that the Fed should have been lending cash to the commercial banks to ease their liquidity plight, it had barely budged. Why?

The Federal Reserve Act had stipulated that each Reserve bank would maintain a gold reserve ratio of 40% of the value of its liabilities (notes and deposits) at a statutory rate of $20.67 per troy ounce. In order for a Reserve bank to create additional money to lend to the commercial banks, it would need more gold reserves in its own vaults. However, the Act gave the Board of Governors authority to circumvent this rule. In times of crisis, the Board could suspend all gold reserve requirements for the Reserve banks for an indefinite period, enabling them to create an unlimited amount of cash. But before they could begin manufacturing Federal Reserve Notes and freely lending the new money to commercial banks, the Fed banks had to address one complicating factor: foreign investors, who were experiencing economic calamity in their own countries, had begun to redeem their Federal Reserve Notes for gold.

Rather than sit idly as its gold reserves were depleted by the repatriation, the Fed raised interest rates to entice the foreign investors to keep their money in dollar-denominated investments. In one sense, the maneuver worked beautifully: the higher interest rates attracted new gold inflows into the Reserve banks, causing the Fed's stockpile of bullion to rebound. Regrettably, the higher rates created tighter credit conditions in the U.S. economy and sent the debt deflation spiral on another leg downward.

After a modest 2% decline in 1930, the U.S. money supply collapsed in successive waves of bank runs over the next four years. In 1931, it fell by 7% and was followed by 17% and 12% declines in 1932 and 1933, respectively—a total drop of 33% from 1929 levels. As the banking system hemorrhaged the monetary blood, the productive organs of the economy shut down. Real output collapsed by 26.5% from 1929 to 1933; unemployment rose from 3% to a staggering 25%. The velocity (or "heart rate") of money also fell by nearly one third ($M \blacktriangledown V \blacktriangledown = P \blacktriangledown Y \blacktriangledown$).

The Great Contraction of 1930-1933:
America loses 1/3 of its economic lifeblood

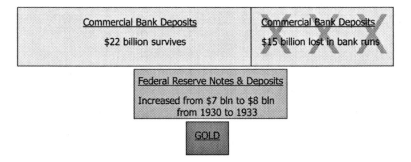

The deplorable state of the economy in 1932 enabled Franklin D. Roosevelt to defeat incumbent American President Herbert Hoover in a November landslide. FDR's first year in office was marked by a bevy of reforms which provided both liquidity and capital to the beleaguered commercial banks.

Additionally, the government also injected liquidity into the Federal Reserve banks via the Gold Reserve Act. The dollar, which had been pegged at $20.67 per ounce of gold, would henceforth be valued at $35 per ounce—a 40% debasement. By reducing the value of its liabilities (the dollar), the Fed was now awash in gold reserves and free to create new money.

With the advent of government bank deposit insurance and a now-accommodative Federal Reserve in early 1933, the bank runs halted, and the money supply stabilized. No longer forced by frightened depositors to call in their loans in a mad scramble for cash, banks were free to lend again, and the economy went on a tear. From 1933 to 1936, the U.S. economy grew at an average annual rate of 9.4%. Total output reached an all-time high, surpassing the previous record set in 1929. The unemployment rate fell from a high of 25.6% in 1933 to a low of 11% in 1937. After falling at an average rate of 6.7% per year from 1930–33, consumer prices rose by an average 2.7% per year from 1934–37 as the stock market increased fourfold.

As the economy mended, bankers added to their cash reserves in a precautionary move against a repeat of the bank run episodes earlier in the decade. By 1936, they were holding reserves at 20% of deposits, more than twice the regulatory-mandated level. In an attempt to boost public confidence in the banks, the Fed decided to raise the reserve requirement between August 1936 and May 1937.

Unfortunately, banks responded to the Fed's move by hoarding even more reserves. As the stockpiled cash sat fallow in bank vaults, lending dried up—and so did economic activity. In 1938, real output fell by 3.4% as unemployment climbed to 19%. A robust recovery was underway by 1939, but the market's natural healing process was soon overshadowed by war mobilization in the wake of the Pearl Harbor attack in December 1941.

As Friedman sifted through the historical data on the Depression, he noticed the same phenomenon that he had observed in other periods in American history: changes in the demand for money (as measured by velocity) were highly correlated with changes in the money supply. During episodes of consumer price inflation, velocity rose as the demand for money declined. In periods of money destruction, velocity declined as the demand for money rose.

A Monetary History of the United States made a convincing statistical case that changes in the money supply and the attendant availability of credit were a major cause of depressions. Yes, money demand rose modestly during recessions, but it did not increase exponentially unless banking institutions were imperiled. Keynes had believed that bankers stopped lending and businesses quit borrowing to invest simply because they had lost their nerve due to melancholy "animal spirits." But Friedman's data brought to light a major omission of Keynes's analysis: during depressions, banks are severely encumbered by capital and liquidity constraints. They aren't simply *scared* to move, they literally *can't* move. *Sudden swings in the demand for cash were due to forced debt repayment by borrowers to their banks and by banks to their depositors*, not a nebulous "failure of aggregate demand" as Keynes had claimed. In the absence of war, demand for money was fairly steady as long as the banking system had a strong foundation.

If indeed commerce shut down on the whims of the market's animal spirits, then the Keynesian prescription of timely government spending could be justified. But if Friedman's diagnosis was correct, *government could play a more valuable economic role simply by ensuring that financial institutions were liquid and well-capitalized.* There would be little need for the drug of budget deficits as long as the economy didn't hemorrhage its monetary blood.

The postwar decades continued to bear out Friedman's hypothesis. In the absence of bank runs, the demand for money held remarkably stable from 1950 to 1980. Fiscal policy also turned out to be less important in determining economic growth than Keynes's followers had believed. When fiscal policy was at odds with monetary policy, the latter consistently proved to be the deciding factor. As far as economic conditions were concerned, decisions made at the Federal Reserve building mattered much more than what transpired on Capitol Hill.

The concurrent phenomena of high unemployment rates and high inflation rates in the 1970s dealt another blow to

Keynesian theory, which had posited that recessions and elevated unemployment resulted from an increase in cash preferences. According to the Keynesians, greater economic uncertainty should cause more people to hoard their money, creating downward pressure on consumer prices. How could the demand for money be falling (as evidenced by the high inflation rate), if unemployment was high?

Simple, Friedman explained. Due to Federal Reserve policy, the money supply was growing faster than the real economy. The natural result of more money chasing a relatively flat volume of goods and services was an increase in the price level ($M \blacktriangle V = P \blacktriangle Y$).

Later in the decade, the Fed finally began to follow Friedman's prescription by slowing money supply growth. After an acute recession, inflation was bridled and robust economic growth resumed in the early 1980s, exactly as Friedman had predicted.

Keynes' theory ignored one leg of the economic triangle....

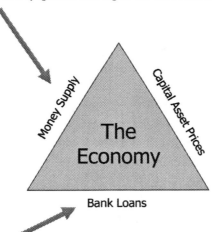

....and neglected the role of liquidity and capital constraints in another leg!

The analyses were conclusive: the Depression of the 1930s and the "stagflation" of the 1970s were not due to fractures in the Invisible Hand. In both cases, the true blame lay at the clubbed feet of the Federal Reserve as it mismanaged the money supply. Deficit spending was not an economic salve, but only a mechanism for diverting capital away from the private sector, creating superfluous bureaucracies and encumbering future generations with debt. "The government solution to a problem," Friedman wrote, "is usually as bad as the problem."

Due in large part to Friedman's efforts, free market ideology enjoyed a robust resurgence in the 1980s. Americans had justifiably learned to place limited faith in their government for having mismanaged the nation's money supply. But in the next two decades, they would learn that private bankers were just as human as the central bankers at the Fed, and the fallout of their mistakes could prove every bit as severe.

$$\$\$\$\$\$$

Of all of the unique individuals that I waited on during my six months at Waffle House, one customer's attire stands out in particular: lime green dress, wide-brimmed white knit hat, faux pearl necklace, and plastic wrist bangles. A gaudy ensemble, to be sure, but the drag queen could have probably still passed for a woman had a gray beard not blown his cover.

"You must like that lady at the high bar," Edward said in a hushed tone as I replenished the beans in the coffee grinder.

"Why is that, Edward?" I asked in a tired voice. I had grown accustomed to him maligning my sexual orientation when I bantered at length with any male acquaintance. By waiting on this guy, I was walking into a veritable minefield of harassment.

"Well, I see you keep licking your lips every time you talk with her."

I had cut the inside of my lower lip during a recent sparring session and had spent most of the shift subconsciously massaging the wound with my tongue. Edward was reticent to accept my explanation on the grounds that adopting such a suggestive mannerism while serving a transvestite could not have been a total coincidence. According to him, this was consistent with an observed pattern of behavior.

"There's a lot of things I've noticed about you, Jimmy. For instance, every time you mess up an order—which is something you do pretty often—it's always a gal's. I have yet to see you screw up when it's a man you're waiting on. Now why would that be?"

"Well, I'm not sure I know, Edward. Perhaps you've formulated a hypothesis of your own."

"Yeah, I got a hypothesis. My hypothesis is that you like dudes more than gals."

"So what might I do to convince you otherwise, Edward?"

"Well, that would make for a pretty long list, and I ain't got that kind of time. Maybe if you were to give first-class treatment to a man *dressed* as a woman, it would actually represent a small sign of improvement. By getting comfortable with a fake gal, you would be better prepared to handle orders from bona fide females."

With no other customers to attend to, I elected to wipe down my tables and cast the occasional furtive glance at the drag queen as he quietly consumed his omelet. I had never seen a real live one before. Admittedly, I didn't know a lot about cross-dressing, but it seemed like it was something people should do at home, or perhaps at a club that catered to that interest. More than anything else, I was intrigued by his age—he had to have been sixty-five years old if he was a day. I guess I had assumed that most practitioners would outgrow their habit by the time they received an AARP card in the mail.

It was only a matter of time until Edward nudged me again on the arm.

"I see you still got your eye on that rough-looking broad at the high bar."

"I was noticing the earrings she . . . he's . . . it's wearing—those gray studs."

"And you're thinking, 'hey, he looks cute in 'em, but I'd wager that they'd look even better on my ears.'"

"I was thinking that they look exactly like the Tahitian pearl earrings I bought my wife for Christmas last year. I'm going to ask her never to wear them again."

$$$$$

"An insurance company," an industry executive once told me, "is a hedge fund in drag." I didn't know what he meant at the time. After a few more years in finance, I began to get the picture. Insurers, banks, and other financial intermediaries all have the same mission: borrow at one rate and lend at a higher rate. It doesn't matter who you borrow your money from, or in what form. Those are details.

At some point in their lives, most people will purchase an insurance policy on their car, home, or life. But despite its ubiquity, few people understand how the insurance business works. The easiest way to think about insurance companies is to consider them as a special type of bank.

A bank, you will recall, earns its profits by borrowing from its depositors, lending out their money at a higher rate, and pocketing the difference.

An insurance company uses the same business model, except that instead of borrowing money from depositors, it borrows from its policyholders. When you purchase an insurance policy, you agree to make a regular payment called a **premium** to the insurance company. In exchange for the premium, the insurance company agrees to pay you a specified sum of money (the **claim**) in the event that the **insured risk**—a car accident, house fire, or untimely death—comes to pass.

By insuring (or underwriting) the risk, the insurance company is making a bet that the insured event will not transpire before the policy matures. Insurance companies use copious data and a team of actuaries to help them assess these risks, but they can never be 100% certain about what the future will bear. The uncertainty about the amount of money that will ultimately be paid out for insurance claims is known as **underwriting risk**.

The premium is the insurance company's compensation for assuming the policyholder's risk. The insurer tries to make a profit by charging a sufficient premium to compensate for the probability that the accident will occur. If the insurer charges an adequate premium, it earns an underwriting profit. If it charges too little relative to the risk it assumes, it will incur an underwriting loss.

Important as they are, underwriting profits are not how insurance companies earn most of their money. Rather, they earn it by lending out the policyholders' premiums—just as a bank lends out its depositors' money. But whereas banks lend out most of their money in the form of bank loans, insurance companies invest most of their money by lending to commercial real estate developers and purchasing bonds issued by large corporations. Once again, a chain of debts is forged.

	Owe money to		*who owe money to*
Developers & Corporations	▶	Insurance Companies ▶	Insurance Policyholders

As a de facto bank, the insurance company faces the same set of challenges faced by banks, namely, credit and liquidity risks. If too many corporations default on their bonds, the insurance company's capital will be depleted, rendering it insolvent. And where a bank must maintain sufficient cash on hand to satisfy deposit redemptions, an insurance company needs to keep adequate cash levels to pay out its claims.

Whereas banks are contractually obligated to redeem the value of checking and savings accounts on demand, insurance companies charge steep penalties and require advance notice for customers that want to cash in their policies. This arrangement has made insurance companies much less prone to liquidity crises (i.e., bank runs) than commercial banks.

The major disadvantage of running an insurance company instead of a commercial bank is the greater uncertainty of liabilities. A bank knows exactly how much it owes each of its depositors. In contrast, an insurance company can never be precisely sure about the ultimate size of its liabilities due to underwriting risks. Accordingly, the most likely reason for an insurance company to collapse is if a large number of accidents occur simultaneously across the country. But should such broad destruction actually occur, it is probable that Armageddon has commenced and the claims department staff won't be showing up for work, anyway.

A nontraditional form of insurance known as credit default swaps (CDS) has proliferated in recent years. CDS are essentially bets on whether or not a particular "reference" bond (or loan) will make its scheduled payments of interest and principal. "Selling" default protection is akin to insuring the reference bond against default. "Purchasing" default protection is buying an insurance policy that pays a claim if the reference bond defaults. In most cases, neither the seller nor the buyer of credit protection actually owns the reference bond.

Selling default protection creates the same economic effect as purchasing the bond referenced by the CDS contract. If the bond defaults, you owe your counterparty money—the same amount you would have lost if you had actually purchased the bond itself. It's sort of like betting on the heavy favorite in a basketball game—you receive a small premium for doing so and, in most cases, your bet will pay off. But when the bet goes against you, the loss is fairly large. The main difference is that in the CDS market, you are wagering on corporations or home mortgages rather than the New York Knicks. (And Goldman Sachs is your bookie.)

When I started in the insurance business in August 2001, the CDS market was still in its infancy. Within three years, it had eclipsed the market for "cash" corporate bonds—i.e., the actual debt obligations issued by the companies themselves. By early 2009, the market had reached a notional value of $40 trillion, nearly three times the size of total U.S. annual output.

When I left the bond market in January 2009, five-year credit default swaps on McDonald's corporation traded at 50 basis points, meaning that you could earn $5,000 per year for insuring a million dollars worth of McDonald's debt until January 2014. On the same date, five-year CDS on U.S. Treasury bonds were trading at 65 basis points. Writing a comparable insurance policy on Uncle Sam's debt would garner an annual payment of $6,500.

This was perhaps the most horribly disconcerting set of price quotes that I ever saw during my bond market tenure. The Street was telling you that Ronald McDonald and friends had a better chance of surviving the economic holocaust than the United States Treasury Department. It seemed ludicrous at the time, but then again, who was to say that Timothy Geithner wouldn't be grilling Big Macs before the nightmare finally ended?

$$$$$

If the Waffle House occasionally manifested elements of *Hamlet* on the weeknights, the early Saturday morning shenanigans of mischievous young lovers were more reminiscent of Shakespeare's *A Midsummer Night's Dream*. Girls really made themselves up for a night out on the town in the hopes of landing a man. A few of them skipped the clubs altogether and headed straight to the Waffle House after party, where they could mingle without the nuisance of paying a cover charge. I could appreciate the rationale, but something about donning a slinky neon dress and a pair of stilettos for the avowed purpose of eating biscuits and gravy struck me as inherently absurd.

As a pretty girl in a short-hemmed pink dress took a booth seat, Edward leaned over my shoulder.

"There's a lot of beef on that cow," he stated.

Startled, I wheeled around to face him. "Edward, that girl has a perfect figure. What are you talking about?"

"What is a man supposed to do with beef?"

"What?"

"Beef, Jimmy. What do you do with beef?"

"I suppose that's not a rhetorical question."

"No, it ain't rhetorical. It's not even multiple choice. It's a question that every man your age should know the answer to by now."

The heat was on.

"Well, I suppose that one grills beef to the temperature he pleases, douses it with his favorite array of condiments, and then dines."

"That's right." He paused, waiting for me to draw the appropriate conclusion.

"So you're saying that a 'beefy cow' is an expression for a beautiful woman?"

"I'm glad to see your education hasn't entirely robbed you of your capacity to reason."

"You might be surprised, Edward. It's just that I've never traveled in circles where 'cow' was anything other than a pejorative term for a woman. I spent ten months in Romania, and it's considered quite an insult over there."

"It's also several thousand miles away. Is it time for another geography lesson?"

"That won't be necessary, Edward. I will gladly defer to your judgment." It stood to reason that challenging Edward on his use of idioms would be as utterly futile as questioning his position on Japanese cultural norms.

As we were bantering, another attractive female entered the store and joined her friend at the table.

"That girl makes the blood change directions," Edward said.

"I'm pretty sure I catch your drift on that one," I said.

"Yeaauuuh. You a smart man. You ain't 100% there yet, but you're coming along."

$$$$$

When coupled with effective flirtation, a lady's provocative dress frequently culminated with a male admirer offering to pick up the tab for her hashbrowns.

"Oh, sweetie, you shouldn't have," she'd reply, embracing him with all of the zeal of a silhouette in a DeBeers' commercial. In a few more minutes they would leave the store with their arms wrapped around each other's waists.

It was touching to see romance blossom. Hashbrowns, unlike diamonds, are not forever. But they're an indisputably cost-effective way to garner the love of a woman. At least at three in the morning. Cupid really is a knavish lad, thus to make poor females mad.

While our customers were busy offering, accepting, and rejecting romantic overtures, I spent every spare minute that I had washing plates, glasses and silverware in the dish pit underneath the high bar. Although convenient for maintaining productivity throughout the shift, the location had one major drawback. If the pressurized water struck a plate, pot, or cup at an awkward angle, several customers could be completely drenched by the consequent ricochet. (I made this mistake myself on several occasions.)

Although the volume could be daunting at times, I usually found washing dishes to be a very therapeutic exercise. There was only one element of dishwashing that I didn't appreciate: no matter how thoroughly I scraped the plates before spraying them, food particles always found their way to the bottom of the sink, clogging the basin. As the store had no dishwashing gloves, I was left to remove the grits, hashbrowns, and meat chunks with a bare hand from the ten-inch-deep drain. After several handfuls of the detritus had been extracted, the remainder had to be gently cajoled down the drain with my index and middle fingers. And if that wasn't sufficiently grotesque, when I finally retrieved my hand from the abyss, stray grits clung to my forearm hair like fleas on a dog's back.

After they had been cleaned manually, we ran the dishes through a high-temperature industrial dishwashing machine. But despite our thoroughness and high marks from state inspectors, many patrons still requested a glass of hot water to sterilize their own silverware before eating. Others eschewed metal silverware altogether, demanding instead the plastic utensils that we generally reserved for take-out orders. While I could empathize somewhat with the germaphobes, I couldn't understand why so many of them were more concerned about the bacterial threats from our silverware than from the strangers that they took back to their apartments after dining with us.

Most of the romantic liaisons forged inside the walls of the Waffle House were made between patrons, but every so often a grill operator or server was the object of a customer advance. In our store, the preponderance of female attention was garnered by Tommy, the server who had shielded me from a bowl of hot grits. Not only did his good looks and congeniality win him two hundred dollars worth of tips on most Friday nights, he usually went home with several phone numbers, as well. If I was ever mildly envious of his monetary success, the drawbacks of Tommy's popularity became manifest at 4 A.M. on a balmy summer morning as he tended to a rotund lady at the cash register.

"Tommy, when do you think it's gonna clear up in here?" I called from the dish pit.

"Why, you need to be somewhere?"

"No, Man, but I'm starving. I'm feeling a double hashbrown all the way. When do you think the grill op will have time to make some for me?"

"Don't worry about it. I'll make 'em for you myself after it dies down."

"Thanks, I'd appreciate that."

I spent the next several minutes scrubbing iron skillets as Tommy exchanged playful banter with his admirer at the register. I couldn't hear most of the dialogue over the din of the dish hose, but it was quite evident from their facial expressions that she was throwing him a lay-up. While I'm not generally disposed to eavesdropping, I couldn't resist the opportunity to see if the portly lioness was going to catch her prey.

"That will be eight forty-nine. You payin' cash or credit?" he asked.

She reached a hand down into her low-cut blouse, fished around for a moment, and withdrew a credit card. The gesture was clearly intended to be seductive, but I have to say that it would only have had the intended effect on the most nearsighted of men. Although television commercials proclaim that "Visa is everywhere you want to be," let me assure that the card has also been at least one place to where no sober fellow would electively venture.

Tommy asked her for a driver's license to verify the credit card ownership. None of the servers ever bothered with this gesture unless they had some ulterior motive.

"It says here you're twenty-nine years old. You don't look it."

"On the inside, I'm twenty-one and holding. But I am twenty-nine years old, legally."

Just as I was turning off the dish sink water, she delivered the coup de grace.

"Hey, baby, did I ever show you my tattoo?"

"Yeah, once before I think."

"Well, let me show you again."

I had already observed part of the tattoo when the woman had dug her fingers into her blouse. The top of her left breast had the words "Mess with my heart," scrawled in cursive lettering above a graphic that I couldn't make out. I could discern a few circles, but the whole picture was an enigma. I would have been perfectly content to leave my curiosity unsatisfied.

Alas, she promptly yanked down her blouse and brassiere, causing an enormous boob to crash land on top of the cash register with an audible thud. The five circles I had noticed earlier constituted the chambers and barrel of a revolver pointed directly at the reader. Underneath the gun, I could read the rest of the phrase, "and I'll kill you."

A firm message. And if appearances were any indicator, decidedly firmer than the mammary on which it was engraved. For a woman ostensibly so worried about getting her heart broken, she sure was putting herself out there. Tommy politely refused her entreaty, chatted with her pleasantly for another minute, and sent her out of the store with a gentle wave.

After I had recovered from the stupor that the spectacle had given me, I spoke.

"Tommy?"

"What's up, Man?"

I had originally meant to ask him if our female patrons usually came on to him so strongly, but suddenly my mind switched gears.

"Never mind about those hashbrowns. I'm not so hungry, anymore."

$$$$$

I had to hand it to Tommy. While his customer's sales pitch had rendered me catatonic, he had played it perfectly cool. Perhaps I shouldn't have been surprised by his poise. In our five months working together, I had yet to see it waver. No matter how severe the antagonism he received from customers or other employees, he simply could not be provoked to respond.

As I discovered in a conversation with him, Tommy had a very strong legal incentive to maintain his composure: he had been convicted of felonies on three separate occasions. Two of the convictions were for drug dealing; another was for breaking and entering. While he admitted his culpability on the former counts, the latter had been a special situation. The tenants had stolen some property from him a few weeks previously, so he spent several hours in the bushes outside their house waiting for them to leave so he could reclaim his possessions.

Given his criminal record, the smallest legal infraction (e.g., an assault charge) would guarantee Tommy thirty more years in a state penitentiary. He had no intention of spending the rest of his life behind bars and believed that amiability was his best defense against another term there. Should his disposition fail him, Tommy had also purchased an insurance policy that would prevent him from going back to prison.

During my five years in the insurance industry, I had never encountered the idea of insuring against a prison term. I knew that Lloyd's of London had some esoteric product offerings (Tina Turner has a Lloyd's policy on her legs), but this was beyond me. Before I could ask if he was sending premium checks to Travelers every month, Tommy explained that the "insurance" in question was more of a figure of speech.

"See my car over there?" he said, pointing to an old Cadillac in the restaurant parking lot. I nodded.

"Well, I got three guns in that trunk. Two of 'em are fully automatic. And I've got a couple hundred rounds of ammunition in there, too."

"I don't quite follow you," I said. "You're afraid of being cited for jaywalking, and yet you're comfortable with keeping automatic weapons in the trunk of your car?"

Tommy explained that he would never dream of brandishing the rifles unless he found himself in a situation wherein law enforcement officials were going to haul him back to the clink. In such a circumstance, he was fully prepared to go out in a blaze of glory a la Butch Cassidy.

"If it's going down, it's really going down, Man. I told the po-lice, if they ever have to come for me again, they better bring a whole army with 'em. 'Cause I am going doing swingin,' Baby."

It was a fairly convincing argument. Tommy didn't have an MBA or a CFA charter, but when it came to managing risk, he was unquestionably canny. If the whole purpose of insurance is to protect yourself against risks, at some point it makes sense to take matters into your own hands rather than depending on a potentially unreliable counterpart. Unlike many hedge funds that traded insurance derivatives with Bear Stearns and Lehman Brothers before their collapse, Tommy would be able to cash in his policy when it was most needed. I couldn't help but wonder how different his life would have been had he been raised in an affluent family and had attended the right prep school.

"Tommy, you could have been one heck of a mortgage bond salesman."

He smiled and blushed with pride. I didn't have the heart to tell him that he was doing a lot less damage to society by serving hashbrowns.

$$\$\$\$\$\$$

Although Tommy's disposition was generally quite pleasant, I couldn't help but be moderately concerned about his private arsenal in the parking lot. But if it was an unconventional approach to hedging, it was probably still an effective one. An acquaintance of mine had adopted a similar self-insurance program to hedge against skyrocketing gasoline prices by storing several drums of fuel in his suburban garage.

I had pointed out to him that gasoline fumes are highly flammable and that the potential savings from his hedging scheme were probably offset by the increased risk of his house burning down. I asked him to instead consider purchasing shares of Exxon, which would provide comparable protection against $200 oil without concurrently threatening the life of his infant daughter.

My friend's investment philosophy was also decidedly unorthodox. Rather than channeling his savings into stocks, bonds, or real estate, he had funneled his cash into another market. While I devoted my days to combing through broker research reports looking attractive securities, he carefully sifted through flea market tables in search of vintage auto parts and highbrow pornography. He believed that scarce, quality items like '67 Ford Mustang mufflers and *Penthouse Forum* issues from the early 1990s were likely to appreciate over time. Like stocks and bonds, they could also be readily sold for cash on short notice. But they were better than securities in that you could also find practical uses for them in the interim.

When my friend first articulated this investment strategy, my reaction was incredulity followed by internal scoffing. Recent events have humbled me. I have to admit that if I did the math, his retirement fund has probably outperformed mine. I'm not ready to embrace the approach myself, but I would still really like to read a broker research report which contains a paragraph like this: "Broadly speaking, we do not perceive value in domestic equities. Rather, we advocate an overweight to emerging market debt, with a particular emphasis on Latin American sovereign issuers. However, we do find compelling pairs trading opportunities in domestic adult magazines. We recommend going long the June 1979 *Playboy*, offset by a short position in any Larry Flynt publication of the same era."

$$$$$

Beyond self-insuring against incarceration, Tommy was also conscious about managing the risks attendant with his personal life. To facilitate a high rate of girlfriend turnover, he maintained an inventory of five cell phones. This practice enabled him to broadly distribute his contact information while providing his exes with an alibi for why they were no longer able to reach him—he had changed his number.

Perhaps the tactic was somewhat reprehensible, but given the sort of women that were coming on to him, the strategy struck me as a complete necessity. When a woman tattoos herself in a preemptive threat to kill you over a broken heart, you really have to exercise the utmost caution when philandering. Hell hath no fury like a woman scorned, indeed.

"Yeah, baby, I'll be at the store 'til seven tomorrow morning," he said into phone #3. "Stop by anytime. Alright. Holla."

"Who's the lucky lady?" I inquired.

"You remember that gal that was in here a few weeks ago? The one with the tattoo?"

Given that most of our female patrons had at least one visible tattoo, I really wanted to give him the benefit of the doubt. Surely it couldn't be.

"You don't mean the one with the revolver inside her triple-D cup."

"That's the one. You remember her?"

I nodded slowly. How could I forget? Since her visit, I hadn't been able to eat a plate of hashbrowns without being interrupted by a harrowing vision of her .38 special. I couldn't understand why a man who was beloved by all of our female patrons would pursue this woman, whom I shall henceforth refer to as "Gunshot."

"I don't get it, Man. What's the appeal?"

Tommy offered a long-winded explanation whose rationale I could only partially follow. His sentiments echoed George Mallory, the English mountaineer whose burning desire to scale Mount Everest was justified with the succinct phrase, "because it is there." Given the size of his latest romantic quarry, the metaphor seemed to fit Tommy's situation only too well. (Mallory, by the way, died in close proximity to the summit; historians are still unsure whether or not he actually attained it. I could only hope that Tommy would have better luck in his climb, which I figured may prove comparably perilous.)

In addition to dating large women, Tommy's amorous nature had also once led him to romance a dwarf.

"Don't let the size fool ya," he testified. "Midgets is strong *everywhere*."

I had to take his word for it.

Tommy was convinced that pursuing Gunshot was a worthwhile endeavor, so I wasn't going to waste my breath enumerating reasons to the contrary. For my part, I just couldn't envision any fruits from laboring in that field. Perhaps I simply lacked his intestinal fortitude. Then again, he had scars from two bullet wounds on his stomach and another on his leg, so he probably found her tattoo decidedly less intimidating than I had.

"That girl's alright," he continued. "The only thing else she wants from me is to see my papers."

While 'papers' evoked thoughts of passports or thoroughbred pedigrees in my mind, Tommy explained that Gunshot was looking for impeccable results from a blood test before she would agree to a second date.

This woman was really something else. Apparently, she had been giving him the full court press in the weeks since she had compromised my appetite. But despite her aggressiveness, the warning engraved on her chest and her demand for a clean bill of health evidenced a genuine commitment to hedging her bets. I wondered if she had previously worked as an options trader for Lehman Brothers.

I had the opportunity to ask Gunshot about her career path later that night as I waited on her at the high bar. Tattoo notwithstanding, she was very pleasant and highly complimentary of my capacities as a server. She had relocated to town a few years ago after earning an accounting degree from a college in Florida. So much for stereotypes about that profession.

"You seem a bit extroverted to pursue a career in accounting," I said.

"Yeah, I didn't enjoy that so much," she confessed. "Now I work in customer service."

After she retired from the store at 5 A.M., I asked Tommy about the state of their relationship. Despite his initial zeal, the night's dialogue had dampened his enthusiasm for their prospects together.

"She's twenty-nine and wants to have a baby before she's thirty. And she wants me to do the honors. But I already got enough mouths to feed. I don't need any more right now."

Tommy's love life was really none of my business, but I was still relieved for him. He had already fathered five children with three different women, so his reticence to augment his brood was probably a wise decision.

While I concur with Thomas Paine's dictum that "That government is best which governs least," some of the events I witnessed on third shift occasionally caused me to reconsider the merits of public sterilization campaigns. Gunshot was amicable enough, but I just couldn't envision her brandishing that tattoo at parent/teacher conferences or bake sales at her child's school.

I sincerely hope that if and when she does birth a child, Gunshot elects to sustain her baby on formula rather than mother's milk. Granted, I'm not a trained psychologist, but I can't help but worry that a child who breastfeeds on the muzzle of a revolver may exhibit debilitating emotional effects down the road. That is, if playing a round of Russian roulette serves as a casual reminder to call your mom, you are probably in need of some serious psychotherapy.

Chapter 8

MEA CULPA

"False principles are more fatal than even intentional misconduct;
because they are followed up with erroneous notions of self-interest,
and are long persevered in without remorse or reserve."
—Jean-Baptiste Say

Shortly after I marked my fifth month at the store during the second week of July, Sharon delivered some bad news. Edward had been reassigned to the airport location, where he would remain for the foreseeable future. I was devastated. How could the third shift crew maintain its esprit de corps when our captain had been taken from our midst?

Edward's replacement only made the void left by his transfer even more conspicuous. The new grill op was very courteous, but his passive demeanor really left me at a loss. After months of listening to Edward's ribald observations and extemporaneous diatribes, the newfound decorum was positively unnerving. Yes, Edward had his defects—a critical temperament chief among them—but they were happily overlooked on account of his astronomical entertainment value.

Jennifer and I both agreed that the store just wasn't the same in the absence of our witty and charismatic ringleader. Despite constant bickering during their shifts together, Edward had still been gracious enough to provide Jennifer with a lift back to her apartment when she required one. Although she had initially been reticent to defer to his counsel, Jennifer had to acknowledge that her quantum leap in professional competence was largely due to his mentorship. More than anything, she had been greatly impressed by his indifference to her feminine wiles as she tried to deflect his reprimands. (While Edward was no pushover, I'm not sure her methods were quite as persuasive as she imagined.)

Amongst its other effects, the exodus also left me with the responsibility of training new servers, one of whom had recently relocated to North Carolina from Wyoming. For the first few days, most of our conversations revolved around the distance between the two states. My rookie maintained that he had logged exactly 38,000 miles on his odometer over the course of four days of driving. I observed that his route must have been especially circuitous given that a 38,000-mile drive would have enabled him to circumnavigate the earth one and a half times.

Normally, I wouldn't let that sort of comment perturb me, but the precipitous decline in the quality of the banter was downright disgraceful. Granted, many of Edward's break-room anecdotes contained a fair amount of hyperbole, but he never said anything so patently ludicrous. But if most of the fallout from Edward's departure was tolerable, the abrupt sea change in the balance of power was not. No sooner had the transfer occurred than a grill operator named Larry began to posture himself as the Supreme Pontiff of Waffle House.

As Edward explained to me, most grade school bullies learn abusive behavior in their own homes before applying the same principles in the schoolyard. Larry was no exception. He had the meanest old lady in the Tarheel State. In Edward's words, describing the woman as "an extremely hard broad" didn't even begin to account for her brutality. In addition to the verbal abuse Larry took from her directly, she had two surly children from a previous relationship who followed their mother's lead in endlessly belittling him.

I witnessed the domestic abuse firsthand as Larry's girlfriend dropped him off at work. Sitting inside the store, I couldn't hear any of the dialogue exchanged in her minivan, but the body language was unmistakable—he was receiving a serious browbeating. After enduring two minutes of her lecture, he reached for the car door, muttering a retort. The defiance was promptly acknowledged with a backhand to his face.

Although he had been emasculated in his personal life, Larry had recaptured a modicum of his dignity with his recent promotion to the position of relief manager. Unfortunately, Larry interpreted this new assignment from "Miss Sharon" (of whom he now spoke in the most reverent tones) to mean that he should mercilessly criticize other employees whenever the slightest opportunity presented itself.

The gravity of Larry's rapid-fire chastisements was under-mined by an acute lisp resulting from his total absence of canine and bicuspid teeth. The best way I can explain his speech is by challenging you to imagine how Daffy Duck would have spoken had he hailed from Queens and been under the constant influence of methamphetamines.

I first bore the brunt of Larry's unrighteous dominion as I dined on two chocolate chip waffles at the low bar. At the conclusion of an intense Friday night shift, the warm plate was nothing short of ambrosia. And then Larry walked in.

"Jimmy, what are you doing eating at the low bar? You're never supposed to eat on the restaurant floor while you're in uniform! It looks unprofessional to the customers."

Making my head motions as deliberate as possible, I glanced around the store. It was completely devoid of patronage.

"Larry, you're absolutely right. The minute I see a customer, I'll be sure to abide by that policy." I took another bite.

"Don't be disrespectin' me," he said. "I'm a relief manajuh and I won't hethitate to write you up to Mith Sharon."

$$$$$

Prior to his promotion, my only interactions with Larry had been brief exchanges during shift changes. Now he had gotten in the habit of relieving the third shift grill operator at 5 A.M., which meant that I had to spend the last two hours of my workday calling in my orders to him. A prosaic request for hashbrowns needlessly became a source of contention.

"Drop me two scattered please, Larry."

"Drop two what?" he asked antagonistically.

"See if you can guess, Larry. What's the only thing we ever deliberately drop in the Waffle House?"

Larry made it quite clear that he was in no mood for riddles and that all order calling protocols were to be respected when we were working together. Not only had I failed to specify my drop item, I was standing eighteen inches away from the colored floor tile from which all orders were supposed to be called. Thoroughly reproved, I took his demands to heart.

"I'm sorry, Larry, let me try this again from the top," I said as I walked over to the designated mark. I took a moment to clear my throat and started again.

"My good sir, wouldst thou drop me two cupfuls of hashbrown potatoes?" I bellowed in an intonation that I generally reserve for addressing the British House of Lords.

"Now there's no need for smart mouthin'," he retorted. "You betta wath yo step or yo gonna find yoself in Mith Sharon's offith."

$$$$$

The full brunt of Larry's indignation came the following Thursday evening. No sooner had I arrived at the store than he handed me a document citing me and two other servers for neglecting our side work on a previous shift. To my chagrin, the other defendants had already signed the sheet, thereby conceding that the accusation was true.

Customer volume had been very slow on the Sunday morning in question. Energy that the servers would have devoted to waiting tables was instead applied towards thoroughly cleaning the restaurant. The three of us had actually taken a minute to compliment each other on how our elbow grease had left the place looking fabulous.

I was apoplectic. I would have signed a document that cited me for insolence, but this was simply a dishonest indictment of great work performance. Using a tone I have never before used at the workplace, I called Larry a bold-faced liar in front of the other employees. He promised to immediately notify Sharon of my insubordination and lobby for my early termination.

As with any other job, working Waffle House meant enduring some hard times with customers, other employees, and managers. But in the aggregate, it had been a great adventure, and I had no intention of concluding my six-month tenure on a sour note. Before Larry could press the issue any further, I gave Sharon my two weeks' notice. She gave me several plaudits on my performance and assured me that I was welcome to work for her again in the future.

Although my contention with Larry may have provided the impetus for my resignation, I had been contemplating retiring my apron ever since my mentor's departure. As far as I was concerned, my technical education in the art of table waiting was more or less complete. The most important thing now was to meticulously record the financial lessons learned during my stint in foodservice.

$$\$\$\$\$\$$

A popular introductory economics text written nearly a century ago explained that "a cautious and conservative policy in the giving of credit is essential to the stability not only of the banks and their allies, *but of the whole industrial community.*" More than any other profession, bankers play a governing role in the body of commerce. Not only are they responsible for allocating capital to organs so that they may continue to produce, bankers also create money, which enables production to circulate from one producer to another. In short, bankers have a sacred trust which cannot be understated.

Unfortunately, bankers are inclined to break this trust during prolonged periods of economic comfort. As with most people, prosperity causes bankers to succumb to lapses in judgment and self-discipline. In their state of complacency, they begin to lend imprudently and assume higher debt levels on their own balance sheet. But despite the poor underwriting and greater debt, banks can get away with the heightened risk level until collateral values experience a large decline. In the interim, stockholders are content with the situation. After all, the upside to their share price is unlimited.

Bank depositors have a different view of the increased risk taking. For them, the best possible outcome is simply getting their money back. That is, their investment has negligible upside potential with a very large amount of downside risk. The reckless loan underwriting, coupled with insufficient stockholder capital, can quickly wipe out their life savings.

The fallout from irresponsible banking is not limited to shareholders and depositors. When a bank's solvency is imperiled by a souring loan portfolio, another group of people is soon hurt: business customers. Liquidity and capital constraints force banks to call in their loans, depriving even profitable businesses of financing. Were banks not so leveraged, the survival of good businesses would not be compromised.

Lastly, the general public suffers greatly from bankers' mistakes. When a large component of the money supply is lost in bank runs, the body of commerce goes into cardiac arrest. Output grinds to a halt as the economy hemorrhages the medium of production exchange. The worst two depressions in America's history, the Panic of 1837 and the Great Depression of 1929–1932, were both exacerbated by 30% declines in the nation's money supply.

With the advent of deposit insurance in 1934 and a generally accommodating Federal Reserve policy subsequent to 1938, the United States did not face a bank run for the seven decades ending in 2007. While the nation endured numerous recessions as resources were reallocated from one sector of the economy to another, each of the episodes paled in comparison to the acute deflations of the late 19th and early 20th centuries.

In 1971, the Federal Reserve ceased to redeem its Notes for gold, enabling it to issue more dollars without concern that a run would occur on its gold reserves. Unencumbered by gold reserve requirements, the Fed consistently increased the volume of its liabilities over the next four decades. By doing so, the Fed provided commercial banks with the means to increase the money supply through the fractional reserve process. Presently, cash only constitutes about 20% of the U.S. money supply; the remaining 80% consists of commercial bank liabilities (checking and savings accounts) and money market funds.

As the money supply has steadily grown, inflation (rather than deflation) has become the rule for consumer prices. ($M \blacktriangle V = P \blacktriangle Y \blacktriangle$) While economists and politicians debate the optimal amount of inflation for a healthy economy, there is general agreement that a 2–4% annual increase in the price level is far preferable to the twenty or thirty percent price declines experienced during 19th-century banking crises.

All things considered, the monetary system has worked pretty well since the Great Depression. Until recently.

$$\$\$\$\$\$$

As explained in the last chapter, insurance companies are really a special type of bank that borrows money by selling insurance policies. Like commercial banks, insurance companies earn profits by lending at a higher rate than their cost of borrowing. In addition to insurers, there are a myriad of other bank-like entities that simultaneously borrow from one group of investors and lend to another. These financial institutions have been suitably named "shadow banks" by a prominent investment manager. Here's a sampling:

Type of Shadow Bank	Example
Insurance companies	AIG, Allstate, Nationwide
Student loan companies	Sallie Mae
Commercial finance companies	CIT, GE Capital
Wall Street broker/dealers	Lehman Brothers, Goldman Sachs

Credit card companies	Capital One, MBNA
Private Mortgage Companies	Countrywide
Gov't-sponsored Mortgage Cos.	Fannie Mae, Freddie Mac
Credit hedge funds	Long-Term Capital Management

(I have omitted pension funds, money market mutual funds, endowments, and sovereign wealth funds from this list. Unlike banks, they act as agents investing directly on behalf of their shareholders and beneficiaries. As a result, they cannot be forced to sell assets to raise liquidity or capital because they do not borrow money to finance their lending activities.)

The main difference between commercial banks and shadow banks is their mix of investments and methods of borrowing. You can find the types of loans and funding sources used by banks and shadow banks listed on their balance sheets, listed under "assets" and "liabilities," respectively. But make no mistake: *it's all the same game*.

Assets/Loans	Liabilities/Funding Sources
Corporate bonds	Repurchase agreement (Repo)
Business loans	Asset Securitization
Residential mortgages	Bond
Mortgage-backed securities	Checking/Savings Account
Student loans	Certificate of Deposit
Commercial mortgages	Insurance Policy
Equipment leases	Annuity
Credit card receivables	Funding Agreement

In addition to borrowing directly from creditors, shadow banks also use derivatives contracts to bet on the performance of an investment without actually purchasing it. Traditionally, if a commercial bank wanted to invest in the debt of IBM Corporation, it would use cash proceeds from customer deposits to purchase a bond issued by IBM corp. Today, a hedge fund can write a credit default swap (CDS) on IBM and obtain exactly the same economic effect—a leveraged bet on IBM's ability to repay its debt.

Instead of borrowing money from a depositor, the hedge fund is effectively borrowing the money from its CDS counterparty—typically a Wall Street broker/dealer. Through the derivatives market, the hedge fund has effectively become a bank. Nearly anyone can start one of these de facto banks as long as a Wall Street dealer is willing to face him as a derivative counterparty.

<table>
<tr><td></td><td>make bets with</td><td></td><td>who owe money to</td></tr>
<tr><td>Hedge Funds</td><td>▶</td><td>Broker/Dealers ▶</td><td>Money market funds</td></tr>
</table>

The number of shadow banks has increased exponentially in the past thirty years. In the early 1980s, commercial banks accounted for 70% to 80% of all the loans made in the United States; shadow banks accounted for the remainder. By 2008, the positions had reversed: 70% of the country's total loans were either originated or held by shadow banks, leaving commercial banks with only a 30% share. The trend was pervasive: even large commercial banks had established shadow banking subsidiaries known as "structured investment vehicles."

As with conventional banks, shadow banks were susceptible to the same risks, namely: (1) Insufficient capital to absorb loan losses; and (2) insufficient cash reserves (i.e., liquidity) to repay nervous depositors.

Moreover, shadow banks faced the same temptations that commercial banks encounter during the upswing of a credit cycle: making riskier loans and using more financial leverage.

"A sound banker," Keynes wrote in 1931, "alas, is not one who foresees danger and avoids it, but one who, when he is ruined, is ruined in a conventional way along with his fellows, so that no one can really blame him." Somewhere, he must be smiling.

Shortly after the close of the 20th century, many bankers— both commercial and shadow—began to notice that on a nationwide basis, housing prices had never declined year-over-year since the Great Depression of the 1930s. Admittedly, there had been a number of regional housing busts since then. But if an individual bank maintained a residential mortgage portfolio with sufficient geographic diversity, the total credit risk should be manageable.

As with all other asset booms, the housing bubble was the result of a self-reinforcing feedback loop of naive optimism. Speculator demand was fed by a large cadre of bankers, who were increasingly confident that the bloated volume of credit devoted to the housing sector would prevent any dramatic price declines. Besides, the bankers reasoned, even if housing prices experienced a widespread precipitous drop, most of the American banking system would become insolvent. The country would be plunged into a severe recession, if not an outright depression. And while the public could pillory the financiers *collectively*, no single organization could be blamed for the entire debacle. In hindsight, they were exactly right.

Most commercial banks lent the money to borrowers directly:

	borrowed from		*who owed money to*	
Home buyers	▶	Commercial banks	▶	Bank depositors

Most shadow banks lent the money indirectly through mortgage-backed securities (bonds backed by pools of thousands of mortgages):

	borrowed from		*who in turn owed*	
Home buyers	▶	Mortgage securitization cos.	▶	Insurance cos.

Other shadow banks—particularly broker/dealers, hedge funds, and insurance companies—placed side bets with each other by selling credit default swaps (CDS) written on mortgage pools:

	Placed bets with		*regarding*		*who had borrowed from*	
Hedge Funds	▶	Broker/Dealers	▶	Home buyers	▶	Mortgage cos.

The actors and assets had changed, but it was the same story as in 1907:

	had borrowed from		*who owed money to*		*who in turn owed*	
Speculators	▶	Trust cos. & Brokers	▶	Banks	▶	Bank depositors

1929 hadn't been too different, either:

had borrowed from   *who owed money to*

Stock market speculators   ▶   Brokers   ▶   Banks   ▶

who in turn owed

Bank Depositors

Rather than recycling savings into productive investments, bankers had once again misallocated capital to finance speculation, this time in the housing market. As these loans were made and derivative bets were placed, chains of debt were forged across the entire financial system. In some cases, there were four financial intermediaries between the borrowers and the savers that ultimately provided the capital for the loan.

Here's a not-so-hypothetical illustration: A southern California resident borrowed money from a mortgage company to purchase a million-dollar home with no money down. After lending him the money, the mortgage company sold the mortgage (along with many others) to an investment bank, which bundled the loans into a mortgage-backed security. The investment bank then sold the mortgage-backed security to a hedge fund. The hedge fund borrowed the money to buy the mortgage-backed security from a broker/dealer using a repurchase agreement. The broker/dealer borrowed the money to lend to the hedge fund by issuing commercial paper to an insurance company. Lastly, the insurance company borrowed the money from its policyholders to lend to the broker/dealer. (Got all that?)

Every month, the flow of borrower payments went something like this:

Homebuyer   ▶   Mortgage Co.   ▶   Hedge Fund   ▶

Broker/Dealer   ▶   Life insurer   ▶   Policyholder

Despite the large number of middlemen, each of the shadow banks was able to earn a positive net interest spread (the lending rate less the borrowing rate) because the borrowing costs were progressively lower for each link in the debt chain:

- The homeowner borrowed the money from a mortgage company at a 6% rate.

- After a 0.5% servicing fee to the mortgage company, the hedge fund earned a 5.5% yield on its mortgage bond.

- The hedge fund paid a 5.2% rate on its repurchase agreement financing with the broker/dealer.

- The broker/dealer sold its short-term debt to the life insurance company at a 4.7% interest rate.

- The life insurance company credited its policyholders' accounts at a 4.0% rate.

	Asset Yield	Cost of Funds	Net Interest Spread
Hedge Fund	5.5%	5.2%	0.3%
Broker/Dealer	5.2%	4.7%	0.5%
Insurance Co.	4.7%	4.0%	0.7%

While the interest spreads were relatively small (ranging from 0.3% and 0.7%), each shadow bank could still earn a handsome return on its stockholders' capital. You can probably guess how they did it: by dialing up the leverage.

Remember, return on capital is calculated as: Asset yield + (Net interest spread x Leverage).

	Asset Yield	Net Interest Spread	Leverage	Return on Capital
Hedge Fund	5.5%	0.3%	20	12%
Broker/Dealer	5.2%	0.5%	25	18%
Insurance Co.	4.7%	0.7%	15	15%

In the short term, this arrangement benefited everyone. The homeowner got the money he needed to purchase the house, the mortgage company earned a nice fee for servicing the loan, and three financial intermediaries each earned attractive returns.

Of course, leverage has a major downside: it greatly reduces an investment's margin for error. As chains of debt were forged across the financial intermediaries, the potential for unfathomable disaster was set. A few bad mortgage loans could quickly metastasize into global financial ruin: one set of loans backs another set of loans, which supports yet another group of loans. When each participant's liability is someone else's asset, "upstream" problems can have sudden adverse effects on everyone living "downstream."

Participant	Asset		Liability		Capital
Homeowner	House	1,000,000	Mortgage	1,000,000	0
Hedge Fund	Mortgage	1,000,000	Repo agreement	952,381	47,619
Broker	Repo agreement	952,381	Corp. Bond	915,751	36,630
Life Ins. Co.	Corp. Bond	915,751	Insurance Policy	858,516	57,234
TOTAL		2,868,132		2,726,648	141,484

In this example, the bankers had created $2.7 million of liabilities against the same real asset, a $1 million house which was overvalued in the first place! Little did the father of three realize that a wave of mortgage defaults in Phoenix, AZ and Stockton, CA could ultimately compromise the insurance policy he purchased to protect his family.

Before the 2008 crash, I once tried to justify this sophisticated layering of debt to my wife, who has spent the past five years laboring in hospital Intensive Care Units. It's really honest work, which has afforded her many incredible experiences. Regrettably, her vocation has left her completely intolerant of b.s., which renders her completely unsuited to appreciate the theoretical nuances of finance.

"This system sounds an awful lot like a Ponzi scheme," she observed.

I tried to explain that several really smart guys who had won Nobel Prizes in Economics (and who presumably understood risk and leverage much better than she did) were perfectly comfortable with these arrangements.

The credentials failed to impress her. She had just spent the afternoon explaining to a physician that despite a computer report indicating solid vital signs, a patient's condition is not "stable" if he also requires two pints of blood every hour to replace the amount he has been hemorrhaging. The (ostensibly) well-educated M.D. couldn't seem to appreciate that the computer data was neglecting to tell the whole story. In hindsight, I believe that the doctor should have pursued a career in economics, a field where a math fetish and a penchant for ignoring the obvious frequently earns you that coveted trip to Stockholm.

As usual, my wife's intuition was dead-on. The only thing that separates a bank from a Ponzi scheme is a thin layer of stockholder capital. The more leverage that each bank employs, the more quickly it becomes insolvent. And the more linkages between highly leveraged banks, the greater the potential for a system-wide catastrophe.

Most of the time, the system works because the vast majority of the "upstream" bank borrowers are able to pay their debts. But when borrower delinquencies reach a critical mass, the chain reaction goes off, and the entire scheme unravels. And that's exactly what happened during 2007–2008. Cash-strapped homeowners found themselves unable to service their loan obligations. Powerless to refinance their mortgages amidst rapidly deteriorating housing prices, the borrowers began to default en masse. In the pattern of a 19th-century bank panic, commercial and shadow banks quickly found themselves simultaneously strained for both capital and liquidity.

Hamstrung by their own debts, the banks were forced to raise cash and capital by calling in loans and selling bonds. As the financing for capital assets (like real estate) was withdrawn, asset prices declined further, and the pernicious cycle of debt de-leveraging began to snowball. The situation was horribly reminiscent of the initial stages of the Great Depression.

The De-Leveraging Carousel:
Where it stops, nobody knows...

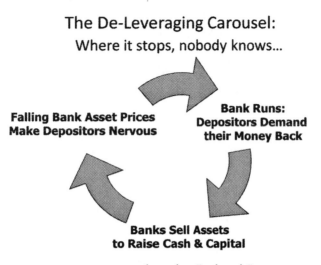

**Falling Bank Asset Prices
Make Depositors Nervous**

**Bank Runs:
Depositors Demand
their Money Back**

**Banks Sell Assets
to Raise Cash & Capital**

...except, maybe, the Federal Reserve.

Fortunately, actions taken by the Federal Reserve and U.S. Treasury during 2008 were able to prevent a total implosion of the financial system. Fed chairman Ben Bernanke had spent much of his academic career studying the Depression, basing much of his own research on Milton Friedman's *Monetary History*. The "Bernanke Fed" implemented numerous emergency lending facilities to provide liquidity to the banking system and slashed short-term interest rates in an effort to raise asset prices and lower banks' funding costs.

While the Federal Reserve furnished the banks (both commercial and shadow) with liquidity, the U.S. Treasury concurrently provided much-needed capital. In some cases, the government facilitated the acquisition of insolvent banks by larger competitors by agreeing to absorb a share of failing loans. In other instances, the treasury assumed majority ownership stakes in failing banks in exchange for replenishing their equity cushions which had been depleted by large loan losses.

After proceeding in fits and starts, the measures ultimately worked. By providing liquidity and capital to imperiled financial institutions, government checked the debt deflation cycle before it spiraled completely out of control. But while the credit market turmoil was not magnified by the destruction of the money supply, the economic damage—steep production declines and a spike in unemployment—was acute nonetheless.

Constrained by credit losses and liquidity concerns, commercial and shadow banks severely rationed credit, resulting in a precipitous drop in investment spending. Beginning in the last quarter of 2007, private investment declined for seven consecutive quarters, the longest stretch in the postwar era. Responding to the heightened economic uncertainty and a dearth of credit, production fell dramatically. Between January 2008 and June 2009, total U.S. output (as measured by changes in real GDP) declined by nearly 14% as the national unemployment rate spiked from 5.0% to 9.5%.

By June 2009, U.S. residential real estate values had declined roughly $4 trillion from their zenith in 2006. Although the losses were considerable, they had been less than half those of the March 2000–October 2002 bear market in stocks, in which $10 trillion in wealth vanished in a comparable time frame. During that episode, however, the fall in output and rise and unemployment had been much milder. From April 2000 through December 2002, total U.S. output fell in only three of eleven quarters (the largest decline was a modest −1.4% in Q3 2001), while unemployment rose from 4.0% to 6.0%. The recession had been relatively brief and painless.

During the real estate bubble, banks and mortgage companies had often financed 90–100% of the purchase price of a home. In contrast, the vast majority of stock market investment during the dotcom bubble had not been financed by intermediaries like banks and insurance companies. Because the decline in stock prices never posed a serious threat to their capital and liquidity cushions, the banking system remained strong. Viable businesses were able to retain access to capital (albeit at occasionally higher interest rates), and the structure of production could readily adjust to a dynamic change in the marketplace.

In the depths of the Great Depression, Irving Fisher observed that "overinvestment and overspeculation . . . would have far less serious results were they not conducted with borrowed money." His remark had proved eerily prescient. Here, then, was the difference between the 2000–2002 stock market collapse and the 2007–2009 real estate collapse: debt.

The problem with debt is its manic tendencies. It plays servant one minute and master the next. When asset prices are rising, debt paves the road to fast riches for speculators and their bankers. But in a bear market, debt quickly becomes a debilitating fetter. Despite heavily discounted selling prices, potential buyers cannot bid because they themselves are encumbered by their own financial liabilities. Having bound themselves in chains of debt, market participants can no longer move. The "free market" is no longer free at all.

Imagine a lakeside community where each resident is responsible for disposing of his own garbage. Most of the homeowners pay a modest fee for a trash collection service. But one enterprising individual finds a way to keep his expenses down. Under cover of darkness, he quietly disposes his trash in the lake. After a few months, several neighbors discover his scheme and confront him. He explains that he is just trying to keep his expenses down and that because he is just one person, the environment is unlikely to be materially affected by his waste.

The sympathetic neighbors acknowledge that any detrimental effects are insignificant in such a large body of water and agree to turn a blind eye. They return home and begin to contemplate his reasoning. Trash collection is an unnecessary expense, they tell themselves. They soon decide to follow his lead. The number of polluters gradually increases, and the dumping continues unchecked.

After several uneventful years, the residents suddenly begin to feel the effect of the lake's changing chemistry. Children become ill after swimming. Dead fish appear on the water's surface. The residents summon an ecologist to examine the water. Sure enough, he finds that it contains a high level of toxins. The once-beautiful lake has been compromised. Thanks to a few corner-cutting individuals, the entire community is now deprived of a precious resource.

In an unfortunate deviation from Adam Smith's vision of capitalism, the pursuit of selfish behavior has failed to produce a beneficial outcome for society. The lake dumping temporarily helped a few residents balance their household budgets; but in the end, the practice cost everyone else their quality of life.

Pollution imposes costs on others without their consent— in this case, the loss of use of the lake. Economists refer to these third-party costs as **externalities**. Essentially, externalities are a subtle form of theft that generally occur over long periods of time. Whereas you will be immediately aware of the costs associated with someone stealing your car, it may take several years to realize the costs arising from pollution.

One individual act of pollution often has a negligible effect on others. However, once enough polluters join the bandwagon, the ecological damage reaches a critical mass, forcing all of society to pay for the indiscretions of an irresponsible minority.

As the primary role of government is to protect private property rights, the state has a legitimate role to play in addressing externalities like water pollution. Regrettably, externalities prove a difficult problem to manage objectively. That is, deciding how much garbage each resident can safely dump in the lake before public safety is threatened quickly becomes an arbitrary matter. Some polluters will argue that their particular form of waste is biodegradable, and therefore more benign than their neighbors.'

Conceding the point, the government determines which types of refuse are the most ecologically hazardous and then establishes permissible dumping levels for each. It's a rational approach for a regulatory regime, but it allows little margin for error. By the time it is discovered that some varieties of trash are causing unacceptable damage to the ecosystem, it's too late. The lake can only be cleaned up at great expense to the public.

Permit me to disclose one of the most important, but least understood, principles of capitalism: *foolish investment, coupled with financial leverage, is a form of pollution.* Sooner or later, one man's bad debt becomes somebody else's big problem. If it is not preemptively contained, the cost of misused leverage is borne by all of society. As with other market externalities, government has an important role to play in regulating financial leverage.

Adam Smith recognized the dangers of debt and advocated banking regulation. He wrote that "those exertions of the natural liberty of a few individuals, which might endanger the security of the whole society, are, and ought to be, restrained by the laws of all governments. . . . The obligation of building party walls, in order to prevent the communication of fire, is a violation of natural liberty exactly of the same kind with the regulations of the banking trade which are here proposed."

State governments and federal agencies have constructed various sorts of "firewalls" by creating a myriad of financial regulators. Each of these entities attempts to manage financial leverage by establishing liquidity and capital requirements and restricting the types and terms of loans that each institution can offer.

Currently, the Federal Reserve Banks (in conjunction with its Board) supervise approximately 900 state member banks and 5,000 bank holding companies. However, oversight of the commercial banking system is shared amongst three other federal regulators: the Office of the Comptroller of the Currency, the Federal Deposit Insurance Corporation (FDIC), and the Office of Thrift Supervision. In addition to Federal oversight, most commercial banks are also subject to regulatory supervision by state agencies.

Insurance companies are regulated by a separate commission in each state in which they write policies. The regulations of the fifty state insurance commissions are somewhat standardized by the National Association of Insurance Commissioners (NAIC). Insurance holding companies, however, are not subject to any regulatory supervision.

Student lenders and commercial finance companies are both typically subject to state and federal banking regulators. Typically, student lenders also fall under the regulatory purview of the Department of Education, while commercial finance companies may be additionally supervised by the Small Business Administration and/or the Financial Industry Regulatory Authority.

Credit card companies are frequently overseen by Federal Reserve Board, FDIC, and state bureaus. Government-sponsored Mortgage Companies were formerly supervised by the Office of Federal Housing Enterprise Oversight but as of 2008 are now regulated by a new entity called the Federal Housing Finance Agency.

Broker/dealers like Goldman Sachs have capital requirements mandated by their regulator, the Securities and Exchange Commission (SEC). Most hedge fund advisers are also registered with the SEC, although the organization currently imposes no liquidity or capital constraints on any hedge fund.

Inasmuch as the regulatory regime is highly fragmented, it is also markedly inconsistent in its approach to capital requirements. State commissions require insurance companies to hold a relatively small amount of capital against "AAA"-rated corporate bonds issued by companies like Exxon-Mobil or Johnson & Johnson. In contrast, bank regulators view mortgage securities much more favorably than corporate bonds. A bank must hold five times as much capital against a triple-A corporate bond relative to a comparably-rated bond backed by subprime mortgages. Think about the reasoning implicit in this requirement: it is five times more likely that 5,000 subprime borrowers will make regular payments on their no-money-down mortgages than it is that the rest of the world will continue to fill their gas tanks or apply band-aids to skinned knees. In addition to disparate risk assessments of investment assets, leverage limitations vary greatly across industry regulators. Most life insurance companies entered 2008 with total leverage of 10–20 times their capital base. Most large broker/dealers like Bear Stearns and Lehman Brothers had precrisis leverage in the range of 30 times capital (in 2003, the SEC had raised permissible levels from 10 times). The most unapologetic use of debt occurred at the government-sponsored enterprises (GSEs), better known as Fannie Mae and Freddie Mac. Adjusted for off-balance sheet obligations, these mortgage market behemoths were leveraged in excess of 50 times their capital base at the beginning of 2008.

As a young analyst, I had asked a mortgage securities portfolio manager how the GSEs could possibly justify such astronomical debt levels.

"The first bill everyone pays is their mortgage, and Fannie and Freddie both have high underwriting standards. It doesn't get much safer than that," she explained.

I conceded that the relative risk of the loans was safer than corporate junk bonds but pointed out that fifty times leverage didn't give the agencies much room for error.

"You worry too much," she said.

On September 7, 2008, their capital bases depleted by loan losses, Fannie and Freddie were placed into federal government conservatorship. The U.S. Treasury assumed a 79.9% ownership stake in the institutions in exchange for guaranteeing $5 trillion of their liabilities. The action ensured that investors holding Fannie and Freddie mortgage bonds would not lose one cent of principal. The portfolio manager had been right after all. As an investor, there really is no need to worry when the American taxpayer covers your losses. (To date, the government has absorbed $90 billion in GSE losses. The Congressional Budget Office estimates that Fannie and Freddie will suffer combined losses of $370 billion over the next ten years.)

Repugnant though it may be, bailing out large financial institutions is far preferable to enduring the financial pandemic unleashed by their failures. Had the government not shored up beleaguered banks during the crisis, the United States would have undoubtedly endured large-scale bank runs and destruction of the money supply, just as it had in the 1930s. Domestic production losses would have been much steeper, and the investment losses to

large international institutions—including foreign central banks—
would likely have fomented a serious geopolitical crisis.

Society also pays for bankers' mistakes in another, more
subtle form: inflation. Between January 2008 and January 2010,
the Federal Reserve purchased a substantial amount of government
bonds, mortgage-backed securities, and loaned money to a number
of embattled commercial and shadow banks. As it did so, the Fed's
liabilities (i.e., the monetary base) grew from $890 billion to $2.2
trillion, a 150% increase.

Inasmuch as the spike in the monetary base replaces
disappearing bank liabilities which had previously functioned
as money, the Fed's actions do not present a great threat of
consumer price inflation. However, if a large amount of the cash is
subsequently reloaned by commercial banks, the fractional reserve
process will cause the money supply to increase. At a ten percent
reserve requirement, the 150% increase in the monetary base could
theoretically translate into a 1500% increase in the money supply.
Should that transpire, a tidal wave of consumer price inflation
would inevitably result.

The Fed has repeatedly stated its position that it would rather
maintain an "easy money" policy for an extended period of time
at the risk of raising inflation, rather than move to a "tighter"
policy which would hamper employment growth. While the easy
money policy may marginally help the unemployed by lowering
borrowing costs for businesses, any consequent rise in consumer
prices hurts people living on fixed incomes, particularly senior
citizens. Effectively, the inflation serves as a tax on savers to the
benefit of the borrowers (and, of course, their bankers).

Lastly, American citizens cover the bill for bankers'
transgressions in the form of Keynesian stimulus programs. As
loan losses force the private banking system to tighten the credit
spigot, companies lose investment funding and lay off large
numbers of employees. The declining business revenue and rising
unemployment create political pressure for increased government
spending designed to "bridge the gap" between a higher consumer

savings rate and a falling level of private-sector investment. The intent of the stimulus is to buy time for the banks to strengthen their balance sheets. When their capital reservoirs are replenished, the government can pass the torch of investment spending back to the private sector.

Some of the government spending occurs automatically in the form of unemployment insurance, which enables individuals to continue a moderate level of spending when their income streams are otherwise compromised. Other forms of Keynesian stimulus, such as the American Recovery and Reinvestment Act of 2009, require new legislation. The Act provided a $500 billion expansion of federal spending coupled with $275 billion in tax credits and deductions.

When all of its forms are considered—bank recapitalizations, inflation, and stimulus programs—the ultimate cost of the economic rescue is likely to exceed one trillion dollars. Given their massive scale, the bailout packages have drawn considerable populist angst and demands for banking reform.

Returning to the lake metaphor, proposed regulations have centered around increasing restrictions on the types and volumes of trash that are permissible for dumping. In financial terms, a restriction on the type of trash would necessitate more stringent credit ratings methodology for mortgage securities held by banks. A curtailment on "quantities of trash" would involve limitations on the size of financial institutions and their use of leverage—in both conventional and derivative forms.

Despite Congress's best efforts, I have little doubt that the banking lobby will ensure that the leverage limitations are not sufficiently onerous to prevent another disaster. Whatever the form and implementation of new regulations, a cadre of smart guys in lower Manhattan will comb them for loopholes. Within 48 hours of the new legislation's descent from Capitol Hill, Wall Street banks will begin creating new derivative instruments enabling them to employ more leverage while respecting the letter of the law. When questioned about their behavior, the bankers will justify their actions by arguing that they are fighting Congressional tyranny in the name of increasing market efficiency.

I remember observing this sort of self-serving churlish behavior when I was nine years old. My mother had taken a friend and me to the local public swimming pool. At the entrance, management had placed a large sign about four feet from ground level. Written in large red letters were the words:

"Welcome to our OOL. Notice there is no 'P' in it. Please keep it that way."

Although subtly couched in clever word play, the message was quite straightforward. All pee was supposed to be deposited in the bathroom. It seemed like a fair rule that everyone should adhere to. I, for one, didn't want to swim in someone else's urine.

After an hour of swimming, my friend waded over to me and whispered something in my ear. In a shameless act of civil disobedience, he had just violated the 'P' rule. He felt that any ordinance that restrained him from urinating in a body of water was clearly an all-out assault on his civil liberties. The water was too cold, he explained, and his discharge had provided a welcome respite from the frigid temperature. If the pool staff really intended to keep the water clean, he reasoned, they should have turned up the pool heater. Besides, he added, anyone ingesting his pee probably wouldn't notice the taste, anyway.

In his own mind, he was Gandhi, defying a tyrannical British empire on a salt march.

To any casual observer with a cerebrum, however, he was just a bratty kid too lazy to walk thirty feet to the bathroom. I don't know what ever happened to that boy, but I can't help but wonder if he eventually found employment in the capital markets group of a Wall Street bank.

I really shouldn't throw so many stones at bankers without disclosing the fact that I was once building a glass house of my own. During my last ten months with Alpha Managers, I was assigned the task of creating a particular type of shadow bank known as a "Mortgage Real Estate Investment Trust (REIT)."

There are several Mortgage REITs which trade on the New York Stock Exchange. They're pretty simple businesses and work as follows: Issue a bunch of stock to investors. Use the cash from the stock sales to purchase mortgages issued by Fannie Mae and Freddie Mac. Then borrow a lot of money from Wall Street dealers using repurchase agreements to buy 5–8 times as many mortgages as you initially purchased outright. Your profit is the difference between the interest earned on the mortgages and the interest cost of borrowing from Wall Street. It's a bank without a physical branch. All you really need is a telephone and a Bloomberg terminal.

The neat thing about Mortgage REITs is that they don't really have customers. They simply create another link in the chain between borrowers and savers:

Homeowner (Borrower) ▶ Fannie Mae (Shadow Bank) ▶ Mortgage REIT (Shadow Bank) ▶ Broker/Dealer (Shadow Bank) ▶ Money market fund (Saver)

Another favorable aspect of this particular type of shadow bank is the total absence of credit risk. I didn't have to worry that the REIT's mortgage bonds would default—they were effectively guaranteed by the Federal government, which owns most of Fannie and Freddie. I wasn't concerned about our creditors demanding their money back, either. If the financial system got in a severe pickle again and broker/dealers quit lending money against Fannie and Freddie bonds, the Federal Reserve would probably create a new lending facility that provided the same service.

The only major risk the REIT faced was a sudden change in interest rates; all of the others would have been covered by the American taxpayer. But that's not even the best part. As long as management told the truth in our accounting statements, we faced no regulatory scrutiny whatsoever. It was a wholly unregulated bank, whose assets and liabilities were tacitly insured by Uncle Sam, but whose profits were entirely private. It was beautiful.

Or, rather, it would have been beautiful. In late 2008, I had all my ducks in a row, ready to launch the new venture. In another eighteen months, I would be an officer of a publicly traded company, making a few hundred thousand dollars per year. But as fate would have it, I was laid off before my firm could secure the seed investment before going to the stock market for more capital. I spent the first several weeks after my layoff contemplating just how close I had come to pulling it all off. But as more time passes, the less I lament the forgone wealth. If it represented anything at all, the deal's collapse was an act of grace. For whatever legacy I may leave to the world, at least it won't be forging another layer of debt in the global financial system.

As I entered the store to begin my last series of weekend shifts, I reflected on what had been the most extraordinary chapter in my professional life. Wherever I might next tread on my career path, it was highly doubtful that a future road would be replete with such interesting characters.

"What are you doing here?" a grill op asked. "You're not slated to work tonight."

I checked the schedule in the back room. Sure enough, my name was nowhere to be found.

"Well, I suppose that's it then," I said sullenly. "I guess I'll just go home." It was certainly an anticlimactic conclusion to a journey that had been punctuated by so much excitement. Then the store phone rang.

"Yes, he's here now," the grill op said into the transmitter. "Alright, I'll tell him." He hung up and turned to me.

"Jimmy, you need to report to the Airport. That's where you're going to spend your last three days. Say hi to Edward for us while you're out there."

So I was going to have one last hurrah with the World's Greatest Short Order Cook after all. I drove out to the airport, ecstatic about the propitious turn of events. When I arrived there, Edward explained that Sharon had transferred him to replace a lethargic and unreliable predecessor as relief manager. His commute had been lengthened by ten minutes, but he was amenable to the move as long as he was guaranteed a workweek of at least forty hours.

The only real drawback to Edward's new gig was that his new coworkers, while congenial, were decidedly less interesting than the crew at our old store. Accordingly, he had spoken to Sharon and personally arranged my reassignment. As her longest-standing and most dependable employee, she was happy to oblige his request. I was genuinely flattered.

While we had never worked together in that location, we hit our stride immediately. My calls were on point, Edward's callbacks were flawless, and volume was healthy, yet manageable, with nary a churlish customer in sight. It was the sort of picturesque scenario envisioned by *The Waffle House Way*.

"Marking two chocolate waffles. Yee-hee!" Edward yelped in a high pitch. He had been adding Michael Jackson sound effects to his order callbacks in homage to the recently late King of Pop. In between orders, we passed the hours debating whether the Linebacker or the Giantess (another formidable dame who had recently joined the crew) would win in a fight, and how much pay-per-view revenue such a televised event could garner. We had come a long way since February.

During the lull before the Friday night rush, I was eating a cheeseburger in the break room when Edward suddenly volunteered information about which I had been curious for some time.

"I never told you why I went to prison," he began.

Nearly thirty years ago, Edward had committed a robbery which culminated in an accidental death. Despite being only seventeen, he was tried as an adult and received a twenty-five-year sentence. He spoke of the event with a degree of sobriety and regret that I had never heard anyone express before. He didn't weep as he related the account, but the sincerity of his remorse was unquestionable. Edward made no efforts to exculpate himself or assign the blame to his parents or society. He freely acknowledged his guilt and had sought God's forgiveness for his crime on many occasions since.

It was a terrifying and yet strangely inspiring account. I don't know why he shared it with me. Maybe he just wanted me to appraise him as a fundamentally honorable man, despite his past mistakes. Whatever the reason he imparted his history, I was grateful that he did.

"The main thing I learned in prison," he concluded, "was that if you want anything in this world, you got to work for it in the first place. Greed will never take you anywhere good."

Later that night, Edward asked if he could borrow twenty-one dollars. I was surprised by his request. He had never tried to borrow money from me before, and I knew that he had a general aversion to debt. I wondered briefly about the use of proceeds but didn't bother to ask. I trusted him, so it didn't matter. I slipped him the two bills, all too eager to get rid of a banknote featuring a portrait of Andrew Jackson.

$$$$$

As I drove home, I pondered Edward's words. "If you want anything in this world, you've got to work for it in the first place." It was a poignant restatement of a now very familiar principle, one which we had both violated. I hadn't transgressed as overtly as Edward had, but I had clearly been an accessory to the crime in my role as a financier. I had provided capital to enable people who tried to consume more than they had produced. In hindsight, the blowback was clearly unavoidable.

Speaking of the Ten Commandments, acclaimed film director Cecil B. DeMille said: "It is impossible for us to break the law. We can only break ourselves against the law." And that's exactly what Edward and I had done: we had broken ourselves against the Law of Markets.

While I can't speak on Edward's behalf, I can at least plead some degree of personal ignorance in the matter: it's difficult to respect a principle that you've never been taught. My freshman economics class at Wake Forest University employed a textbook entitled *Economics: Principles and Policy*, by William J. Baumol and Alan S. Blinder. The book devotes a paltry 25 of its 900 pages to the banking system. John Maynard Keynes is featured prominently in a page-long biographical note; his theories comprise roughly ten percent of the text's total content. Page 559 contains a typical illustration of his doctrine: "Recessions and unemployment are often caused by insufficient aggregate demand."

No one who understands Say's Law would ever make such an assertion. If some fool uttered this ludicrous claim at a cocktail party, I'd laugh at the man and reprove him by dumping my drink right on his blazer. But when the fool in question is a former vice chairman of the Federal Reserve Board of Governors, the statement is more disconcerting than humorous.

Recently, I examined four contemporary undergraduate economics textbooks to find that Say's Law is mentioned in only one of them. Regrettably, the concept is amateurishly explained as "supply creates its own demand," and the author then proceeds to praise Keynes for liberating economics from the antiquated fallacy.

How far we've fallen. In the mid-19th century, Say's *Treatise on Political Economy* was the preeminent economics textbook at American institutions of higher learning, including Harvard University. Instead of learning sound doctrine, today's undergraduates are inundated with principles that will not bear the scrutiny of common sense and experience. Then again, common sense never proved a sufficient impediment to stop a determined economist.

In economics, as in other endeavors, we are often more inclined to embrace a principle based on its convenience rather than its veracity. Keynes's ideas of economic prosperity through government profligacy are very comforting ones. It's easy to blame recessions on "demand failure" and then prescribe a regimen of tax cuts and government spending. It's a fun medicine to take, and one that politicians have become only too happy to administer. Unfortunately, it's a bad prescription based on a lousy diagnosis of the symptoms.

As individuals, Americans tried to violate Say's Law by elevating household debt levels to unsustainable levels. As a country, the United States is now attempting to break it collectively. In 2009, the federal budget deficit exceeded 10% of the nation's total output for the first time since World War II. It is expected to remain above that level throughout fiscal 2010, then fall to the 5% range for the rest of the decade. Our spendthrift approach is a lamentable deviation from the discipline of our ancestors.

The United States government ran a budget surplus in 67 calendar years of the nineteenth century. When the country was not at war, the country was in surplus 75% of the time, with the deficit never exceeding 1% of the nation's output. The trend continued for the first thirty years of the 20th century. Budgets were balanced or in surplus 80% of the time, with large deficits being run only in 1918 and 1919 to fund military expenditures during World War I.

The track record worsened in subsequent decades as the government borrowed to finance FDR's Depression-era New Deal programs, World War II and wars in Korea and Vietnam. From 1931 to 1965, the U.S. Treasury ran deficits in more than three years out of every four. 1965, you may recall, was the same year that *Time* magazine declared the hegemony of Keynesian economic theory. The observation was prescient: the United States government has been a net borrower in nearly 90% of the years since then.

The unavoidable consequence of embracing the short-term gratification that Keynes championed has been a gradual erosion of the American economy's long-term stability. An ever-larger share of capital that could have been devoted to investing reproductively for tomorrow is now earmarked for expenditure today: in 2010, 7% of federal tax receipts will be used for debt payments. By 2013, the number climbs to nearly 11%.

As of May 2010, U.S. national debt—the accumulation of years of deficits—stands at roughly 13 trillion dollars. When unfunded entitlement programs (e.g., Social Security, Medicare, and Medicaid) are included, the number rises to a staggering $62 trillion. If the status quo does not change, mandatory government spending on entitlements and interest on the national debt will exceed tax revenue sometime between 2030 and 2040, leaving no resources for national defense, law enforcement, education, and other "discretionary" items. At that point, the Treasury will need to issue new debt just so that it can keep paying interest on its outstanding obligations. The U.S. government will have become a Ponzi scheme.

In recognition of this threat, Moody's ratings service has recently warned that America is at risk of losing the "AAA" rating status which has enabled it to borrow cheaply from foreign investors. Given that Moody's had also assigned the coveted Triple-A rating to countless pools of subprime mortgages which now trade for twenty cents on the dollar, we should probably be in a state of outright panic.

In a 1938 essay entitled "My Early Beliefs," Keynes offered a description of his undergraduate peer group at Cambridge: "We repudiated entirely customary morals, conventions and traditional wisdom. We were, that is to say, in the strict sense of the term, immoralists . . . we recognized no moral obligation on us, no inner sanction, to conform or to obey." Nowhere was this ethos more manifest than in his refusal to genuflect before the first law of economics.

But whatever else can be said of him, Keynes was surely right on one point—we are all dead in the long run. The question before us is whether we want to die of a self-inflicted overdose of his medicine. We can continue to follow the spurious doctrines of an economic pied piper, or we can acknowledge the simple truth that a burgeoning federal debt only postpones our inevitable arraignment before the Court of Economic Justice.

Neglecting to contemplate the negative consequences of short-sighted behavior will not make them any less likely to come to fruition. As it stands, the U.S. Treasury is on a collision course with Say's Law. I don't know when the crash will occur, but I have no doubt as to which of the two entities will survive the wreckage unscathed.

When I reported to sing my swan song at 9 P.M. Saturday night, Edward was nowhere to be found. Something was wrong; he was never late for a shift. He had mentioned that he had been investigating another job opportunity, so perhaps he had taken me in to his confidence only to borrow some cash before disappearing forever.

I tried to put the matter out of my head as I prepared an egg and cheese sandwich for myself, but I couldn't resist the temptation to repeatedly glance at my watch as my dinner cooked on the grill. 9:45 came and went. Still no Edward.

"I believe this belongs to you, suh," a familiar voice said behind me.

No sooner had I wheeled around than Edward placed two ten-dollar bills and a single in my hand.

"Edward, you're always at least fifteen minutes early for work. What gives?"

"They cut my hours back a little bit. My shift doesn't start 'til ten." He ran his eyes over my face. "Was you afraid you weren't gonna get your money back?"

"That never crossed my mind."

"I can tell you're lyin'."

"Maybe a little bit," I conceded. "It's not about the money, Edward. Losing twenty-one dollars doesn't hurt. But misjudging a man whose character I respected . . . now that would have stung a lot."

After another pleasant ten-hour shift, I decided that cheese eggs and hashbrowns would be the perfect coda to my six months in the restaurant business. While I had served hundreds of orders of cheese eggs, I had never cooked or eaten an order of them myself. But they were such a popular menu item, and I wanted to see what all the fuss was about.

As I scrambled my eggs and flipped my hashbrowns, I permitted myself one final flirtation with Keynesian economics. My stomach had indicated a desire for food, which had led to the subsequent production. So maybe demand really did drive supply after all.

Before my meditation could go any further, a muscular arm reached across my chest and placed a hamburger patty on the grill.

"Excuse me, Jimmy. I'm just gonna fix a quarter cheese plate," Edward declared.

"Would you like me to make it for you?" I offered.

"No suh, that's alright. I'll make it myself. I've been eating my own cooking for thirty years, and I don't intend to break that habit this morning. But I thank you, anyway."

I'm going to eat my own cooking. I'm going to eat my own cooking. I repeated the mantra in my head. I had experienced a myriad of flashes of economic revelation in the past few months. But on this, my last day, the epiphany was particularly forceful.

I like to imagine that a six-month stint at Waffle House would have prompted Keynes to recognize that "demand," in the economic sense, implies more than a simple desire for a good. No one will sell you an item just because you want it. True demand means that you are willing to pay the price of production. It means that you must produce before you can consume. We can only eat inasmuch as we are willing to cook for ourselves or produce *something of value* in exchange for another's cooking. Sure, you can borrow a few bucks for a meal if you're short on change, but only if you're of sound character and have a willingness to produce to repay your creditor.

Jean-Baptiste Say had been right all along. Production drives consumption, not vice versa. I wonder why 20th-century politicians had forgotten this simple dictum which had been so long revered by the Classical economists. In a global economy with large-scale division of labor, perhaps we are so dependent on the production of others that we forget the necessity of our own efforts. While contemplating a purchase, we often look first to a credit card rather than the sweat of our own brow. But Say's Law is best learned viscerally, by harvesting crops or cooking your own food. Most 19th-century American farmers must have understood the Law of Markets intuitively, just as Edward did.

We put the food on our plates and retired to the low bar. I suggested that a toast was in order, though I had absolutely no idea what to drink to. Robert thought for a few seconds before finally raising his cup.

"To the meltdown," he said.

After five months together, he still had the ability to catch me completely off guard.

"The meltdown? Why should we drink to that?"

"Think about it, Man. What are the chances that you woulda spent any time working at Waffle House if the market hadn't collapsed?"

"Slim to none."

"And you've learned a lot since you been here, haven't you?"

"That's a gross understatement, Edward."

"So your journey was worthwhile."

"It certainly was."

"And on my end, it's been a real pleasure traveling together with you." He offered me his hand, which I gladly accepted.

"Well, I guess it's about time to roll out," he declared.

"Edward, could you wait here just a second? I've got something I want to give you before we part ways." I returned from my car a few minutes later and presented him with a DVD.

"Look at that there. Now that's alright," he said, holding his new copy of *The Shawshank Redemption*. "I love this movie and that boy Morgan Freeman, he's a fine actor. Now what are you giving this to me for?"

"Think of it as a memento of our time together. After all, it's a lot like our story, isn't it?"

"How do you figure?" he asked.

"A young banker is thrown into a tough new environment. A veteran of the institution, doubting the tenderfoot's prospects for survival, takes him under his wing. Despite their differing backgrounds, the two form an unexpectedly strong bond as they confront the demons of their past. In the end, hope and tenacity finally pay off. Escaping the chains of past transgressions, they move on to better lives as their friendship carries them through to their redemption."

Edward smiled at me, then studied the DVD case for a few seconds. "You *do* kind of resemble this boy," he said, pointing to Tim Robbins's picture. "See you around, Jimmy Mac."

"Hey, you didn't call me Jimmy Jam or Jimmy Dean."

"No. You've been the Mac for several weeks now. Take care and beware."

After a final handshake, we retired to our vehicles. I waved to Edward as I drove out of the parking lot. As I pulled on to the interstate, I found myself suddenly overcome with a profound sense of gratitude. He was right to have toasted the meltdown. Had I not been laid off, I would never have met him, let alone the Repo Men, the Linebacker, and Crazy Kathy. Except for other finance nerds, my best career-related anecdotes would fall on deaf ears. No grandchild wants to hear lame anecdotes from the bond market about "the great yield curve inversion of aught five" or "the time LIBOR spiked to six percent in two days." My biography, while still bland in many respects, became markedly more exciting thanks to those six months.

For most people, "recession" carries a negative connotation. For me, however, the recent episode has come with a lustrous silver lining. I have learned a life lesson in true capitalism. As originally expounded by Adam Smith, capitalism works. It is a moral and just system of organizing human behavior. It promotes political freedom. It rewards creativity, initiative, and alacrity. It affords us with a higher standard of living than any alternative economic system. At its heart, its ethos is one of serving others. When earned honestly, profits are merely a byproduct of diligent service.

True capitalism means that capitalists and financiers gracefully bear the consequences of their misallocated capital. The cure for recession isn't government profligacy; it is to reallocate labor and capital to where they are most needed. And if you have an ounce of daring, the reallocation process can provide you with the experience of a lifetime.

I learned more about the true nature of productivity and economic organization by observing Edward's work ethic and pondering his casual restatements of Say's Law than I did from all my time in the bond market and from studying Keynes's half-baked theories during my undergraduate years. It is wonderfully ironic that the example and common sense of a paroled short-order cook could decimate the reasoning of the 20th century's most influential economist. But perhaps I shouldn't have been surprised. After all, irony is the fundamental organizing principle of the universe.

One realization was painful, however. The next time I dined at Waffle House, I would have to pay full price for my food. But, I reflected, that was an acceptable state of affairs. The triple hashbrowns were worth at least $2.25 to my palate. The restaurant would turn a profit on the sale, and my waiter would undoubtedly garner a healthy tip. Everyone would win in a confluence of culinary excellence and laissez-faire capitalism. Undoubtedly, Adam Smith and Jean-Baptiste Say would heartily approve. There was only one unresolved question in my mind: how would the Fathers of Capitalism take *their* hashbrowns?

ARTICLES OF ECONOMIC FAITH

1. Production is the source of all consumption. No good or service can be consumed without first being produced. Society's wealth can only grow by adding more workers and/or increasing their productivity.

2. Money is only a mechanism through which society's producers exchange their productions. Any large, sudden increase or decrease in the volume of money inevitably creates adverse consequences on the volume of real production.

3. Capitalism operates on principles of freedom and mutual edification for producers, consumers, capital, and labor alike. Ergo, it is a fundamentally moral system of production arrangements.

4. The primary responsibility of governments is to ensure the protection of private property for all citizens.

5. Productivity enhancements result from individuals' willingness to defer consumption and invest their savings into reproductive investments. The role of the financier is to facilitate and direct these transfers of capital. Capital should only be entrusted to persons of sound character.

6. Because the vast majority of the money supply is supported by the assets of commercial banks, bankers have a sacred responsibility to ensure that their capital is loaned prudently.

7. Bankers will be tempted to make riskier loans and employ more financial leverage when asset prices are rising. The worse the loan underwriting and the greater the leverage employed, the more profound the economic fallout when the credit cycle turns.

8. Recessions and unemployment result from changes in the structure of production as it shifts to meet changes in the structure of demand. The key to maintaining output and employment at high levels is to produce goods and services in correct proportions to each other.

9. When financial intermediaries like banks misallocate capital using an excessive volume of leverage, the miscalculation imposes costs upon third parties without their consent. It is the proper province of government to prevent this imposition from occurring by regulating financial leverage.

REFERENCES

Akerlof, George A., and Robert J. Shiller. *Animal Spirits: How Human Psychology Drives the Economy, and Why It Matters for Global Capitalism*. Princeton: Princeton, 2009.

Barbera, Robert J. *The Cost of Capitalism: Understanding Market Mayhem and Stabilizing Our Economic Future*. New York: McGraw-Hill, 2009.

"Banking Unsound Practices." *TIME*. April 29, 1991.

Baumol, William J. *Microtheory: Applications and Origins*. Cambridge, MA: MIT, 1986.

Baumol, William J., and Alan S. Blinder. *Economics: Principles and Policy*. Orlando, FL: Harcourt Brace, 1994.

Bernstein, Peter L. *Against the Gods: The Remarkable Story of Risk*. New York: John Wiley & Sons, 1996.

Bernstein, Peter L. *The Power of Gold: The History of an Obsession*. New York: Wiley, 2000.

Bremner, Robert P. *Chairman of the Fed: William McChesney Martin, Jr., and the Creation of the Modern American Financial System*. New Haven, CT: Yale, 2004.

Bruner, Robert F., and Sean D. Carr. *The Panic of 1907: Lessons Learned from the Market's Perfect Storm.* Hoboken, NJ: John Wiley & Sons, 2007.

Buchholz, Todd G. *New Ideas from Dead Economists: An Introduction to Modern Economic Thought.* New York: Plume, 2007.

Clay, Henry, and Eugene Ewald Agger. *Economics: An Introduction for the General Reader.* New York: Macmillan, 1921.

Cooper, George. *The Origin of Financial Crises: Central Banks, Credit Bubbles and the Efficient Market Fallacy.* New York: Vintage, 2008.

Ebenstein, Alan O. *Milton Friedman: A Biography.* New York, NY: Palgrave Macmillan, 2007.

Ferguson, Niall. *The Ascent of Money: A Financial History of the World.* New York: Penguin, 2008.

Foley, Duncan K. *Adam's Fallacy: A Guide to Economic Theology.* Cambridge, MA: Belknap of Harvard, 2006.

Fraser Management Associates. "Money Trust Investigation. Subcommittee of the Committee on Banking and Currency, House of Representatives, Washington, D.C., Thursday, December 19, 1912." Retrieved August 2010 from http://fraser.stlouisfed.org/publications/montru/issue/3642/download/53582/montru_pt15.pdf.

Friedman, Milton. *An Economist's Protest.* Glen Ridge, NJ: Thomas Horton, 1975.

Friedman, Milton. "Commanding Heights: Milton Friedman on PBS." PBS interview. Retrieved 22 July 2010 from http://www.pbs.org/wgbh/commandingheights/shared/minitext/int_miltonfriedman.html.

Friedman, Milton, and Anna Jacobson Schwartz. *The Great Contraction 1929–1933.* Princeton, NJ: Princeton, 2008.

Friedman, Milton, and Rose D. Friedman. *Free to Choose: A Personal Statement.* San Diego: Harcourt Brace Jovanovich, 1990.

Greenspan, Alan. *The Age of Turbulence: Adventures in a New World.* New York: Penguin, 2007.

Griffin, G. Edward. *The Creature from Jekyll Island: A Second Look at the Federal Reserve.* Westlake Village, CA: American Media, 2002.

Hazlitt, Henry. *The Failure of the "New Economics": An Analysis of the Keynesian Fallacies.* Auburn, AL: Ludwig Von Mises Institute, 2007.

Kates, Steven. *Say's Law and the Keynesian Revolution: How Macroeconomic Theory Lost Its Way.* Northampton, MA: Edward Elgar, 1998.

Keynes, John Maynard. *The Collected Writings of John Maynard Keynes.* Edited by Donald Moggridge. Vol. 4: *A Tract on Monetary Reform.* London: Macmillan, 1971.

Keynes, John Maynard. *The Collected Writings of John Maynard Keynes.* Edited by Donald Moggridge. Vol. 7: *The General Theory of Employment, Interest, and Money.* London: Macmillan, 1978.

Keynes, John Maynard. *The General Theory of Employment, Interest and Money.* Amherst, NY: Prometheus, 1997.

Lewis, C. S. *The Complete C.S. Lewis Signature Classics.* San Francisco: HarperSanFrancisco, 2002.

Lewis, Hunter. *Where Keynes Went Wrong: And Why World Governments Keep Creating Inflation, Bubbles, and Busts.* Mount Jackson, VA: Axios, 2009.

Lowenstein, Roger. *When Genius Failed: The Rise and Fall of Long-Term Capital Management.* New York: Random House, 2000.

Mankiw, N. Gregory. *Principles of Economics.* Mason, OH: South-Western Cengage Learning, 2009.

O'Rourke, P. J., and Adam Smith. *On the Wealth of Nations.* New York: Grove, 2007.

Paul, Ron. *End the Fed.* New York: Grand Central, 2009.

Rosenbaum, S. P. *The Bloomsbury Group: A Collection of Memoirs and Commentary.* Toronto: University of Toronto, 1995.

Rothbard, Murray N. Classical Economics: *An Austrian Perspective on the History of Economic Thought.* Vol. II. Aldershot, UK: Edward Elgar, 1995.

Say, Jean Baptiste. *A Treatise on Political Economy.* New Brunswick, NJ: Transaction, 2001.

Skidelsky, Robert Jacob Alexander. *Keynes: The Return of the Master.* New York: Public Affairs, 2009.

Smith, Adam, D. D. Raphael, and A. L. Macfie. *The Theory of Moral Sentiments.* Indianapolis: Liberty Classics, 1982.

Soros, George, and George Soros. *Open Society: Reforming Global Capitalism.* New York: Public Affairs, 2000.

Woods, Thomas E. *Meltdown: A Free-Market Look at Why the Stock Market Collapsed, the Economy Tanked, and Government Bailouts Will Make Things Worse.* Washington, D.C.: Regnery, 2009.

INDEX OF ECONOMIC TERMS